*Teaching and Talking With
Deaf Children*

WILEY SERIES IN DEVELOPMENTAL PSYCHOLOGY AND ITS APPLICATIONS

Series Editor
Professor Kevin Connolly

The Development of Movement Control and Co-ordination
J. A. Scott Kelso and Jane E. Clark

Psychobiology of the Human Newborn
edited by Peter Stratton

Morality in the Making: Thought, Action and the Social Context
edited by Helen Weinreich-Haste and Don Locke

The Psychology of Written Language: Developmental and Educational Perspectives
edited by Margaret Martlew

The Psychology of Gifted Children: Perspectives on Development and Education
edited by Joan Freeman

Children's Single-Word Speech
edited by Martyn D. Barrett

Teaching and Talking with Deaf Children
David Wood, Heather Wood, Amanda Griffiths and Ian Howarth

Further titles in preparation

Teaching and Talking
With Deaf Children

David Wood, Heather Wood, Amanda Griffiths and Ian Howarth
with Contributions by Margaret Tait and Sue Lewis

JOHN WILEY & SONS
Chichester · New York · Brisbane · Toronto · Singapore

Reprinted October 1991
Reprinted April 1992
Reprinted February 1993

Library of Congress Cataloging-in-Publication Data:
Main entry under title:

Teaching and talking with deaf children.

(Wiley series in developmental psychology and its
applications)
   Bibliography: p.
   Includes index.
   1. Children, Deaf — Education — Great Britain.
2. Children, Deaf — Great Britain — Language.
3. Children, Deaf — Language — Study and teaching —
Great Britain. 4. Deaf — Education — Great Britain.
I. Wood, David. II. Series.
HV2443,T43 1986   371.91'2   85-26553
ISBN 0 471 90827 4 (ppc)
ISBN 0 471 93327 9 (pbk)

British Library Cataloguing in Publication Data:

Teaching and talking with deaf children.—
   (Wiley series in developmental psychology and
   its applications)
   1. Children, Deaf — Languages   2. Deaf —
   Means of communications
   I. Wood, David
   362.4'2   HV2471

ISBN 0 471 90827 4 (ppc)
ISBN 0 471 93327 9 (pbk)

Printed and Bound by Dotesios Ltd, Trowbridge, Wiltshire

We dedicate this book with affection, gratitude and many fond memories to two past colleagues and great friends Pat Howarth and Jack French, MBE

Contents

Foreword

Over the last two decades there have been growing doubts about some of our long-held notions of development; in particular, work from the life sciences and the social sciences has led to the questioning of assumptions of constancy and continuity across the lifespan. Despite the evident regularity and similarity in patterns of development between members of the same species it is plain that we are dealing with an open system which exhibits plasticity at several levels from the molecular to the socio-cultural. Whether we are dealing with abnormal or damaged systems or with normal healthy ones the same principles of development apply, though of course the processes and the outcomes may well differ. The notion of plasticity implies that the development of living organisms can be modified by manipulation of the environment, and this is important not only theoretically but also practically because it permits us to plan interventions designed to improve the human condition.

For a number of years the Nottingham group have researched the development of deaf children. Their aim has been a better understanding of this group of disabled children with a clear view to improving life for them. Atypical development is as much a model for normal development as normal development is for the atypical but abnormality offers a probe with which to explore a system and unravel significant contributions to the processes of development at particular times. The capacity to communicate and the development of speech and language are generally thought to be closely bound up with the growth of intelligence and competence. Does this mean therefore that the deaf are different, and if so why and how? If language is the primary means whereby we transmit our culture what consequences does deafness have for the acculturation of the young? These and other questions form the backdrop against which the Nottingham group's work was conducted. Their concern is not with methods of teaching but with understanding the processes of intellectual development in deaf children, but of course a knowledge of the latter has implications for the former.

All too often psychologists have done little more than pay lip service to the significance of individual differences. So far as our theories are concerned they have often been more of an embarrassment than a help, yet they are plain enough for all to see. The investigations described in this book have made much of individual differences both between children and between teachers because they offer a further probe with which to explore systems and unravel processes. The work of the Nottingham group is important for a number of reasons. It is a sustained and skilful enquiry into aspects of the development of children suffering a particular disability and it focuses on what actually happens to deaf children. It is concerned largely with common place happenings in the lives of the individuals and from a psychological point of view these are likely to be the most important since they form the basis for the growth of human mentality. The book is written in a straightforward and engaging style and the authors succeed in reporting original research in a manner which commands the interest of practitioners working with deaf children, other specialist researchers and the wider group of those interested in the broad issues of development.

Kevin Connolly

Preface

In the mid-1970s, the British Medical Research Council set up two working parties to look into the possibilities for new approaches to research into deafness. The brief of one was to consider clinical problems and the other to examine social and rehabilitation needs of the deaf. Ian Howarth was Chairman of the latter working party, which identified a considerable gap between knowledge of the development of deaf children and the growing literature and new insights that were emerging from studies of hearing children. The time seemed right to try to bridge the gap by stimulating research into the intellectual and linguistic development of the deaf. Our research programme and this volume are products of that belief.

When we began our research, about nine years ago, a number of important developments were taking place in the study of children's language acquisition and intellectual growth. The dramatic expansion of work in the study of children's language, inspired largely by Chomsky's revolutionary ideas, was well underway and alternatives to his theory were also being formulated and explored. We were influenced in particular by findings on the nature of adult speech to children and by ideas about the roles played by adults in helping children to acquire their mother tongue (e.g. Snow and Ferguson, 1977). One of us had previously worked for a number of years with Jerome Bruner, first at the Center for Cognitive Studies at Harvard University and then with the Preschool Research Group at the University of Oxford. Bruner's ideas on the nature and origins of communication and, more generally, on the role of informal and formal instruction in helping to form children's understanding exerted a profound influence on our own work. His emphasis on the importance of social interaction and everyday encounters between adults and children in ensuring the transmission of knowledge and culture from the mature to the immature offered, we felt, an approach to the study of deaf children and their development that had not been hitherto explored. We believed that such an approach might not only enrich our knowledge of deaf children but also help us to understand the challenges facing parents and teachers who are entrusted with their care and education. We hope that we succeed in this book, not only in establishing the value and importance of this approach to understanding deaf children's education but also in generating some new ideas about how we might better meet their needs in the future.

Since our approach stresses the importance of children's everyday experiences in fostering their psychological development, it led us inevitably into homes and classrooms. Although we are not opposed to the use of formal tests and experimental investigation in research, and make use of such techniques in our studies, we feel that the information these yield becomes so much more powerful and revealing when we understand how it relates to children's daily lives and educational experiences. When we were embarked on the early stages of research, Conrad's (1979) important survey of the linguistic achievements of deaf children in England and Wales was published. This proved an invaluable source of information, ideas and issues. In particular, it led us to ask the central question that has directed our research and which pervades this book. Why, after years of dedicated teaching, do so many deaf children leave school unable to communicate effectively with hearing people and with such low levels of literacy?

In asking this question, we soon became aware of the usual answers to it. These, of course, revolve around the issue of mode of communication. We felt, however, that the answer might lie, wholly or in part, elsewhere—not arising so much from the mode of communication being employed in homes and schools but, rather, in the quality and productiveness of the *processes* of communication and teaching that deaf children experience. Such processes and their effects on children's development are the main focus of our book.

A veritable army of people have contributed to the research, findings and ideas presented in this volume. We thank them all. We owe a special debt to the principals, teachers and children in the many schools for partially hearing, deaf and normally hearing children who have been the focus of our studies. Without their goodwill, support and interest it would obviously have been impossible to undertake our investigations. We have always made it clear, throughout our research, that we will never identify teachers, children or their schools by name in any of our publications. This, coupled with the fact that there are simply too many people to list, makes it impossible for us to convey our thanks individually. However, we offer both our gratitude and underline our respect for them for taking part in what were often, for teachers, potentially threatening investigations.

We must also thank past and present members of the Deafness Research Group who have been joint architects of our work. In particular, we owe a large debt to Marian Kingsmill, who has undertaken hours of transcribing and analysis and managed to remain sane and cheerful. Susan Gregory, Kay Mogford and Juliet Bishop have been involved in countless hours of discussion with us, and their own research with very young children has provided us with many important insights. Jean Lees, who studied with us for a number of years, not only helped to form our views on the nature of conversations with oung deaf children but often managed to make us laugh. We also thank our colleague, Geoffrey Underwood, for discussions and arguments about reading and its development. To these and all our other colleagues we offer our thanks.

Outside the confines of our own group, many other academics, teachers, speech therapists, parents and other professionals have played an important part in shaping our ideas. In the United Kingdom, Mark Haggard, and from Australia, Des Power, Gordon Elias, Ray Jeanes and Heather Mohay, have all read drafts of chapters and taken part in long and informative discussions about the education of hearing-impaired children. Visits by Sheila White from the United States and Christiane Lepot-Froment from Belgium gave us opportunities to gain insights into deaf children's education outside our country and provided new perspectives on our own work.

We are grateful to Paul Arnold who commented on several draft chapters of the book and offered much useful advice. We would also like to thank Maureen Copley for reading and commenting upon an early draft of the book and making a number of important criticisms and observations. We also owe a great deal to our present secretary, Irene Jackson, and our past one, Penny Radcliffe, for their support, patience and hard work.

Finally, we express our gratitude to the Medical Research Council for their financial support for our research.

CHAPTER 1

Introduction: Theory, Issues and Methods

WHAT THE BOOK IS ABOUT

A great deal has been written, particularly in the last few years, about the education and development of deaf children. Extensive educational research in different countries has been reported in many papers and books, and these have been (and are being) used to refuel longstanding and seemingly irreconcilable arguments about the educational needs of deaf children and the political rights of deaf people.

Psychological research undertaken through formal testing and laboratory experimentation has been dedicated to exploring and describing how deaf people think and, to use Conrad's (1979) term, has tried to discover what 'stuff' deaf people think in. Whilst the nature of this mental 'stuff' still remains obscure, there has emerged an increasing body of evidence showing that the majority of very deaf people do not think in words or 'internal speech'. Reasons—psychological, neurological and cultural—as to why this should be the case have been formulated and are still being debated. Psychologists, and members of other academic disciplines, have not been backward in coming forward with both criticisms of and suggestions for educators of the deaf. In particular, psychological and linguistic research findings have been used as a basis for recommendations to teachers about what methods of communication they *should* use to educate deaf children. However, surprisingly little attention has been given to the question of how teachers actually *do* teach and communicate with the deaf child.

This question is the main subject of our book. We explore it with a number of other questions in mind. Foremost amongst these asks: 'Why, despite years of teaching, do so many deaf children leave school essentially illiterate, with lower educational achievements than hearing children, and unable to understand or communicate with hearing people?' Educational, linguistic and

1

psychological research has provided many insights into the problems facing those who attempt to prepare deaf children for life in the 'hearing world', but not much consideration has been given to the issue of how and why these problems actually emerge and manifest themselves in classrooms. How *do* deaf children's communication and learning problems originate and what influence do these have on the processes of education and teaching?

One aspect of the problem of providing for deaf children's educational needs is the diverse nature of children labelled 'deaf'. There are marked individual differences not only in degree of deafness and vulnerability to additional learning, emotional, social and personal problems, but also in levels of academic and linguistic achievement. Whilst some of the 'organic' factors associated with levels of achievement, such as level of intelligence and cause of deafness, have been explored and measured, environmental factors have been less intensively studied. This is not surprising when one considers that even *describing* the social and educational environment in ways that might reveal potentially important developmental influences is a complex theoretical and empirical exercise. What do we look for in classrooms, for example, that might help to explain why a particular child is or is not progressing? What do we mean by 'progress'?

This book is also concerned with the study of individual differences both in the abilities and achievements of children and in the philosophies and 'styles' of teachers. Furthermore, we explore the relationships between these to see if we can gain some insights into aspects of teaching style that accompany and might be causally related to the *creation* of different children's linguistic and educational achievements. The pursuit of this aim is a far more ambitious, problematic and uncertain affair than that of identifying learning problems. We will often be cautious and even circumspect when we discuss educational 'causes' of achievement, since we are aware of the fact that many factors beyond our control (and that of teachers) and even outside our current knowledge might be far more important determinants of individual differences than those we are about to study. However difficult the task may be, we feel that it is time to start looking in detail at what actually *happens* in the education of deaf children and to try to sort out some of the social influences on children's development. Although we adopt a cautious stance we will draw on our observations, results and experiences in many different schools to give our views on changes or developments in educational practice that teachers and others can consider and, we hope, act upon, to discover for themselves whether or not any promise of progress materializes.

Throughout our work we have tried to keep an open but critical mind about the variety of practices we have encountered and sought to analyse. Of course, even with a will to be 'open-minded', we cannot escape all the presuppositions, assumptions and 'biases' that constrain the very fabric of our perceptions and thoughts. Consequently, we need to say a little about our own theoretical background and our working assumptions.

Our theoretical 'roots' are to be found in the ideas of Vygotsky (1962) and

Bruner (1966, 1983). We do not intend, however, to make this book an introduction to theories of child development nor consider the differences of opinion between various theories in any detail, although we shall, specifically in Chapter 9, consider the implications of major developmental theories for the formal education of deaf children. The central feature of both Vygotsky's and Bruner's approaches to the study of the human mind is a fundamental emphasis on the role played by adult–child interaction in the formation of intelligence and competence. Everyday interactions between parents and infants, for example, lay the foundations for the acquisition of language. Formal instruction in schools is the basis for the cultivation of rational thought and scientific understanding. Culture is transmitted from one generation to another through communications between those already embedded in that culture and new arrivals to it.

We bring this general perspective to bear on the study of deaf children's education. What impact does deafness exert on the processes of cultural and educational transmission? How are interactions between the mature and immature affected by the handicap? Our view is that many features of the development of communication and spoken language and of ways of thinking and understanding are threatened by childhood deafness. The study of disrupted adult–child interactions and the effects of such disruptions on the child's linguistic and educational development provide a major theme that runs throughout our writings. However, we are not only hoping to identify 'special problems' facing teacher and child. As we shall see, teachers adopt very different philosophies, methods and strategies when they interact with preschoolers (Chapter 3), talk to school-aged children (Chapters 4, 5, 7 and 8) and try to teach reading (Chapter 6). By exploring differences between teachers and their effects on children's learning, we gain some insights into educational approaches that work relatively well and those that do less well. The reasons why some approaches work better than others are theoretically interesting and educationally important and will be discussed as we go along.

WHAT THE BOOK IS NOT ABOUT

Anyone looking for a comparison of, or discussions about, different methods of communication in this book will be disappointed. We are only concerned with children who are being educated in 'oral' settings: special schools and units attached to ordinary schools. Our neglect of other methods of communication is *not* due to ideological bias. It arises from more mundane, practical limitations. First, the work we will discuss involves long periods of involvement in schools and the development of relationships based on mutual trust with teachers. The very nature of our approach to the study of education demands attention to *details* and a great deal of time transcribing, classifying and evaluating videotaped classroom interactions. Only by maintaining a relatively narrow focus on one method of communication were we able to find enough resources to complete these analyses. More recently, however, we have turned our attention to the study of other methods of communication. A second, practical constraint acting on us was the fact that, when we began this work ten years ago, few schools in the United Kingdom were using other than oral approaches to communication with young deaf children.

Anyone interested in different methods of communication will, we suspect, find themselves wanting to explore several lines of thought and debate should they bother to read this book. 'Would this problem happen if you *signed* to children?' will, we think, be a question raised in each of our chapters. Only rarely will we pursue such lines of enquiry here. There are a number of reasons for adopting this strategy. First, we did not want to make the book too long, nor to 'obscure' its main message. We believe that many arguments about *methods* of communication have taken place in the absence of sufficient knowledge about the *processes* of communication that they create. This is reflected in the often polemical and even irrational arguments that all too often characterize talk about 'methods'. By drawing attention to important features of communication and teaching processes we hope to provide new ways of evaluating different methods. In the final chapter, we consider a range of questions and issues that need to be addressed in arguments about methodology. Answers to these, we suggest, will provide more effective ways of deciding whether or not a particular approach to the education of a given child is or is not working well.

But the main reason for postponing discussion of communication is that we are still in the process of extending our analyses to children in schools using Signed English and sign support for English, both in the United Kingdom and Australia. When the information provided by these studies is analysed, digested and evaluated, we will return to discuss and compare methods of communication currently being used in different schools.

Another limitation of the book is its 'audio-centric' orientation. We will be considering children's problems and capacities in relation to sound, talk and text. Although we will place considerable stress on the importance of pre-verbal and non-verbal communication in development, these will be discussed within a framework provided by knowledge of spoken language. It is important to acknowledge that analyses based on different frameworks and assumptions (e.g. on a theory of sign language and its structure) would probably reveal *different* insights into the processes we will explore and, perhaps, lead to different implications. No analysis, however 'objective' it may seem, can escape constraints imposed on it by the implicit and explicit assumptions on which it is based. We accept this view of scientific analysis and try, insofar as we can, to articulate some of the assumptions that shaped the way in which we looked at classroom interaction.

Finally, this book does not embody a detailed review of the literature on the development of deaf children. Good, contemporary, evaluative overviews already exist (e.g. Quigley and Kretschmer, 1982; Quigley and Paul, 1984), and we have no intention of trying to do what they have already achieved. We will concentrate on our own studies and their educational and theoretical implications, drawing, when appropriate, on other research both to explain and discuss our own work. Our main audience in addition to our colleagues (we hope) will be teachers of the deaf, speech therapists, educational psychologists and, perhaps, parents of deaf children.

ASSUMPTIONS AND HYPOTHESES

Articulating one's assumptions is a far more difficult task than announcing one's objectives. In this section, we try to spell out our own in terms of a series of propositions about the nature and development of deaf children. Thus, the reader may challenge our evidence not simply on the basis of its internal consistency, representativeness or robustness, but also in terms of the basic assumptions which attribute it with significance. In the book, we will examine both our own evidence and that provided by other studies in an attempt to show the force and value of these assumptions. Sometimes, we will argue that the evidence should compel us to accept their value but, at other times, we will be more speculative and discursive where the evidence is, in our judgement, less than compelling.

Proposition 1: Deaf Children Face Special Problems

To one outside the field of hearing impairment, this might sound like a self-evident and uncontroversial assumption. Why write a book about deaf children's education or provide special equipment, teachers and schools for them if they have no special problems? The issue is much deeper and more complex than such questions imply. Indeed, the stance one adopts in relation to these questions (as Freeman, Carbin and Boese, 1981, have pointed out in some detail) betrays one's basic image of the deaf person.

Many of the practical arguments about the educational needs of deaf children, such as where they should be educated, by whom they should be taught, what kind of syllabus they should follow and what methods of communication they should receive, are really based on answers to, or attitudes towards, certain key theoretical issues. Is the deaf child basically like all other children? In comparison to hearing children of the same age, are the 'lower' levels of educational and linguistic performance of deaf children simply the result of slower but essentially normal development? Or does profound deafness result in a different 'psychology' and a unique developmental path? If so, what are the special characteristics of this psychology, what needs does it give rise to and how might these be met? And when is a child to be considered 'deaf'?

Conrad (1979), for reasons explored later in the book, suggests that a child with an 'average better-ear loss' of 85 dB is unlikely to develop functional speech or literacy. Others (e.g. Meadow, 1980) argue that the threshold should be 70 dB, whilst some put the figure at 105 dB. Quigley and Paul (1984), who discuss the issue of classification in some detail, offer 90 dB as 'the most defensible criterion' (p. 3). In this book, most of the children we will be studying have losses around or in excess of 85 dB. When referring to these children en masse, we will employ the collective terms 'severely or profoundly deaf' or, by way of shorthand, 'deaf'. However, we fully accept that classifying a given child as 'functionally' deaf or partially hearing is not an easy task. It is even more difficult to determine whether any special learning problems created by deafness occur only with a specific degree of deafness or whether deaf and partially hearing children suffer similar problems with differing degrees of severity. If the latter, when do we start making special provision for the child?

Another set of important questions about proper provision for children reflects one's views on the relationships between speaking and thinking. How important is language and, specifically, speech for intellectual functioning? Is speech the basis for various intellectual activities, such as mathematical computation, or simply one medium in which thinking can take place? We will consider these questions and discuss some of the proposed answers to them in the later chapters of the book. For the moment, we introduce them to underline the fundamental connections that exist between practical consider-ations such as educational provision and teaching methods on the one hand and difficult theoretical issues on the other.

What do we mean, then, by saying deaf children face 'special problems' and what educational implications stem from these? Well, imagine for a moment a child who is totally deaf. Such a person is indeed rare, since very few 'deaf' children are born with absolutely no hearing. Suppose our totally deaf individual is but six or seven months old. As we shall see in the next chapter, at this age, adults and hearing babies are already involved in structured interactions and are embarked on the early stages of communication. When involved in feeding, bathing or some other interaction, the adult tends to follow the flow of the baby's attention and to put into words what she thinks he is experiencing or feeling. From the first days of life, the hearing infant's activities are suffused with the sounds of human speech that overlay and often interpret his experiences.

Consider now the totally deaf infant. When he turns from the adult's face to an object, say, what sign does he have, not simply that the adult is still in existence (perhaps through touch, warmth and smell) but also that they are sharing and commenting upon the object of his attentions? Logically, the infant faces a problem of discovering what is largely given for the hearing baby. When the infant turns back to the adult, how does he construe the visible reactions he sees? Is it a new event? Or is it a comment that relates to what he has *just* experienced? How is the adult to help coordinate his experience of reality with the act of communication? Will this achievement not take more time and need more maturity and intelligence on the deaf baby's part than is demanded of the hearing baby? Will there not be, at least, some delay?

This is a logical point and derives any force it has both from a consideration of a very rare individual, the totally deaf baby, and from findings (largely Piagetian) about the cognitive capacities of young infants (i.e. that they find it difficult to coordinate experiences that take place at different times). When we come to consider hearing-impaired infants with hearing aids on, the issue ceases to be a logical one and becomes empirical. What level of assisted hearing is needed before sound intrudes into the baby's consciousness? What information does an infant with a given level of hearing get from any sounds he hears? How far does the faintest murmur help him to discover the relationships between reality and communication?

These issues are taken up in Chapters 2 and 3. For the moment, we provide this example as an illustration of one problem that many hearing-impaired children face, not simply at this stage of development but throughout life. To be sure, all the children we shall consider have some degree of hearing, so the problem they face may not be as severe as that faced by our hypothetical, totally deaf child. But, we will argue, many do face problems of this type.

A consideration of these and other specific problems facing the deaf child are a major focus of the rest of the book. The central questions to which they lead ask if, how and when they can be helped to overcome such problems.

Proposition 2. Many Problems that Deaf Children Face are 'Secondary' Consequences of Their Handicap

Deaf children, throughout their development, are likely to evidence an increasing gap between what they know, think and feel on the one hand, and what they can express, negotiate and communicate about on the other. This growing gap between knowledge and communication often dislocates processes of social interaction, teaching and learning. One problem facing teachers is, so to speak, to decide whether they should address and instruct the 'intellectual' child or the 'linguistic' child. To understand many of the problems that deaf children face, we need to examine the effects that their handicap exert on those hearing adults who are significant influences in their development.

This assertion, too, may seem relatively uncontroversial, but it is not. Indeed, there are many possible bases for argument, as we shall see. For example, unlike Piagetian psychologists, notably Hans Furth (1966, 1971), we afford social interaction an important role in determining not simply what the child thinks about but also *how* he thinks. Piagetians argue that social interaction and language play no important role in determining the structure of thinking. We will be exploring the view that they do play such a role and that any problems of communication between adults and children are likely to have far-reaching, 'secondary' consequences on development.

More importantly, however, we will argue that such secondary effects, though a product of the handicap, are not inevitable. Here we will also find ourselves enmeshed in arguments about the role of social factors in the development of language. For instance, it is reasonably well established that in our sort of society, one finds close links between a child's stage of linguistic development and the language addressed to him by more competent speaker-hearers (e.g. Cross, 1978; Snow, 1979; Bruner, 1983; Wells, 1984) The issue is this: is such a close connection a *necessary* condition for linguistic development? If so, is it the child who paces the adult or the adult who leads the child? Such questions are of more than theoretical interest in any study of children with language problems. If the answer to the question just raised lies in the child, then adults may play a relatively minor role in mediating the effects of handicap on development. However, if adults lead, then any disruptions in their normal styles of interaction and communication may be causally involved in at least some of the problems the child faces.

We will explore this issue later in the book. We do so largely through the exploitation of two basic concepts—control and contingency. This is not the place to explore these concepts in depth, but a brief consideration is necessary to establish the basis for our third proposition.

Children learn most readily and generalize what they learn most effectively when the help they are offered is *contingent* upon their developing competence. Stated boldly, such a principle sounds commonplace and even banal but its achievement, as we shall see, is hardly commonplace in schools. To be contingent upon a child, one must offer help and control when he faces difficulty, and relinquish control and provide opportunities for initiative when he shows signs of success. Consider what this involves. First, one must be aware of what the child is attempting to achieve, and be able to diagnose success and failure. This itself is not nearly as easy as it may sound. It demands attention to the child, observation and listening, both of which may be difficult to achieve in the classroom. Further, many 'errors' that children make are not due to inattentiveness, stupidity or ignorance. Rather, they are a natural product of their stage or phase of learning and must be interpreted as such. To take a specific example: if we look at a piece of writing from a deaf child, can we say with any confidence how far his departures from standard English are due to his stage of language development? Can we spot those 'errors' that are the product of a 'child grammar'? If so, when is the time right for control and corrective feedback? The issue is not easy. To diagnose and interpret the significance of errors and successes by a given child, we must have a valid psychological model both of the learner and what it is he is learning. Thus the way we interpret linguistic errors is determined by our theory of language and its development. Demanding corrections that are too far beyond the child' current level of mastery serves to demoralize him. Conversely, demanding too low a level of response is likely to bore him. The achievement of contingency is often formidably difficult in schools and especially so with the deaf child.

Proposition 3: Secondary Problems Can Be Ameliorated

This proposition, certainly no less controversial than the preceding ones forms the pedagogical 'heart' of the book. We will show first that the incidence of control and contingency often varies from teacher to teacher. More important, we will identify several predictable effects of different teaching styles on children's learning and their use of language and will try to tease apart cause and effect to show that teaching style and not simply factors 'in' the child mediate these effects. We will also look at individual differences between children of similar hearing loss and intelligence to reveal some marked differences in language ability and educational achievement. Although such studies demonstrate that degree of deafness and intelligence are not the only determinants of success, it will be left to the reader to judge how far our evidence supports the view that teaching philosophies and styles are other important determinants. Our evidence is not compelling, but it is highly suggestive and consistent with knowledge about the course of human development.

SIGNPOSTS

The next two chapters chart children's transition from largely pre-verbal to verbal communication. They also consider aspects of the relationship between language and learning in deaf children, and identify important ingredients of linguistic development. Chapter 3 considers some aspects of children's experiences in nursery school in the light of research into the relationships between pre-verbal and verbal communication. In Chapter 4 we move on to the study of conversations between linguistically more advanced deaf children and their teachers, where language is being used to talk about events and experiences not located in the 'here and now'. We examine teaching styles and their effects on deaf children's language. We then move on, in Chapter 5, to examine the effects of changes in teachers' style, when the notion of control and the role of adults in language development come to the fore. We also offer our views on the role and structure of productive conversations with young deaf children.

Our attention then shifts to the development and assessment of literacy and to a critique of both the teaching and measurement of reading skills in deaf children (Chapter 6). We question the value of reading tests and ask what they tell us about linguistic competence and linguistic development in deaf children. This, in turn, leads us to ask the question: 'Do deaf children really develop a generative linguistic competence or simply a rag-bag of language-related tricks?' (Chapter 7). We conclude both on the basis of our own work and a review of the relevant literature that they do develop a generative linguistic system, but one that is usually extremely limited in power. This leads us back to the classroom in an attempt to explore the child's experience of language. We ask a deceptively simple question: 'Do deaf children actually experience language that violates their own limited grammatical competence?' 'If not, wherein lies cause and effect?' (Chapter 8). This discussion leads to some detailed considerations of the nature of deaf children's linguistic problems and some speculations about why these come about. In Chapter 9 we discuss reasoning in deaf children and, in particular, their mathematical competence. This relates back to the fundamental issues already raised about our 'image' of the deaf child, and to a consideration of the school curriculum. Finally, Susan Lewis, who has attempted to use some of our research materials in teacher training, comments upon their uses and limitations in the transition from research to practice.

FOOTNOTE: SEXIST PRONOMINAL REFERENCE

Throughout the book, unless we are making reference to a 'known person' we will refer to teachers and adults as 'she' and a child as 'he'. We have attempted a number of different strategies for pronominal reference, such as always using plurals (which becomes ungainly and stilted) or s/he (which runs into problems when one needs to use possessive pronouns such as his or hers). We apologize to male teachers and female pupils for this misrepresentation. It is difficult, particularly when talking about social and linguistic *interactions*, to find a readable and equitable solution to the 'pronoun' problem, but, after some discussion, we decided to adopt the strategy just outlined and to make this apologia.

CHAPTER 2

The Preschool Child:
From Communication to Language

In the next two chapters we will identify and discuss some of the stages that young deaf children pass through as they make the transition from 'pre-verbal' communication to when they begin to understand what is said to them and to produce words themselves. We will also be looking more widely at the deaf child's experiences in nursery school, examining some aspects of the impact of deafness on teaching–learning interactions. We attempt to outline and discuss observations of young children in school and start to 'measure' their school experiences against their communicative and wider developmental needs.

In this chapter, we begin by discussing the early stages of language development in hearing children. Why, one might ask, start with hearing infants? Well, in the first place, recent studies have shown how the emergence of a child's first words represents the *culmination* of a process of communication that begins at birth. The importance of this work, for our purposes, is the lessons it holds for the management and teaching of young deaf children. When the hearing baby is developing the pre-verbal foundations of communication he is largely immobile, attracted to human faces and limited in his thinking to what fills his senses. As we shall see, many deaf preschoolers are still in the pre-verbal stages of development when they enter nursery school. They are mobile, interested in many things and likely to have plans and intentions. Establishing the conditions for contingent interactions to foster the development of verbal communication is far more difficult when a child's intellectual maturity is so far in advance of his communicative development.

The acquisition of speech involves much more than the ability to hear others talk. Communication between infants and 'significant others' (e.g.

11

parents and siblings) is established *before* the infant begins to understand or produce speech. We shall argue, following Bruner (1983) and others (e.g. Lock, 1980), that such pre-verbal communication provides the child with 'keys' to unlock the meanings of speech.

Although the importance of pre-verbal communication is becoming widely recognized amongst educators of young children, we will argue in the next chapter (and later ones) that many features of teaching *practice* are still at variance with this knowledge. In short, teachers often attempt to get deaf children to 'listen' and 'speak' without due regard for the processes of *communication* which lend sense and significance to language.

One way of looking at research into early language development is as an illustration of its 'multisensory' and 'interactive' nature. For words to take on meaning for a child, they must be integrated with what he sees, feels or in some other way 'senses' in the world. To take on communicative *significance* words must refer to something perceived, remembered, imagined or felt. Words are also 'shared symbols' and for successful communication they must invoke similar percepts, ideas or conceptions in both a speaker and listener; they are 'socially constructed, shared symbols'. Thus, to understand what a word means to a child and to study its acquisition by that child, our observations must be rooted in social interaction. Similarly, the study and evaluation of the deaf child's experiences of language must look beyond what the child is saying or doing to consider the social practices in which he participates. If language arises through communicative interaction, then problems in acquiring language may reside, in part, in the nature and structure of such interactions. Here, too, we will be arguing that teachers are often concerned with the quality of a child's language or his ability to comprehend speech without paying due regard to the social practices that lend meaning and significance to utterances.

Finally, towards the end of the chapter, we consider two issues that are central to the educational concerns of our classroom research and this book. How far or in what sense do adults 'teach' children language or provide the basis for its development? Is there an 'appropriate' way to talk to children to assist language learning? More specifically, should the immature speaker be exposed to relatively 'simple' speech in order to foster that learning?

These, then, are some of the principle reasons for beginning our study of the spoken language development of deaf children by considering the transition from pre-verbal to spoken communication in hearing children.

SOUNDS AND MEANINGS

In this section, we examine some of the achievements made by young hearing babies in their first year of life. We cannot hope to provide even a modest overview of the voluminous research into this period of human development; rather we shall examine some important 'landmarks' in the growth of infant competence.

Systematic observations of babies within hours of their birth have demonstrated their remarkable powers; powers that are soon exploited in their contacts with adults (usually, of course, their mothers). Newborn babies, or neonates, show considerable powers of *discrimination* and *organization* that are either present at conception or developed in the womb. They react selectively and (often) predictably to many sensory experiences very early in life. For instance, a touch on the neonate's cheek will usually elicit a 'rooting reflex'; any ensuing contact with a suckable object will then evoke highly organized sucking behaviour. Although not so predictable in their effects, sounds will also occasion movements of the (supported) head and, more often than chance allows, the infant will turn *towards* the sound source, showing both that he can hear and that the ability to locate sounds is innate or developed during intrauterine experience (Crassini and Broese, 1980). The baby also responds selectively to different sounds. Loud, percussive noises startle whilst gentle, low frequency, repetitive sounds tend to soothe. Although the baby's responses to sound are not totally predictable (depending, for example, on how alert he is) they are at least partially structured (a fact that is exploited by microprocessor-controlled units such as the Linco-Bennett cradle for neonatal screening for deafness) (see Stratton, *Psychobiology of the Human Newborn*, in this series).

The neonate is also selective in his responses to certain smells. Offered a choice between his own mother's breastpad and that of another lactating female, the infant will usually turn to his mother's. Similarly, although the neonate can only focus on an object a few inches from his face, he is able to bring both eyes into focus on an object at that distance and show marked preference for the sight of the human face. The human voice is also accorded preferential treatment. The *combination* of human face and speech, for a baby who is reasonably alert, is almost irresistibly attractive (Brazelton, 1982).

Adults soon 'exploit' the privileged status afforded them by their look, smell and sound. When they hold the baby, bring their face close to his and talk to him, they are likely to be rewarded by intent attention. They may also exert some control over the infant's state of being—helping to rouse the sleepy baby with movements, an animated voice and face, and to soothe the agitated one by holding him close and uttering low, soft, repetitive sounds.

Because babies are, so to speak, functioning on all sensory cylinders, there are many 'avenues'—touch, smell, sight, sound and taste—whereby they can become attached to and familiar with those in frequent contact with them. Perhaps this is one reason why sensory handicaps in young babies are so difficult to detect: the infant always has other ways of coming to know the world and of establishing interactions with others.

The infant's 'love affair' with the human face lasts until around four months of age when his attention becomes monopolized by objects. Those long, sustained periods of looking at faces decline and the characteristic responses of the adult change in ways that reflect the baby's interests. During the first few months, when adult and infant are *en face*, the baby shows a pattern of engagement/disengagement. He may look intently at an adult's face for time, then turn away for a period before coming back into eye contact. The adult, meanwhile, is likely to be looking at the baby all the time. When she addresses the infant, it is usually to talk *about* him. The baby's changing facial expressions, movements and sounds are likely to be *interpreted* as 'meaningful' events by the adult and put into words. By making their reactions and sounds *contingent* upon the baby's initially spontaneous activities, adult help to endow these with 'meaning'. The infant begins to reciprocate by *repeating* a movement, gesture or sound which 'caused' an adult response. If this, in turn, leads the adult to respond again, the baby may try again, thus building up the foundations for *communicative* exchanges.

Once the baby produces an action and shows clear signs of *expecting* a response, he must have at least a rudimentary *knowledge* of the likely action of another person. By three months of age the infant has almost certainly built up such expectations since, if his partner (usually the mother) does *not* respond as she usually does, the baby shows signs of unhappiness, withdrawal surprise or alarm (Cohn and Tronick, 1982). Well before the emergence of the first word the baby is thus playing a part in communicative exchanges in which he 'expects' certain things to happen as a consequence of his own *actions*.

When, at about four months, the infant's attention turns to objects and happenings in the environment the patterns of interaction change. Typically when adult and baby are together, the infant's visual exploration of the environment is 'mirrored' by the adult, who probably looks where the baby looks and talks about what is being looked at (Collis and Schaffer, 1975). By following the infant's line of attention, drawing inferences about what he is looking at and may be feeling, the adult may put into words that which is likely to be of interest to the baby. More remarkably, at around the same age the baby begins to follow the *adult's* line of gaze when they break eye contact (Scaife and Bruner, 1975; Butterworth and Cochran, 1980; Churcher and Scaife, 1982). How babies achieve this feat is not known, but it increases the probability that adult and child will be looking at the same things.

Such shared attention to common objects and events has been called the 'reference triangle' and identified as the basis for the development of shared meanings and, eventually, words. If both partners look at the same thing whilst one talks about it, then the chances that the baby will discover the relationships between words and things is increased. The adult spontaneously helps to bring the infant's experiences into conjunction with language. Even before the baby recognizes or produces words, the intonation or 'mood music' supplied by the human voice, which has already become significant for the infant, may play a part in providing an *interpretation* of the significance of different experiences. Sounds of surprise, caution, delight, fear or whatever may 'infect' the infant's feelings whilst he looks at the object of communication. Thus, the beginnings of verbal meaning reside not so much in the significance of individual word sounds but in the personal, social and emoonal 'tone' that is communicated by the intonation of the voice. Put another ay, the baby is introduced to 'interpretations' and not only single ord–object relationships. Because the infant's state of being can be conolled by the tone of voice, so his feelings can be affected in the presence of ifferent objects and events. We can thus communicate feelings of security, ar, surprise to the infant before he understands individual words.

In the first few months of life, then, the infant is playing an active, ciprocal role in interaction. He has come to recognize and respond selecvely to the voices of familiar people, such as those of mother and father. In is sound making, early coos and gurgles are giving way to babbling. Comarisons of the sounds made by babies in different cultures reveal that the itonation patterns found in the six-month-old's pre-speech sounds begin to semble those of his host language (e.g. Menyuk, 1971). Thus, by six months lere is already some convergence between the infant's sound making and spects of the speech system that he will eventually master. Similarly, by eight lonths of age babies respond differently to various patterns of intonation ddressed to them. They react in different ways, for instance, to questions and atements. Though they may not recognize words, they show some discrimiation between intonation patterns (Kaplan, 1969).

After a period of rapt attention to the human face and the beginnings of iterest in things and events in the immediate environment, the infant begins) 'integrate' the world of people and objects. For example, when, around ten lonths or so, the infant looks at the mother whilst *pointing* to an object, he most literally 'draws' a 'triangle of reference', which involves the object of ference and two minds trained upon that object. Similarly, in 'give and take' ames, an object plays a role *within* a social exchange. As both Lock (1980) id Bruner (1983) have argued, the emergence of such gestures and games is i indication of the development of intentional acts of communication by the aby. Thus the scene is set for the acquisition and use of vocal symbols. A ord or utterance that is used in response to or in parallel with such in-verbal gestures is likely to be interpreted by the baby as a reference to e activity that is uppermost in his mind (and that of the speaker).

Before moving on to look in a little more detail at the emergence of speech the child, we pause to draw attention to some general features of pre-verbal mmunication that will figure in our analyses of teacher–child interactions ith pre-verbal deaf children. First, an obvious but important point: during e early interactions we discussed the infant was drawn 'naturally' to the man face. During most or all of the period we have been discussing, babies e incapable of moving their bodies around in space. They are not easily ored' by repetitions of simple routines. The natural attraction of faces lends e adult significance and provokes the necessary attention for the growth of mmunication with the baby. His immobility means that the adult, in teractions with the infant, is likely to find the object of the child's interest bvious'. The infant's stage of development is such that what he is aware of ill be present in the immediate context. Infants' 'tolerance' and enjoyment simple, repeated sequences of interaction also provide a 'natural' starting place for the discovery of regularity and predictability in their experiences which forms the basis for communication.

If the child's development of pre-verbal communication is 'delayed' for any reason, each of these conditions is likely to be violated. If the face has to compete with other, more attractive objects; if the child is able to formulate relatively long-term plans and desires; if he is mobile and difficult to follow or easily bored by simple repetition, then the problem of achieving mutually satisfying pre-verbal communicative exchanges becomes increasingly difficult.

Two other points need to be raised as preliminaries to our considerations of communicative development in deaf children. These concern the achievements which accompany the development of 'reciprocal interaction'. As the baby comes to anticipate the structure of recurrent events like feeding, undressing, playing and so forth, he discovers how to 'take turns' in interactions. Once he expects his actions to result in some predictable reaction from another, he is participating in turn-taking routines in which, so to speak, he leaves 'gaps' or 'pauses' to be filled by the anticipated response. Bruner (1983) has argued that such 'formats' in early interaction engender the development of 'conversation-like' exchanges in which mother and baby take turns. Although there is still debate as to exactly when and how the baby can be said to be a truly 'active partner' in turn-taking, infants have almost certainly mastered the rudiments of this ability before they begin to talk.

One final point concerns a general feature of adult responses to young infants. From the start they respond to the child *as though* he has intention and *as if* the child is controlling them. Similarly, when, later in this period they talk about what the child is looking at, they make what they do and say *contingent* upon their interpretation of what is in the child's mind. Thus, not only do they help to bring the child's experience into conjunction with speech sounds, they also offer the infant an opportunity to *control* what happens next. For the infant, the growth of communication and of 'self-efficacy' are thus closely intertwined—something we return to when we discuss the 'control' of deaf children by parents and teachers.

Having identified some of the more general features of early, pre-verbal communication that will inform our discussions of deaf children, we will go no further into the development of pre-verbal patterns of interaction, although many other achievements occur en route to the development of speech. We turn our attention now to the child who is beginning to talk, to consider the early stages of speech development. Again, the reason for looking selectively at aspects of language development is to identify features of the process that are relevant to our considerations of deaf children.

LANGUAGE: 'TAUGHT' OR 'CAUGHT'?

As Bruner (1983) points out, two theories of language acquisition have dominated research in the past. One (called by Miller the 'impossible' theory) held that language was *taught* by exposing children to simple association etween 'words' and 'things' (Skinner, 1957). The other view (the 'miracle' theory) held that language was simply *caught*, rather like an ailment, by exposure to speech. Because the child was born with an innate 'Language Acquisition Device' or 'LAD' (Chomsky, 1965), there was no need for either teaching or 'privileged communication with another speaker'. More recently, although arguments about the precise roles of innate abilities and environmental influences in promoting language acquisition persist, most students of child language have come to accept an 'interactionist' perspective in which both the child's natural capacities and interactions with more mature speakers are important in development. The child may 'catch' language, but, to abuse the metaphor perhaps, adults tend to make sure he is in the right place at the right time to catch the verbal ball.

When the infant begins to use sounds 'meaningfully' (the first sounds used communicatively by a baby are not, of course, 'adult' words) a number of important changes occur in the reactions he receives from adults. Studies of adult talk to children undertaken in several countries have revealed some common (though perhaps not universal) phenomena. Adults in different parts of the world, when talking to infants, tend to talk about similar things connected with 'universal' aspects of child care such as feeding, dressing and so on. Thus, the vocabulary addressed to babies is similar across many cultures. Adults also begin to use 'simpler' language than they used previously when talking to the pre-verbal baby. Utterances tend to be articulated relatively slowly, they display a fair degree of repetition and are characterized by exaggerated intonation patterns at relatively high speech frequencies in comparison to talk between adults and older children.

Such features of adult talk to infants have been called 'motherese', labelled the 'baby talk register' or described as a child's 'primary linguistic data'. Since adult talk to children tends to become more complex, less repetitive and less intonationally inflected as the child gets older, the term 'grammatical fine tuning' has also been coined to mark the complex 'adjustments' found in adult speech as children become more verbally competent. Similarly, what is *talked about* changes as the child gets older, more knowledgeable and mature.

There has been a great deal of debate and research about the generality, cause and significance of such findings. Some theorists have argued that 'fine tuning', for example, represents a form of indirect language teaching whereby adults present children with examples of language that are just 'beyond' their current levels of production to help 'model' or provide support for the next steps in their progress (e.g. Snow, 1979). An alternative interpretation of the same phenomenon places far more emphasis on the child's naturally developing abilities. Basically, the counter-argument to the 'teaching' view is that changes in adult speech represent *accommodations* to the child's developing competence (Gleitman, Newport and Gleitman, 1984). From this perspective, adults change what they talk about and how they talk to fit in with the child's abilities to understand, but such adjustments follow rather than lead the child on to the next stage.

We enter into this debate later in the chapter. First, however, we consider some of the evidence relating to claims and counter-claims about 'motherese' since the importance we attach to parental speech to children will clearly inform the ways in which we examine attempts by teachers to 'teach' deaf children language.

THE MORE THE BETTER?

Several researchers have studied the language of parents to young children in terms of how often they use certain language structures. Differences between parents are then compared with what their children say some time later in development. Is children's progress in mastering the language structures studied related to how frequently they hear those structures?

Generally speaking, the answer to this question is 'no' (Gleitman and Wanner, 1982). Mere frequency of exposure to grammatical structures does not play a vital role in their acquisition by children. We suspect few people would doubt the fact that some *minimal* level of exposure is needed; however, the implication is that the hearing children in these studies all encountered adequate levels of exposure to various structures and, therefore, all acquired them. We can, however, reject the notion that children who acquire a given structure of language quickly are those who hear it most often; mere 'amount' of exposure is not a good basis for explaining the phenomenon of language acquisition.

Before moving on to consider the lessons we might draw from this conclusion, we need to draw attention to two other important findings that have emerged from child language research. The first addresses the theory that hearing 'simple utterances' is the key to early language acquisition and the second illustrates how the 'natural' working of the auditory system rather than any environmental experiences constrain the way in which children discover aspects of linguistic meanings. Again, this is grist for the 'miraculists'' mill.

THE SIMPLER THE BETTER?

The finding that adults tend to use relatively simple grammatical structures when they talk to young children has been used to support the notion that language is taught; teaching starts with the simple and moves on to the more complex. This proposal, however, is weakened by two lines of evidence: one from studies of talk to children and the other from experiments in computational linguistics (i.e. attempts to program computers to 'understand' language).

Although, as we have just seen, there seems to be no general relationship between the number of times children hear various language structures and how quickly they learn them, one less obvious connection has been found both by researchers who support and those who deny the fine-tuning hypothesis. The finding in question concerns children's acquisition of auxiliary verb phases such as 'I will . . .'. In adult speech, such a combination of a

pronoun and auxiliary verb is often spoken in the contracted form 'I'll . . .'.
Children only come to produce such contractions relatively late in language
development after a period of using the non-contracted forms. Thus, although
children often hear contractions, they do not produce them until they are
ready' to do so (Gleitman, Newport and Gleitman, 1984).

There is one type of utterance, however, in which adults cannot contract
such pronoun–auxiliary pairs. These involve two-choice questions such as
'Will I have time . . . ?' or 'Will you please . . . ?'. Children whose parents ask
relatively large numbers of such questions begin to use *statements* including
the auxiliary earlier than those whose parents ask fewer. The implication is
that children discover or learn how to use auxiliary verbs not by hearing adults
use relatively simple, declarative statements but the grammatically more
complex question form. This finding might also imply that children, in some
intuitive sense, 'understand' the grammatical connections between the auxiliary verb systems in questions and statements. If one accepts this view, then
one is attributing sophisticated, early knowledge of language *structure* to very
young children—something that those who believe in the child's 'natural'
language acquisition capacities are likely to use as evidence for their views.

The point we wish to underline, however, is that children appear to be
exploiting quite *complex* linguistic structures to inform their 'theory' of
language at a very early stage. Thus, the notion of 'simplicity' in adult speech
is not as simple as might appear.

This observation has received support from designers of computer 'language learning' programs (Gleitman and Wanner, 1982). Without delving
into details, they have found that a computer exposed only to simple language
(e.g. Mary hit John, Anne went to town, etc.) is unlikely to 'discover' the
grammar of English because a large number of grammatical rules could
account for such simple constructions. However, if the machine is also
presented with examples of more complex language, these narrow down the
number of possible rules that can 'explain' how the language is structured.
This discovery from computational linguistics, in company with studies of
child language, seriously undermines the view that *exclusive* exposure to
'simple' utterances is the best way to learn language. We will be considering
the general question of simplified speech to deaf children in Chapter 8.

Another line of evidence also questions the 'language is taught not caught'
theory and helps to shed some light onto the specific speech acquisition
problems of deaf children. We have already taken note of the fact that young
hearing children do not utter linguistic contractions like 'We'll . . .' until
relatively late in development. This phenomenon is part of a general feature
of the early stages of language development in which children seem to work
on the assumption that anything that sounds like a *single sound unit* in speech
also functions as a single *element* of meaning. Many words are, of course,
single-meaning elements (e.g. cat, house, large, etc.). Many, however, are not.
For example, words like 'un-friend-ly', 'cat-s', 'un-prepare-(e)d' contain two
or three elements of meaning. Furthermore, the meanings of some of these
elements, like '-ed', are grammatical in nature. Children may utter words

containing such 'grammatical morphemes' early in development (e.g. says, cats, walked, etc.) but only use them generatively or in a 'rule-like' way in all relevant contexts after some time (Brown, 1973; Bowerman, 1982). How and when do children come to appreciate the grammatical significance of prefixes and suffixes?

The answer to this specific question has general implications for language development. One could argue that children learn *first* those prefixes and suffixes which they hear most often. Alternatively, it might be the case that some suffixes or prefixes are easier to learn than others because they express 'simpler ideas'. For example, it might be the case that it is easier for a child to learn the distinction between one/many (cat/cats) than it is to learn the difference between perfective (walked) and progressive (walking) verb forms, because plurality is a 'simpler' idea than the state of actions. Third, children may learn some things before others because they are acoustically more salient. The first explanation—frequency—does not stand for similar reasons to those discussed earlier. The second—intellectual difficulty—may well be true of some features of language development (DeVilliers and DeVilliers, 1979), but the third explanation—acoustic salience—seems to play a major role in the acquisition of grammatical morphemes like '-ing', '-ed', 'un-' and '-s', for example (though most of the evidence comes from studies of languages other than English). Briefly, children appear to learn first those prefixes and suffixes that are most *stressed* in speech (Gleitman and Wanner, 1982). For example, '-ing' is almost always learned before '-ed'.

Such findings add weight to the view that the course of language development is not determined as much by factors 'outside' the child, such as how often he hears things said, as it is by factors 'inside', such as how *salient* things *sound*. The implications of such findings for the linguistic development of deaf children and, in particular, the problems they face in learning about tense and aspect (e.g. progressive versus perfective verb forms) will be explored later.

It seems clear that any theory that seeks to explain language development in terms of *teaching* ignores important, 'natural' factors that are part of human nature. Thus, we are not advocating, and will be arguing against, the idea that language is, in any simple sense, 'taught' to children. However, we shall also reject the idea that all we need to consider in understanding what deaf children understand of language is the view that language is usually 'caught' by children. The relationships between linguistic experience and language development are more complex than either extreme view allows. That complexity, we suggest, is best studied by examining language in use for purposes of communication, i.e. discourse, coupled with attempts to describe the deaf child's 'theories' of language.

COMMUNICATION AND DISCOURSE

Although there are diametrically opposing views about the importance of adult talk to children in facilitating the course of language development, there seems to be widespread agreement that the child's discovery of relationships between sounds and meanings is facilitated by pre-verbal communicative interactions such as those outlined earlier. However, the relationships between *communication*, on the one hand, and grammatically structured *speech*, on the other, are still being debated. Unfortunately, attempts to explicate the relationships between talk addressed to children and rates of language development have been too crude in conception to shed much light onto the processes involved. Whilst ruling out the importance of sheer quantity of exposure as an explanation for rates of acquisition, they have failed to look at the *processes* of language use in ways that might be more revealing. Our own view is that any attempt to study the facilitation of language development that neglects the *structure* of the interaction and discourse within which language is embedded is doomed to failure. We need to consider, for example, not how often parents use a given linguistic structure when talking to children but also *how*, *when and where* they talk and *what* they say in response to children during conversation. Furthermore, we will question attempts to study language development that concentrate on syntax to the exclusion of all else. Studies by Wells (1984), for example, have been far more concerned with the study of how parents *respond* to what their children say and how what they say *relates* semantically (i.e. at the level of meaning rather than syntax) to the child's perceived meanings. Parents who were more likely to respond *contingently* to what their child was trying to say and communicate, to build upon or extend what the child was talking about or to negotiate with the child about what both of them were trying to communicate, facilitated their child's linguistic development more than less contingent parents. Studies by Cazden (1977) have also shown that when children are treated more like 'equal partners' in discourse, where what they say is used as a basis for conversation, children show more rapid language development than do children who have what they say repeated back to them in 'better grammar', for example.

Any attempt to study the acquisition of language without due attention to interactions between speakers, in our view, misses the very thing it seeks to study. Throughout this book, we shall concentrate upon language in use and the structure, content and function of conversations between adults and children for this reason.

Before moving on to the study of deaf children entering nursery school, we undertake a brief review of some of the research into the development of communication between deaf babies and their mothers. It is not our intention to attempt a comprehensive overview of the findings and issues raised by this research, but to provide some sense of 'life before school'. Gregory (in preparation) will be presenting a detailed study of parent–child interaction in the first three years of life, and Bishop and Gregory (in preparation) will discuss the transition of the deaf child from home to school.

SOUNDS AND THINGS

Earlier, we used the medical metaphor of 'infection' to characterize what happens in the infant's experience when people talk to him about what he is looking at or experiencing. Sounds signifying, for example, reassurance, surprise, shock or concern may be communicated to the baby before he understands individual words. Imagine a deaf baby with little or no awareness of sound. Assume that he does not hear (though, eventually, he may be able to listen). When he looks at an object or event, he receives none of the 'mood music' that accompanies the social experiences of the hearing baby. Suppose he looks from an object of his attention to turn to an adult who is 'sharing' the experience with him and the adult talks about what he has just been looking at. Is it obvious to the child that what they are doing is an *act of reference*? Does the infant even realize that *communication* is taking place? To discover the relationships between a word and its referent, the deaf infant has to *remember* something he has just observed and deliberately *relate* this memory to another observation. In short, the deaf child with little or no auditory awareness has to do by intellect, *in sequence*, what 'happens' to the hearing baby in parallel. An adult can take the responsibility for timing and adjusting the act of communication to fit the hearing infant's attention. The deaf baby has to do much more, 'discovering' the relationships between two very different visual experiences that are displaced in time.

The problem of 'divided attention' provides an explanation for a number of features of the deaf baby's social experiences that several different observers have reported. In comparison with encounters between hearing infants and their mothers, those between hearing parents and deaf babies have been described as more likely to be 'emotionally negative' (e.g. Schlesinger and Meadow, 1972). Signs of frustration for both parent and child are more frequent. The reason usually given, not surprisingly, concerns differences in the quality of communication and two-way frustration at not being able to achieve mutual understanding. Gregory's (e.g. Gregory and Mogford, 1981) research indicates that even with babies in the pre-verbal stages, mothers have much greater difficulty in establishing turn-taking and reciprocity when their baby is deaf. The reason for such findings we believe lies in the general role that sound usually plays in establishing and maintaining contact with the infant and in 'sharing' the object of his attention. Unlike the hearing baby, the deaf baby's experience of objects is not 'infected' with human sounds, so the process of communication is more difficult even before we would expect his understanding and use of speech to emerge onto the scene.

One common and perhaps 'natural' response by hearing adults to the problem of achieving mutual understanding with their deaf infant is to become more 'controlling' (Goss, 1970; Mogford, Gregory and Hartley, 1980). We suggest that such control is a byproduct of efforts by adults to 'simplify' the child's task by trying to manipulate his visual attention in some way. They may, for instance, turn the infant's head towards them, try to insinuate their face into his visual field or take objects from him to bring them close to their own mouths. Each of these common responses results in a more intrusive parental style and much higher levels of external control over the infant's experiences. They are, we suggest, consciously or unconsciously designed by the adult to overcome the problem of divided attention. They are also counter-productive. Even when the adult 'demands' or 'grabs' the child's attention or takes objects close to her face the infant still has to *work out* what is going on. Indeed, rather than making the child's task *easier* it renders it more difficult, as we shall see later.

Thus, whereas adults interacting with hearing babies often make what they say and do *contingent* upon their interpretation of what the child is seeing or thinking, when hearing adults interact with deaf babies they often demand that the deaf baby attends to *them* and the baby has to work out what they mean. Put another way, the deaf baby is often 'expected' to make *his* thinking contingent upon the intentions of the adult. We believe that this demand is totally unrealistic and cannot be met by infants of this age or, as we will see, by children who are considerably older. If attempts to 'help', direct and control the child result in frustration and tears, it should come as no surprise, given the difficult demands being placed upon the child. Consequently, we suggest that the deaf child may be frustrated not only by any lack of success in communicating his own needs and intentions but also by the demands placed on him when adults try to help him communicate by overcontrolling his actions and attentions. He is also likely to be frustrated in attempts to achieve his own intentions when the adult 'cuts across' his path of activity by 'distracting' him from his own purposes.

Other researchers have argued, however, that such parental responses to deafness are not universal and that given early diagnosis of infant deafness, provision of good amplification and effective parental support, contingent interactions between very deaf babies and their mothers can be established (Tucker and Nolan, 1984). We will consider the theoretical and educational significance of these arguments in the final chapter when we have described our own work. For the moment, however, whilst we accept that very deaf infants with useful levels of auditory awareness do exist and also acknowledge the fact that such awareness (by definition, in our view) overcomes or at least ameliorates the problem of divided attention, the majority of children whom we have studied and who are the subject of this book are not so fortunate.

Given the fact that very few deaf babies are diagnosed or studied in the first year of life, we have no firm information about their social or communicative development during this period. There is no reason to believe that the deaf neonate will not display the usual attraction to the human face, so initial attachments to parents may take place. However, Gregory (in preparation) suggests that by ten months of age when, normally, the baby begins to integrate the world of people and objects and is participating in activities like 'give and take' games, differences between deaf and hearing infants are detectable. This is consistent with the view that voice sounds have already 'infected' the hearing child's experiences to provide a 'bridge' between objects and people. But what of those deaf children who, aged three years or so, enter special nursery provision? What stages of development have they reached?

CHAPTER 3

The Nursery Years

This chapter is concerned with a number of questions and issues relating to the 'quality' of deaf children's experiences in special nursery school groups. More generally, it reports an attempt to describe the structure of adult–child interactions and to relate these to the child's developmental needs and progress. What developmental 'tasks' are facing severely/profoundly deaf three- to five-year-olds in classrooms? What are their educational, social and linguistic needs and are these usually met? How can we evaluate a child's progress during this period and assess the relevance or value of the experiences he is having?

In an attempt to answer these questions, we have undertaken three lines of research. We have observed children in their classrooms, studied attempts to teach deaf preschoolers a difficult construction task and filmed a group of twelve children at regular intervals in interactions with their teacher. Each line of research has raised common issues concerning the communication and learning problems facing the deaf child and the difficulties and challenges these problems create for teachers. In addition, the longitudinal study of twelve children (Tait, 1984) yielded detailed insights into some of the stages the preschool deaf child passes through in attempting to communicate, acquire speech and learn.

INTO THE NURSERY

Studies of young deaf children in preschool groups are relatively rare, and most of the research that has been done has concentrated mainly on children at play. Since the pioneering observations by Heider and Heider (e.g. Heider and Heider, 1941) a number of studies have painted similar pictures. Their play is often characterized as rather 'literal' and concrete, repetitive, non-symbolic, largely non-social and disjointed. So, for example, whilst one may observe deaf children involved in imitative role play or making 'appropriate use' of toys such as tea sets, hairdriers and cars, one sees little evidence of symbolic or representational play in which objects and toys are exploited for more fanciful or imaginative uses (as when, for instance, a child uses a broom as a horse or a matchbox as a car). The deaf child's play tends to be more solitary than that of similarly aged hearing preschoolers, and any interactions with peers are less likely to be sustained, involve make-believe, negotiation or playthemes not directly related to objects in the 'here and now'.

In our experience of preschool groups, the organization of activities and choice of materials in special nurseries are similar to those in hearing nurseries or playgroups (see Sylva, Roy and Painter, 1980, for a description of life in preschool groups). Children are usually left largely to their own devices in 'free-play' periods. They are encouraged to involve themselves in art and craft activities and to participate in adult-directed group activities: listening to stories, holding group 'conversations' and so on. Whilst the amount of time spent in such activities varies from classroom to classroom (as it does in hearing groups) a similar diet of materials and opportunities are provided.

In our observations, however, we have noted some important differences in the interactions that take place in hearing and deaf nurseries which have been replicated and extended recently in a larger-scale study (Gross, in preparation). The deaf child, throughout his day in school, has many more encounters with adults than is usually the case in hearing groups. The more generous adult–child ratios in special nurseries, coupled, perhaps, with a teaching philosophy amongst teachers of the deaf that puts more emphasis on the importance of adult–child interaction, probably explain such differences. However, whilst the higher levels of contact in the special groups may be consistent with the goals of teachers, more detailed examination of the duration and 'quality' of these interactions shows that they are not, in our view, compatible with the goal of encouraging the development of communicative competence in deaf children. Although more numerous in free-play activities than they are in hearing preschool groups, adult–child contacts in special nurseries are brief (as they usually are in hearing groups too). The majority of contacts do not last over ninety seconds and involve only two or three 'turns' in an interaction (typically, the teacher says or does something, the child responds, the teacher responds and the contact breaks). Such contacts are best described as 'encounters' not interactions.

Encounters *between* children are also generally brief. Extended periods of cooperative play are relatively rare and, in Gross' observations, show little increase over time. In other words, the child who is rising five years is not involved in many more sustained bouts of cooperative play than he was at the age of three. In our earlier observations (which, unlike Gross', were not longitudinal but involved different children at various ages) we found a dramatic increase in the frequency and duration of child–child interactions at around six years of age. This is, of course, the time when opportunities for child–child interactions in the classroom are inhibited by changes in school timetable. More about this later.

In addition to our studies of deaf children in nursery schools, we have also been involved in detailed analyses of interactions between hearing pre-schoolers and adults in playgroups and nurseries (Wood, McMahon and Cranstoun, 1980). Some of the conclusions we drew from our observations in that research are relevant to our considerations of special nurseries. Broadly speaking, many of the relatively brief encounters between adults and children in 'free-play' sessions are managerial in intent, although this is not true of all classrooms. When one records what teachers are saying to children, the focus of the interaction is often to do with activities like putting on aprons to paint, access to equipment, toileting, ensuring fair turns for all and preventing hostility from breaking out. When adults do become involved in children's play or constructive activities and attempt to help or to converse with them, the interactions often become adult dominated and revolve around ques-tion–answer exchanges. We pay a great deal of attention to the issue of questioning children in the next two chapters. For the moment, the point we wish to underline is that, despite advantageous adult–child ratios in special nurseries and notwithstanding the much higher frequency of adult–child encounters, the opportunities for sustained, genuinely cooperative interac-tions between teacher and child are not often exploited. Although there are some important and informative differences from classroom to classroom there is considerable scope for improvement if the goal of the teacher is to promote productive interactions with the deaf child. We return to more specific suggestions about how such opportunities might be seized later in the chapter.

When we were working in hearing nurseries, one response we met to our emphasis on teachers and their interactions with children was an ideological one. There is a strong tradition in British nursery schools favouring non-directed, free-play for children and a view of the preschool child's needs that largely 'prohibits' adult involvement. Although we agree that preschool hearing children enjoy and benefit from interactions with each other and learn through self-directed activity, we also believe that adults have an important role to play in developing the child's communicative and intellectual abilities. Though this is not a relevant forum to debate this complex issue, we raise it to illustrate the ideological constraints that underline any attempt to 'evaluate' educational provision. Our theoretical framework leads to a strong emphasis on the central importance of adult–child interactions in promoting develop-ment. Consequently, we strongly challenge the view that any young deaf child who is manifestly incapable of achieving productive, sustained interactions with his peers can benefit from a 'non-interventionist' approach, for specific reasons that we turn to below. At the same time, however, we are not advocating that teachers adopt a didactic role or try formally to *teach* children language or concepts. The role of the adult in fostering the social, emotional, intellectual and communicative competence of preschool children is a far more subtle, demanding and skillful affair than either the 'laissez-faire' or 'didactic' philosophies imply.

The teachers of the deaf with whom we have worked do seem to share our view that they should play a vital role in helping children to learn and communicate. Indeed, every classroom we have observed used group 'conversation' sessions and many also encouraged one-to-one interactions between teachers and children. So it could be argued that free-play should be relatively 'free' from adult interaction because other activities on the timetable are dedicated to such goals. However, for reasons that we now identify, we question the wisdom and validity of this view. Crudely, we feel that many of the group sessions and one-to-one encounters that take place with young deaf children do *not* meet their communicative or social needs.

CONTINGENT CONTROL OF LEARNING AND COMMUNICATION

In the last chapter, we introduced the concept of 'contingency' to characterize adult responses to infant activities that are likely to foster the development of self-efficacy, understanding and communication in babies. It is a concept that we will use frequently throughout this book and one that we think is central to the facilitation of independence and learning at all stages of development. When we began our work with preschool deaf children, the issue of if and how hearing adults could achieve contingent interactions with deaf children was, and still is, one of our major interests. Since we had already undertaken a whole series of experiments with hearing preschoolers in which we had described and evaluated attempts by parents and other adults to teach them, we decided to undertake similar studies with preschool deaf children. The specific task involved was a pyramid to be built up from 21 square blocks, which fitted together via pegs and holes into five layers of four blocks each (the twenty-first finishing off the top of the pyramid—see Figure 3.1). This task is a very difficult one for preschool children. Eight-year-olds find it far from trivial when they are asked to build it alone with the aid of pictures or filmed instructions (Murphy and Wood, 1982) and three-year-olds can only master it if they are taught well (Wood, Wood and Middleton, 1978).

The first question we asked was whether preschool deaf children aged three to five years could be taught the task at all. In our previous work, we found that adults use frequent verbal instructions with young hearing children, so we were not confident that the twelve very deaf children we worked with, all of whom had severe or profound losses and little or no expressive speech, could be taught how to do the task. Although our experiment involves a rather arbitrary problem, the question it addresses—'Can we *teach* pre-verbal deaf children?'—is a very general one that tests our confidence in the young, pre-verbal deaf child's ability to learn from instruction. It is relevant to the issue of 'expectations' of deaf children. It also provided us with a way of investigating the teaching process that could be related directly to similar

Figure 3.1 The pyramid task

studies of hearing children. Thus, we were able to gain some insights into the effects of deafness on teacher behaviour and explore the impact of the handicap on teaching–learning processes. We ourselves learned a great deal from the experience, not least from the reactions of the teachers who took part, as we shall see.

We asked teachers of nursery-aged children to teach individual children how to do the task (having first shown the teachers how to do it!) and emphasized that we wanted them to teach in any way that *they* felt would help the child to understand. When they had completed the task with the child, the blocks were taken apart again and the child was asked to put them back together with no additional help. The whole process was videotaped for later analysis. Our analyses relate the teaching process in the first stage to the child's successes and failures when he or she attempts the task alone. To make sense of these analyses, however, we need to say a little about our methods for describing and evaluating teacher behaviour.

Table 3.1 Levels of intervention in the pyramid task

LEVEL 1	General verbal encouragement
LEVEL 2	Specific verbal information
LEVEL 3	Assists selection
LEVEL 4	Prepares material
LEVEL 5	Demonstrates

In Table 3.1, we present the outline coding system for the analysis of teacher instruction. Note, as you read down the list, how the categories of instruction become more specific, informative and controlling. If the teacher says, for example, 'Now you have a go' (Level 1), she provides the child with no specific guidance as to what he should do nor how he should go about it. If she says 'Get four big ones' (Level 2), she provides an explicit goal verbally but does not help the child to 'unpack' the instruction, as she does if she points to or helps to select blocks that are implicated in the word 'big', for instance. If she actually chooses material for the child (Level 3), then she solves the problem of selecting what blocks to work with next and the child is left with the more constrained task of deciding what to do with them. Orienting the blocks (Level 4) ready for pushing together obviously solves many more problems! If the teacher demonstrates an operation (Level 5), she takes total responsibility for and control over the particular phase of the task in question. In addition to coding each teacher instruction into one of these categories, we also note whether the ensuing responses by the child are successful or not.

How, then, do we turn this analysis of teacher–learner interactions into a 'measure' of effective teaching? Well, how would you, reader, define effective teaching in such a situation? We define it according to two rules. If, following an instruction, a child does *not* succeed, then he should be given more help, or increased control *immediately*. For example, if a specific verbal instruction fails, the appropriate next move is to indicate the relevant blocks to the child or help him by selecting them. Alternatively, if the child *succeeds* in following an instruction, only general encouragement should be given until he encounters a problem that he cannot solve. At this point the teacher should increase help/control until he is again successful, when she again relinquishes control, and so on. By following these two rules, we argue, the teacher maximizes the chances that a child will be confronting problems at the appropriate level of difficulty. Increasing help when he is struggling gives him a more manageable problem. Stepping back when he has shown some degree of success implicitly demands more of him. This is what we mean, in this context, by 'contingency'. The teacher's instructions should always be contingent upon the momentary successes and failures of the child, thus serving to avoid demanding too much or too little of him, neither over- nor underestimating, overwhelming nor boring him.

We have tested the notion of contingency in a number of different experiments involving parents, teachers and adults unfamiliar with the child-learner, and always found the same result. Children who are taught contingently learn much more about the task than children who are not.

When we observed interactions between teachers of the deaf and their children in this situation we found, as with hearing children, that some of the preschoolers did well after instruction, managing to assemble the pyramid alone, whilst others seemed to have learned practically nothing and managed to do little more than fit pegs into holes as if at random. However, when we employed our usual measure of teaching efficiency we found, for the first time, that it did *not* predict how well children did alone after instruction. Why? We thought it unlikely in the extreme that the more successful children could have figured out how to do the task for themselves since, as we have already said, eight-year-old hearing children find the task difficult even when they have pictures to help them. Teaching must, then, have taken place, but it was evident that our analysis was not revealing *how* it took place. How were the successful teachers getting the message across to their children?

VERBAL AND NON-VERBAL COMMUNICATION OF INSTRUCTIONS

From our inspections of the videotapes it was clear to us that the twelve deaf children who took part in this study were generally more difficult to be 'contingent upon' than most hearing children (about 180 in all) in our previous studies. We considered the possibility that the difficulties presented by some children might be so great that, however well they were being taught, they learned little. If so, this might obscure any clear effects of teaching. Three children in particular showed very different 'styles' of responding to teaching and these styles were a reflection of their different capacities in handling the problem of divided attention.

One child, call him Peter, was 'engaged' in his attentions to the teacher but almost to the exclusion of attention to the task. At one point, for example, the teacher asked him to 'Find four big ones'. His eyes never left her face as he moved his hands around on the floor even, at one point, feeling *behind* his body to locate blocks. Despite being one of the least deaf children (75 dB) he was the most 'teacher bound' in his attention. The teacher managed to overcome the problem he posed by looking away from him after giving instructions to look at something else—at which point he paid attention to the blocks and performed quite well. He was reasonably successful, though extremely reluctant, when he was asked to do the task alone.

Another child, Paul, was 'task bound' and his eyes almost never left the blocks. He was very deaf (102 dB) and showed signs of hyperactivity. He worked furiously with the blocks but to no avail. He never looked for instruction and, at one point, the teacher tried in desperation to get into his field of attention by squirming her head along the floor into his field of view. Given this child's seemingly non-existent knowledge of the process of communication it seemed impossible that, even with the best will in the world, the teacher could achieve a contingent interaction with him. All the teachers who knew this child told us that he was a most difficult child to engage in any interaction.

Our third case study, Stephen, was also very deaf but, unlike his two peers, showed tremendous skill in 'incorporating' the teacher into his activities and exploiting her help. Although he had little intelligible speech at the time, it was quite clear that he was learning from the teacher in this situation. In the early stages of instruction, he would look to the teacher, almost invariably having completed a successful operation, as if 'inviting' her to comment. Similarly, if he got into difficulties he would look to the teacher for help. He provided clear and interpretable openings for confirmation or instruction, into which his teacher could offer congratulations or give further suggestions. His ability to distribute his attention between task and teacher made it possible for the teacher to establish a turn-taking structure in their interaction. Stephen met her more than half-way. After instruction, he managed to complete the task on his own and took visible pleasure and pride in doing so.

Around the same time as our experiment took place, we observed these three children, amongst others, in the classroom for a total of six hours each. What we had observed in the experimental situation was reflected in these observations. Peter, for example, spent almost all his time watching the teacher, even when she was on the other side of the room working with other children. Stephen, on the other hand, occupied himself quite well when the teacher was not attending to him, but, unlike Paul, he almost always responded to her proximity by attending to her and providing opportunities for interaction.

These very different levels of 'teachability' in young deaf children illustrate the interplay between educational 'readiness', the problem of divided attention and the difficulties facing the teachers of some young and very deaf children. As yet, however, our analyses have told us nothing about the nature of the teaching process. Should we conclude that the processes of effective instruction in similar task circumstances are very different for deaf and hearing children?

We were entertaining this possibility when we 'de-briefed' the teachers about the results of the experiment. As part of this process, we produced an edited film showing episodes of each child's session which we called 'the social contract'. This was designed to illustrate the problems of divided attention and its impact on the communication process. Around this time, Margaret Tait (who eventually became one of the research team, completed a doctorate and is joint author of this chapter) made a major criticism of our analyses. Having read a preliminary account of the experiment incorporating the coding system outlined in Table 3.1 she was convinced that we had failed to come to grips with the essential nature of her interactions with children. Specifically, she was critical of our notion of 'general verbal prompts' and 'specific verbal instructions' because she felt that they ignored what she was *doing* when she talked to children. She was conscious of the fact that she gave postural, facial and other non-verbal cues to children to help get her message across when talking to them.

In response to her criticisms, we retreated back to our ivory tower and decided how we might test out her intuitions. The solution was obvious (but took some time to figure out nonetheless). We reexamined the video-recordings with the sound switched off! Immediately we did so (and our response was immediate) we were made aware of a wealth of non-verbal communication that, in our attention to speech, we had overlooked. Accompanying our so-called 'verbal' instructions were non-verbal cues and action sequences that were often readily interpretable to us. Let us provide just two examples to illustrate some aspects of the processes involved.

Stephen has just selected four blocks and is attempting to put them together. He has matched them for size but is attempting to assemble two pieces that will not fit together because he has the wrong combination of pegs and holes. What he needs to know is that he must reject one of the pieces (that has a peg on it) in favour of another that contains a hole. He realizes that he has a problem and looks at the teacher. She says: 'You don't want two pegs. You need one with a hole.'—a 'specific verbal instruction' giving information about 'connectives'. However, whilst she says this, she selects two other pieces of matched size that also have the 'wrong' connecting pieces. She holds these and Stephen looks at her hands whilst she 'taps' the two pegs together. He returns to her face and she smiles and shakes her head. This non-verbal 'display' takes place in the same instructional 'turn' as the verbal prompt but we, in our original analysis, had not noticed the non-verbal component that served to draw the child's attention to the crucial features that he had overlooked. He went on to assemble the four pieces with no further problems and then 'generalized' the experience to another four.

A second example shows how *not* to do it. A child has just selected two blocks but they are not matched for size. The teacher takes the smaller of the two from the child and holds it beside her face. The child points to himself, perhaps intending to communicate the fact that the block belongs to him. Certainly, there was no evidence that he understood the teacher's intended message. The teacher said: 'This is not right. It's too small. You need a big one.' However, when we viewed this instruction without sound, all we saw, ignoring lip-patterns, were several shakes of the head which we might interpret as 'This block—no.' Because there was nothing to compare the block to, the critical feature being discussed—'size'—received no non-verbal definition.

When we reanalysed all the teaching episodes without sound and classified the non-verbal instructions in terms of a revised coding system that paid attention to such phenomena, we found that the children who received the most contingent instructions *non-verbally* were usually the ones who learned more of the task. Therefore, the feature of teacher communication that facilitated mutual understanding and learning—contingent responses to children's signs of success and failure—was essentially the same for deaf and hearing children.

To explore the question of non-verbal communication further, we decided to reanalyse a sample of our original recordings of preschool hearing children being taught by their mothers (Wood, 1980). These, too, were analysed without sound and when we examined them we found similar (though less obvious and more fleeting) examples of non-verbal equivalents of verbal instructions to those used with the deaf. The non-verbal contingency measure was also strongly related to how much the hearing children learned. Indeed, the relationship between non-verbal contingency and learning outcomes was much stronger for the hearing than the deaf sessions. More important, however, were marked differences in the relationships between our *verbal* and *non-verbal* measures. In the teaching sessions with hearing children these were very closely related. In short, a mother who was contingent on the verbal measure was also contingent on the purely non-verbal one. The opposite was true of the deaf sessions—the teacher most contingent non-verbally was least so on the verbal measure. Why should the relationships between verbal and non-verbal aspects of teaching be so very different for deaf and hearing groups? The answers, for there are several reasons, are subtle but important. One reason has already been hinted at above. The separation of verbal and non-verbal control is a symptom of the problem of divided attention facing the child and a consequence of counter-productive responses such as taking material out of its task context to 'talk' about it. When a hearing child faces such problems the adult (mother, teacher or whoever) typically marks her doubt with sceptical 'Hmm's', 'Well's' or explicit comments like 'I don't think that looks right'. If the child is not looking at her, the adult will often point to the problem and perhaps elaborate, saying something like: 'This one is bigger than that. You need two the same size.' Not only can the child hear the explicit verbal instruction but he may also be helped to *understand what is said* by what the adult *does*. Indeed, we have argued that such non-verbal support for verbal instructions illustrates how the task-specific meanings of what is said are transmitted to the child (Wood, 1980). If the hearing child looks up to the adult, verbal instructions are accompanied by slight nods of the head or eye movements which 'point' to the things being referred to. Contrast this with what happened above with a deaf child. By taking the offending block out of its task context, the child was robbed of any *non-verbal* support for understanding the teacher's instruction. He was doubly handicapped in comparison with the hearing child both by not understanding what was said and having no non-verbal cues to support what was being communicated. Another study that we have undertaken showed that hearing children who are taught this task purely verbally with little or no non-verbal support find it extremely difficult (Wood, Wood and Middleton, 1978). Ironically, deaf children are more likely than hearing children to be robbed of such non-verbal communication because of the strategies teachers use to try to overcome the problem of divided attention.

In summary, then, when one simply looks at what teachers *say* to young deaf children, one may obtain a false impression of what is actually being communicated, not simply because the child does not hear or understand what is said but also because the non-verbal cues and signals that the teacher provides may be impoverished, non-contingent and even misleading. Deaf children can be taught quite difficult practical tasks but, like hearing children, need contingent instruction. However, the fact that the child has to divide his attention between teacher and task creates problems for him that are often reflected in the actions of the teacher. However, some teachers are able to bring off successful interactions with children and they do so by making what they *do* contingent upon the child's level of understanding.

We have already acknowledged that the teaching situation we have been considering is artificial and 'unnatural'. However, it provided us with opportunities to explore the impact of what we think is a general communication and learning problem facing the deaf child and to demonstrate that this problem generates a range of teaching strategies, some of which are counter-productive. It also illustrates how hard it is to maintain a teaching role with young deaf preschoolers and draws our attention to the central importance of considering the interplay between verbal and non-verbal aspects of communication.

We turn now to a far more elaborate, 'naturalistic' and telling line of research that arose as an indirect consequence of the experiment we have just outlined. We have already mentioned that Dr. Tait became a member of the research group after we had worked in her classroom for some time. We encouraged her to become involved in research of her own, hoping that she would explore further our mutual interest in the non-verbal foundations of verbal understanding and help to show how these might profitably influence classroom practice. We were somewhat surprised when she decided to do research into the role of singing (no, the 'n' and 'g' are not misplaced) in the education of preschool deaf children. The topic of singing and its roles is the subject of a booklet written by her (Tait, 1985). Fortunately, we were able to persuade her to compare her singing sessions with 'conversations' to see how far the comparisons of children in the two situations might lead to insights into the structure and development of turn-taking in communication (since singing is a form of vocal communication that people do together rather than in turns). In the event, two goals were achieved. One was a detailed analysis of the stages involved in the transition from pre-verbal to verbal communication in preschool deaf children. The other was a demonstration of the multifaceted and multipurposed value of singing for deaf children. We turn now to the stages of development.

FROM PRE-VERBAL TO VERBAL COMMUNICATION IN DEAF NURSERY SCHOOL CHILDREN

In the following quotation, Conrad (1979, p. 4) speculates about the communicative competence of very deaf children when they enter school around the age of five years or so. Note that he predicts not only that such children are likely to be unaware of speech sounds *per se*, but that they will also lack fundamental knowledge about the fact that verbal communication (and its non-verbal accompaniments such as lip movements) exists at all.

(Deaf) children ... reach school age with little concept of the existence of verbal language and effectively no experience of it. They may not even know that the facial gestures centred on the mouth that they see around them are accompanied by sounds and are used to effect communication. ... They will not know that objects have names: that they can be referred to when they are not immediately present.

There has, in fact, been very little systematic, detailed research into the early educational experiences of deaf children and none, as far as we are aware, that has looked analytically at the child's 'knowledge' of communication. We present evidence relevant to this question here. Over a period of four years, every severely/profoundly deaf child entering a special nursery for the deaf in an inner city area was included in a longitudinal study of communicative development. Only children with losses in excess of 80 dB (the mean hearing loss of the group was 104 dB) and suffering from no known additional handicap were included. Twelve children fell into this category and these were filmed at three-monthly intervals beginning after they had been in school for a minimum of three months and ending when they moved on to primary school. Children were filmed with their teacher in one-to-one 'conversation' and singing sessions and also in group sessions. These sessions were not 'special' (apart from filming) but a part of the school routine. The teacher herself (Tait) arranged the video cameras which were in place most of the time. Children seemed to 'forget' the presence of a camera.

Although some of the children were speaking in single words on entry to school most were not. They understood little or nothing of what was said to them. Thus, they were at different stages of linguistic development on entry, despite being a reasonably homogeneous group in terms of hearing loss. Not all the children were at the 'earliest' stage outlined below on entry. Individual differences in levels of communicative competence will be explored later.

What changes occurred in children's communicative competence during the twelve to eighteen months spent in the nursery and what inferences can we draw from these about their progress?

Stages of Pre-Verbal Development

Before we consider some of the results of the study we need to say a little about our use of the term 'stage'. We are *not* using it to denote very clear-cut, independent periods in children's progress. The stages often 'overlap' in the sense that children are at certain stages in some familiar situations while they are less competent in other, less familiar or more problematic ones. Another term we use interchangeably with 'stage' is the notion of 'developmental tasks'. Children have to overcome certain 'tasks' before they begin to talk. But these tasks often recur when they find themselves in new relationships with unfamiliar people in unusual circumstances. If, as we did in the block study above, we place the children into new, difficult and initially stressful circumstances it is likely that they would seem less competent than they do in more familiar and predictable settings. The notion of developmental tasks and their recurrence when new demands are made on children are important ones that we explore later.

Stages 1 and 2: 'Disengaged' and 'Engaged'

Consider the two transcripts given below. (Note that the child's contributions, nonexistent at this stage, are in these transcripts presented in parallel to, and below, the teacher's utterances.) The transcripts involve the same teacher and child and were recorded twelve weeks apart. Initially, we represent only what was said. On this criterion, the child seems to have made no progress.

DISENGAGED:

{ Teacher   Look, let's go—round and round and round and round . . .
{ Child

{ Teacher   One . . . Two . . . tickle! Do it again? . . . Round and round . . .
{ Child

The teacher does all the talking and the child makes no vocalization—a typical state of affairs with this child (age at the time 31 months; hearing loss 110 dB). Now the second transcript.

ENGAGED:

{ T.   You tell it, say 'come on!' . . . I'm going to say 'Come on
{ C.

T. train' ... Ch-ch-ch-ch-ch ... Oo! ... Ow! It bumped me! ... It's
C.

T. going to come and ... bump you!
C.

Again the child remains silent, but the nature of his involvement in the interaction has, in fact, changed considerably and positively. To detect such changes, however, we have to attend not only to what the child says (or, in this case, does not say) but also where and what he looks at. We now reproduce the transcripts with two important additions: representations of where both the teacher and child are looking throughout the interaction. The straight line placed above the speech of either partner remains high when they are looking *at* their partner, and drops down towards the verbal transcription when they look away, when what they *are* looking at is written in above the line.

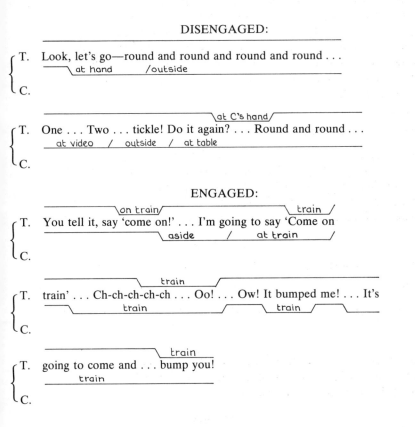

DISENGAGED:

T. Look, let's go—round and round and round and round ...
　　　　　at hand　　　　/outside
C.

T. One ... Two ... tickle! Do it again? ... Round and round ...
　　at video　/　outside　/　at table
C.

ENGAGED:

T. You tell it, say 'come on!' ... I'm going to say 'Come on
　　　　on train　　　　　　　train
　　　　　　aside　/　at train
C.

T. train' ... Ch-ch-ch-ch-ch ... Oo! ... Ow! It bumped me! ... It's
　　　train　　　　　　train　　　train
C.

T. going to come and ... bump you!
　　train
C.

Now the differences between the two episodes should be clearer. In the first transcript, the child's attention patterns are totally unpredictable. He shows no evidence of knowing that communication is taking place, though whether this is due to the fact that he is still new to and overawed by school we cannot say. However, twelve weeks later, his pattern of attention shows a marked change. He is now almost totally 'engaged', either looking at the teacher or at the object/event being talked about.

In both sessions, the teacher's attention is directed almost totally at the child. This may seem a banal point, but it is crucial to the role she is playing in helping him to discover the act of communication. In an early session, for example, when the child was almost totally disengaged, she managed for one brief period to gain his attention and foster interaction. He was given a drum which he duly banged. The teacher feigned alarm and he looked at her. She held a 'shocked' face for a time and he watched her as he banged the drum again. She responded in turn with another expression of shock. The episode only lasted a few seconds, but was made possible by the fact that the teacher was observing the child closely and prepared to respond immediately and contingently to any action that he made which might conceivably be endowed with communicative intent. In the first weeks, she seldom succeeded in earning his attention, however. Her actions and reactions usually went unnoticed by the child because he was not often looking at her at the right time. Eventually, however, he did begin to watch her reactions and started to play a more intentional role in their interactions.

Note what the child is *not* doing on the second transcript. Although he is distributing his attention between object and person, there is little or no correspondence between where he looks and the *structure* of the interaction. For instance, he is almost as likely to look away whilst the teacher is in mid-utterance as he is when she ends her verbal 'turn'. In short, his pattern of attention displays no real appreciation of the 'turn-taking' character of verbal interaction. He is also silent. As we shall see, these two features of interaction are not unrelated.

Stage 3: 'Structured Attention'

In the next episode filmed 24 weeks later we see two new and important features emerging in the interaction. The teacher and child are looking at a picture of an umbrella in a book, and this is used as a springboard into conversation. We will talk about the content of conversation a little later. For the moment note how the child's attention is beginning to reflect the structure of the discourse. When the child looks away during a speaking turn (as he does when the umbrella is *mentioned*) it is usually a fleeting affair and is relevant to the focus of discourse. As we saw in the last chapter, here too we find the emergence of a 'triangle of reference' in the child's distribution of attention. Also note how, when the teacher mentions the fact that they were unable to go outside when it was raining, the child looks outside, again reflecting knowledge of the topic of discourse.

STRUCTURED ATTENTION:

T. My big umbrella, and it's blue.   And . . . Yes,
   _____ \at picture/ ___ \ at picture /
C.   boo   boo

T. it's blue. And you held the umbrella because it
C.   boo

T. was raining.   Yes, it was raining. We couldn't
C.   rai

T. go out, could we?   No. Is it raining
   _____ \outside/
C.   uh (shakes head)

T. today? \outside/   No, it's stopped.
   \ outside /
   \ outside /
C.   'op.

The teacher is still subtly orchestrating turn-taking. Although she usually finishes what she has to say (not, for example, stopping talking when the child glances away) she is prepared to postpone or relinquish what she has to say when she perceives that the child has something to contribute. For instance, when the child twice says 'boo', meaning blue, whilst looking at the book (and hence not hearing the start of the teacher's next contribution 'And . . .') the teacher pauses, acknowledges the child's contribution and only then proceeds to complete her own turn. Establishing such contingent patterns of responding to children is not easy and requires a good deal of vigilance and self-control on the teacher's part.

Another important achievement is illustrated in the transcript. When children show clear signs of having discovered the turn-taking structure of discourse and are able to distribute their attention between the speaker and object of communication, they usually begin to vocalize. There was, in fact, a close relationship across the group of children between the development of visual attention to the teacher during speaking, on the one hand, and the emergence of child vocalizations, on the other. Only when attention to the teacher was sustained and that to objects of discourse relatively fleeting did vocal communication emerge on the scene. The integrated character of attention, turn-taking and vocalizations are compatible with Bruner's theory of the relationships between pre-verbal and verbal communication which we mentioned in the last chapter. Their interrelation is also evidence that, however unintelligible the child's speech may seem to an outside observer, they are beginning to make vocal acts of communication.

Stage 4: 'Structured Vocalization'

Because the development of structured attention and vocalization are closely related and, in some children, almost seemed to emerge simultaneously on the recordings, it is questionable whether we should talk about structured visual attention and vocalization as distinct stages. However, we decided we had to discriminate between them because some children displayed relatively skillful patterns of attention for some time before beginning to vocalize with any frequency. Although vocalizations to the teacher occurred only very infrequently *before* attention patterns were structured with any child (i.e. achieving reciprocal attention was a precursor to the emergence of vocal communication), the 'delay' between structured attention and predictable vocalization varied considerably from child to child.

On the first recordings, made when children had been in the nursery for a relatively short time, they only made a vocal response to the teacher (i.e. took a vocal 'turn' in an interaction) about 25 per cent of the time on average. On their final recordings, as they approached the end of their time in the nursery, this had risen to 75 per cent. Looking at individual children: the most vocal on the early recordings responded to a little over half the opportunities to talk; by the last session, one child missed not a single opening in ten minutes of conversation. At the other end of the scale, five children were virtually silent on the first recordings; by the end, no child was totally silent but two still took up less than half the opportunities given to speak.

Although these children are a relatively homogeneous group in terms of age and hearing loss, there were marked differences both in the readiness with which they developed through the pre-verbal stages of interaction and in the time-lag between the development of structured attention and frequent vocalization.

Stage 5: 'Conversational Partnership'

Children who had clearly reached Stage 5 by the end of the study had become real partners in conversation. Some of what they said was genuinely informative (i.e. not obvious from the context), sometimes amusing, on occasion a blatant lie and occasionally a little rude!

The stage of conversational partnership is marked by the emergence of several quite different achievements, and is best viewed not simply as the product of one development or discovery by the child but as an opening up of many new lines of progress. It is, so to speak, more of a 'watershed' than a single stage. All the achievements that we noted after Stage 4 did not emerge 'immediately' for each child; hence we use the term stage very loosely in this case.

One of the most important things that emerges in Stage 5 is an increase in the *range* of discourse functions or types of linguistic 'move' used by children. For example, one of the most verbal children (aged four years eight months and with a hearing loss of 108 dB in one ear and 104 dB in the other) began to 'disagree with' and 'correct' the teacher, as in the following excerpt. They are discussing a visit that the child (Hazel) had made to a friend's house (Susie). (Note: in these and all subsequent transcripts, the teacher's and the child's utterances are presented in turn.)

CONVERSATIONAL PARTNERSHIP:

C.   Sarah house, Sarah. (shaking her head)
T.   Wasn't Sarah there?
C.   (shakes her head)
T.   Wasn't she? Was Pamela there?
C.   I SUSIE friend (i.e. not Pamela's nor Sarah's who are Susie's sisters).
T.   I know, you're Susie's friend. Was Pamela there?
C.   Pamela school.

Here the child is holding her own in the conversation. When the teacher asks 'Was Pamela there?' (really wanting to know!) the child does not answer immediately, being determined not to let the teacher get away with what she (the child) sees as a misunderstanding. First, then, the child 'refuses' to answer a question because she thinks that the teacher has the wrong end of the conversational stick. Later, she goes beyond the force of the teacher's two-choice question 'Was Pamela there?', not simply saying 'no', a minimal response, but to say where she *was* at the time. Thus, the child starts to argue, attempts to correct what she perceives as a misunderstanding, negotiates rather than 'slavishly' answering questions and elaborates beyond the force of specific questions to provide relevant information. Her role in conversation has become one of initiator and not simply one of acting as a respondent which was a characteristic of earlier interactions. She also shows clear signs of taking conversational initiative. As we will show in the next two chapters, not only is such a display of initiative rare in deaf children, it is also very dependent upon the style and technique of the teacher.

Other signs of autonomy and confidence emerge. These include 'interrupting' the teacher. Whereas, in Stages 1 to 3, any vocalization by the child during a teacher's speaking turn was usually uninterpretable and appeared to have no communicative significance (e.g. a 'spontaneous' noise), the content of interruptions by children in Stage 5 show that they are contributing to the *theme* of conversation. They may lack finesse but they are following the topic.

T.   You'll be a very big girl . . . .
C.   (interrupting) Same as Sarah.
T.   Pardon?
C.   Sarah four.

T. Oh, Sarah's four, of course she is, yes. And YOU'RE four, and when you're five . . . .
C. (interrupting) Susie six.
T. Pardon?

Note not only how the child is volunteering information and showing initiative but also how, characteristically, the teacher is prepared to 'relinquish' the control of the topic, again responding contingently to any offering by the child. Had she not done so, as we will see in the next chapter, it is highly likely that the child would have shut up.

Hazel could speak about 40 to 50 words when she entered school and on the first recording took up about 40 per cent of the openings to speak offered by the teacher. Therefore she was already into Stages 3/4 early in her school life. By the end of the period of study she was taking up about 90 per cent of all openings, but, most important of all, the *range* of her responses changed dramatically from largely *responsive* utterances solicited by the teacher to the use of such autonomous conversational acts as just illustrated.

One final example is taken from the final recording of another child, Andrew, who also became a true partner in conversation before leaving the nursery. Somewhat older than Hazel when he left (five years six months) he had a better-ear loss of 102 dB when he entered school at four years, but this had 'risen' to a 96 dB loss by the time he moved on. Like Hazel, his conversation shows signs of autonomy, initiative and loquacity. He interrupts, elaborates on his answers to questions and volunteers information spontaneously. Here, too, the teacher usually responds contingently to his acts of communication to enable him to hold the conversational floor as much as possible. In the first extract, the child introduces new topics of conversation:

T. Look at what the train's doing now.
C. He happy.
T. Yes, he's happy because he's in the tunnel.

At this point, Andrew starts to point out features of the picture being studied which he thinks are being overlooked. Meanwhile the teacher is saying . . .

T. Look at her (i.e. the train) now! All clean! Isn't she?
C. It my blue.
T. That's you with your blue jumper, yes.

In the next episode he goes beyond the force of teacher questions, interrupting the teacher to continue his answer:

T. What does Lynnette do?
C. She Lynnette cry.
T. She does . . . .
C. (interrupting) She poorly, Lynnette.

Not all children achieved this degree of loquacity, independence and initiative by the time they left the nursery. Two children were still in Stage 3. However, the growth of signs of autonomy in terms of introducing topics, elaborating on answers, interrupting and so on increased across the group as a whole and were clearly evident in the final recordings of several children even though, like Hazel and Andrew, they were very deaf children.

Another feature of Stage 5 conversations, as much to do with the skills of the teacher as with the capacities of the child, is an increase in the volume of 'decontextualized' talk. By this we mean talk about objects, happenings, experiences and the like which are not present in the immediate context. Once deaf children start to play an active role in conversation, there is no reason to suppose that they can only take part in the 'concrete' interactions commonly encountered in schools. Restricted verbal demands such as 'Show me your shoes', 'What colour is your dress?', 'What's this called?', 'Give me the car' are not only likely to inhibit the young child from talking but they also offer little scope for truly *functional* and interesting communication. In our studies of hearing playgroups and nurseries, we found that children in conversation with teachers were likely to be talking about events at home or in the future that had some real *significance* for them. There is no reason to suppose that deaf children would not be similarly motivated about things that matter to *them*. Once children achieve Stage 5, their language begins to catch up with their 'thoughts' and they are 'ready' for genuine conversation. Whilst the teacher may use props or aids (like photographs and toys) to initiate topics there is no reason, once the child has reached this stage of communicative competence, for discourse to remain context bound.

We would like to make one final note about other developments that occur with some children around this time to do with 'auditory awareness'. We have already noted that Andrew's audiogram, like that of several other children, improved with time in the nursery. They were making better use of their hearing in hearing tests and this was reflected in their conversational activities. Some of the children began to look away from the teacher *during* her speaking turns. This was not due to 'regressions' in their stage of development, as they continued to respond appropriately to what she said. We believe that this phenomenon, not found in the less verbally able children, was due to the developing use of residual hearing to monitor voices. Although very deaf, it seems likely that these children were able to hear elements of intonation and stress, together, perhaps, with the start and end of vocal turns. We developed a simple test in which the teacher stood behind the children and asked them to give her familiar objects whose names they already knew. These were included in a set of objects placed on a table in front of the child. Although they could not lip-read the teacher, since she was out of sight, the children who were showing signs of auditory awareness in conversation scored well above chance levels of success in picking out named objects. Thus, they were hearing and understanding something of what was being said to them.

Children who were not showing signs of awareness in conversation could not do this task.

We cannot prove what we are about to say next! We believe the development of auditory awareness, when it occurs, arises in discourse and conversation. One important facet of the teacher's behaviour has yet to be underlined. When we examined the structure of her conversational style on the first and last recordings we found some marked similarities. She was offering very similar numbers of openings to both the non-speaking children and those in Stage 5. She asked similar numbers of questions and so on. Even when children were disengaged, she tended to act 'as though' they were participating in discourse. Studies of interactions between mothers and pre-verbal hearing babies have produced similar findings. Adults orchestrate interactions with babies to produce 'pseudo-conversations'—responding contingently and swiftly to movements and vocalizations from the baby to make it appear that the infant is taking turns in the interaction (Elias, 1983). Thus, both the teacher and parents act out a form of 'self-fulfilling prophesy'. They provide a predictable conversational framework into which the child is eventually 'recruited' as a partner.

Let us return to the children who displayed some auditory awareness. Our interpretation of this finding is that by maintaining a 'normal' conversational framework for children, even with those in Stage 1, the teacher provided conditions for their *discovery* of pre-verbal, verbal and acoustic aspects of language. Some children, even with losses as great as 110 dB, showed signs of making *sense* of what they were hearing and of exploiting it in conversation. It is almost certain that they could not function without lip-reading and other non-verbal cues, but there is evidence that they also exploit their hearing too. We suggest that this is because their experience in discourse with the teacher made what they could hear *meaningful* and significant, because it was encapsulated within interpretable social interactions.

EDUCATIONAL IMPLICATIONS

In both the experimental teaching study and longitudinal observations, we have drawn attention to the importance of sustained, projectful, contingent interactions with young deaf children. We have also argued that we must attend to pre-verbal and non-verbal aspects of what both teacher and child are doing to understand if, when and how communication takes place and to evaluate the value of any activity or interaction. Similarly, if we want to chart any progress made by the child in the early stages of linguistic development, a consideration of his patterns of attention and their relationships to the communicative activities of his partner in interaction are a *sine qua non* for success.

At the beginning of this chapter we commented on the concrete, literal and rather asocial nature of children's encounters with their deaf peers. This is fully understandable and predictable when, as is usually the case with preschool deaf children, they are in Stages 1 to 3 (and, perhaps, 4 too). How can we expect deaf children to maintain extended and productive play themes with each other when they are unable to participate knowingly in interactions with communicatively skilled adults? We also said that we found very dramatic increases in child–child interactions around the age of six years. This is also predictable for those children who achieve Stages 4/5. Once they can develop the ability to construct mutual understanding in communication, they begin to hold sustained interactions with each other. Consequently, we would argue that any benefits likely to accrue to children from peer group interaction and play are most likely to occur not at the age of three or four years but around the age of five years onwards. Paradoxically, however, when children are five or six, they have usually been moved on to more 'formal' educational experiences. In our view, full-time formal teaching, be it concerned with reading, counting or whatever, is only likely to prove beneficial to children who have consolidated their ability to play an active, sustained and competent role in discourse.

Young deaf children can, however, be recruited into 'projectful', constructive interactions in which they help to *do* something with an adult, as we argued in our teaching experiment. The joint completion of projects not only helps to develop and sustain the deaf child's abilities to concentrate, plan and solve problems but also provides a context for reciprocal, contingent interactions. The most important single resource in the classroom is, for us, the teacher and other adults. But are such human resources always used effectively? We think not.

As we also said early on in the chapter, most adult interactions with deaf children in the classroom either take place in groups or tend to be fleeting in character. Group sessions have a role to play but *not* in developing conversational competence in young children. Young hearing children in preschool groups, though relatively fluent verbally and skilled in one-to-one conversations, face considerable problems in 'group talk'. Playing a productive role as listener and contributor in a group demands a range of conversational skills (Wood, McMahon and Cranstoun, 1980) that many preschool hearing children may only just be working on.

Groups have an important part to play in activities like singing (Tait, 1984) and story telling, in which either all participants contribute *in parallel* rather than in turns or all attend together to a drama or story. In the next two chapters, we will look at some of the problems and pitfalls associated with teacher-led group 'conversation' sessions. To our mind, these pitfalls are far too deep for the young deaf child to be exposed to.

The young deaf child needs a great deal of *individual* attention and the kind of experiences in which the more mature create an enabling and contingent framework to facilitate the development of interaction and communication. At the end of the last chapter, we explored some of the problems facing hearing adults when they attempt to communicate with the pre-verbal deaf child. These arise in part, we argued, because of the greater maturity of deaf children (in comparison with hearing infants) when they are in the pre-verbal stages of development. We now examine other factors that are likely to contribute to these problems and inhibit the chances of producing a contingent learning environment for the child. The three most important of these are the fact that children are in groups, with teachers and in school.

Language development in hearing children is a remarkably robust process that is difficult to stop (though it can be impeded). The most formative stages take place in the family and community, in interactions with individuals who are centrally important to the children and who know them intimately. Children are not expected to acquire their mother tongue in groups; nor are they sent to a special room or building to do so. What they communicate about tends to be of immediate significance and personal concern. Topics of talk are not decided by external authority but arise 'naturally' as a consequence of living with other people.

Work with preschool hearing children (Tizard and Hughes, 1984) has shown that interactions between teachers and hearing nursery school children are generally less frequent, less sustained, more context dependent and less linguistically and intellectually challenging than those between mothers and the same children. To a large extent, such differences are likely to be attributable to the less favourable adult–child ratios in school. They also hinge, perhaps, on the philosophy of many educators who hold that an important (if not the most important) experience provided in preschool settings is not adult–child contact but the opportunities provided for peer group interaction. Another important factor stems from the differential nature of the adult–child relationship and the context within which that relationship usually functions. The sustained, verbally elaborated and intellectually stimulating conversations that preschool children have at home revolve around happenings and social practices in their everyday lives and are stimulated by events in their environment. Wells (1979), in a study of language in the home, reports that the three-year-old child *initiates* around three-quarters of the verbal interactions with his parents. *He* chooses what is going to be talked and thought about. In the study by Tizard and Hughes, conversations about such things as 'why Mummy gives money to the window cleaner' led to extended and interesting discussions between mother and child about why people need money, what they do with it, what would happen if they did not have any and so on. The child's induction into monetarism and the language of economics arise out of such seemingly banal events.

In school, such discussions are relatively rare, although, interestingly, we have found that the most common topics for extended conversations between the teacher and hearing preschooler often centre on such familiar ingredients as happenings in the child's life at home (Wood, McMahon and Cranstoun, 1980).

Schools did not evolve as institutions designed to foster language development in children. The education of very young children in groups, looked after by specially trained adults, is still a relatively new experiment in social engineering, conceived a little more than half a century ago. Only recently has the preschool environment been afforded an explicit role in developing children's language and it should, perhaps, come as no surprise to find that it has yet to prove that it can fulfil such a role. Schools were never designed to foster the intimate, two-way, reciprocal and contingent interactions that seem best suited to the development of communication between adults and children. Indeed, they are more likely to achieve the opposite state of affairs by demanding that children 'pay attention' and pursue goals established by adults. The child in such a situation must often make *his* thinking contingent upon that of the adult (Wood, in press), and not the other way round. The history of schools, their curricula and architecture; the teaching role and training of teachers are still rooted in a technology given over to the socialization and education of children which is based on the adult leading and the child learning how to follow. If a child is to be helped to learn how to communicate in a school setting, then many of the implicit and explicit assumptions underlying the historical definition of the teaching role must be questioned and changed. Truly productive use of teacher time with young deaf children will look suspiciously like fun and games to an outside observer. However, the teacher and the more acute observer will realize what tremendous levels of skill and constraint underlie the achievement of any such enjoyable, reciprocal, contingent interactions.

CHAPTER 4

Talking to Deaf Children

In the last chapter, we outlined and discussed several stages in the transition from pre-verbal to verbal communication and found, by Stage 5, that children were starting to participate in conversation. We now move on to study the structure and function of conversations involving children aged from five to fourteen years. In fact, we devote three chapters to the topic. Here, we look at 'pragmatic' aspects of teacher–child conversation, examining both the ways in which teachers manage conversations and children's reactions to different conversational 'moves' and management styles. Analyses and comparisons of the conversational styles of different teachers, talking to both deaf and hearing children, enabled us to identify those features of teacher talk that promote extended verbal responses from children and influence the amount of verbal initiative children display. These results led us to mount a series of classroom intervention studies in which we asked teachers to change their styles of talking to children in order to test our predictions about the effects of different teaching styles on children's receptive and expressive language. These studies, which were designed to help identify strategies for achieving sustained and productive conversations with children, are outlined in the next chapter. In Chapter 8, we look in detail at grammatical features of teachers' talk to children and compare these to aspects of deaf children's understanding of English grammar (which are the subject of Chapter 7). We ask, in Chapter 8, if teachers regularly expose children to examples of language use that might help foster language learning.

CONVERSATION

Why do we allot so much space and time to the study of conversation? What roles does it play in the development of communicative competence that warrant so much emphasis in a book on deaf children?

Conversation is one type of discourse. We do not, for example, regard verbal interactions concerned with naming objects or describing them as conversation. Whilst discovering the names of things and how to analyse and label their properties is obviously an important element of language development, particularly in the early stages, it is not, by our definition, conversation. When talk serves to relate and *share* past experiences, plans for the future, life in other times and places or what might come to be, then it becomes a conversation.

Basically, then, we see conversation as talk about things that are *not* in the immediate environment of the talkers and listeners. Though conversations may, and with young children often do, arise out of talk about objects, pictures or happenings in the shared context, it is when talk moves on to memories, plans, experiences and aspirations that a conversation is born.

Conversation is also to be distinguished from debate and teaching. In 'teaching' discourse, there is an implicit assumption that the 'direction' for and evaluation of what is said will be largely the responsibility of the person in control. In conversation, roles are more 'equal', and what is considered worth saying can be decided by any participant.

Conversation is also different from debate, where there should be a 'tacit contract' accepted by all participants to 'keep their minds' on a specific topic, to 'edit' what they say in order to minimize the introduction of irrelevancies and so forth. In conversation, there are fewer constraints on the topics that may be introduced, and what is considered 'legitimate' talk is less clearly circumscribed. This is not to say, however, that conversations are 'unstructured' or take place without (unspoken or tacit) rules. Indeed, productive conversation is constrained by several types of rules. These include a need to 'take turns', for speakers to make what they say coherent and accessible to their listeners, for listeners to provide indications that what is being said is being *listened* to and to respond to speaker contributions in some intelligible fashion.

Participation in conversation demands knowledge, not only in the construction of intelligible, coherent and linguistically acceptable utterances but also of interpersonal and social skills. Interpersonal understanding is needed to appreciate how one's ideas must be organized and disciplined in such a way that they can be understood. Some things have to be explained before others can be grasped, and so on. It is also necessary for a speaker to monitor his listener's non-verbal and verbal responses for signs of comprehension or misunderstanding, interest and boredom. Thus, participation in conversation provides one route towards an understanding of other people and how they think. A skilled conversationalist cannot be too 'egocentric', taking account only of his own perspective and needs. He must 'put himself in his listener's shoes' and see the situation from their perspective.

To adults who have become practised in the art of conversation, it is easy to overlook the intellectual and interpersonal demands facing the less mature and inexperienced. Preschool hearing children, for instance, find it no easy matter to make themselves understood when they talk to relative strangers, particularly when they are talking in *groups*. Some demands they face are linguistic (e.g. using pronouns appropriately) but others concern the need to relate experiences in a sequence that is comprehensible to their listeners (Wood, McMahon and Cranstoun, 1980). When young children remember a vivid experience or scene they tend to put into words the more salient events that are, naturally, uppermost in their minds. They often do so before 'setting the scene' so that what they say is not easily understood. Coherent conversation contains elements of 'story telling' which help to form a bridge to literacy.

Conversations between more than two people also demand 'group talk' skills which take time to develop. A child will often answer a question addressed to someone else, for example, or interrupt another's speaking turn when a dramatic idea comes to him. Self-restraint, monitoring and listening to others, knowing when to 'come in' and when to wait demand a degree of knowledge and self-control that does not 'come naturally' but demands experience. In short, conversation provides opportunities to discover many aspects of what is involved in 'becoming a person'. It demands not only a grasp of grammatical procedures but knowledge of when, in what manner and to whom one speaks. Many social practices, rules of etiquette and intellectual abilities are implicit in conversation, participation in which promises many developmental rewards.

Becoming a *partner* in conversation demands not only an ability to contribute and question but also the capacity to listen and interpret. For very deaf children, as we saw in Chapter 3, it also demands knowing how and when to maintain one's visual attention on a speaker. Even in two-person interactions where talk is largely about things in the immediate situation and takes place in partnership with a 'skilled' adult, knowing when and how to take turns in talk presents difficult problems for deaf children. When talk moves on to conversation, any support from environmental and non-verbal cues to meaning is reduced (though, as we shall see, they do not disappear entirely). The would-be conversationalist faces a number of intellectual, social and linguistic demands. He must learn what is involved in keeping two or more minds 'focused' on a common topic and discover how to play a part in constructing a shared 'realm of discourse' that 'grows' as conversation develops. He has to learn how to refer, relate and integrate each new item of information to what has already been constructed. This, in turn, involves skills at a number of levels.

At one level, for example, the child must understand how words like pronouns serve to refer back or forward to past and future utterances. He has to realize how words like 'that' can be used to make reference to a previous idea, as in 'I don't agree with that'. He may have to draw implications from what has been said to make sense of a new question or contribution. To take a simple example, if someone has said 'We went to town yesterday (meaning the speaker and another person), we did some shopping and had tea in a little cafe. What did you do?', the 'timeframe' being referred to in the question is established, implicitly, in an earlier contribution. Many, more subtle aspects of meaning rest on the ability of a listener to interpret a new conversational move in the light of what has been said or implied in previous ones. In addition to paying attention and understanding individual utterances, then, a child has to learn how to participate in the construction of realms of discourse.

Most conversations between teachers and children, as we shall see, are characterized by question–answer exchanges, in which almost all the questions come from the teacher and nearly all the answers from the children. One 'advantage' of such a strategy is that it enables a teacher to establish and develop the 'theme' of conversation and to maintain coherence in discourse. Her questions produce the 'framework' into which a child's responses fit and can be related back to preceding utterances. Questions may establish who or what is being talked about (the topic) and then proceed to establish things about that topic, such as who did what, when, to whom and with what consequences. From the child's point of view, this means that he can often participate in the interaction by attending to each question from the teacher as a single event, taking little or no responsibility for the task of constructing a *coherent* conversation.

Questions, by their nature, are 'demanding' and 'controlling'. They have to be listened to and thought about. Indeed, as we shall see in Chapter 7, a child's ability to answer teachers' Wh-type questions (who, what, where, when, why and how) with appropriate and relatively long replies is usually a good index of his linguistic competence, including his reading ability. Eventually, however, if the child is to become a truly 'equal partner' in conversation, he must learn how to attend to longer *sequences* of utterances and discover how to integrate and remember them. He also has to work out how to use this accumulated information as a basis for questions or contributions of his own that are sensibly and coherently related to what has gone before in the conversation. Constant cycles of question–answer exchanges, we will try to demonstrate, are unlikely to provide conditions for a child to learn how to develop such skills and abilities in creating realms of discourse.

Conversation provides a means to many developmental ends, but it is not, educationally speaking, the terminus of communicative or linguistic competence. Being able to attend to and understand teacher 'monologues' when she is 'transmitting' knowledge and information creates a new set of demands which, we believe, grow out of and extend abilities founded in conversation. When the child is exposed to long sequences of monologue (or 'autonomous' speech; Romaine, 1984) he has to maintain his attention on the speaker for relatively long periods of talk and try to recreate from sequences of utterances the structure of the 'story' being told. The information is not 'broken up' into a series of relatively simple utterances, as can happen in conversational turn-taking. Nor are there as many opportunities for mutual checks of understanding that the two-way exchanges in conversation permit. If the child is to be capable of transmitting information himself, he must develop the capacity to present ideas not simply in grammatically well-formed, single utterances but in a sequence that honours his listener's needs. He must learn how to avoid ambiguity in what he says. He must be capable of analysing a task or topic being talked about and of framing series of utterances in such a way that he reflects and articulates the structure of the task. He must also monitor his listener for indices of comprehension and signs of perplexity or misunderstanding. Faced with a breakdown in mutual understanding he may have to supplement, paraphrase or explain what he has already tried to say in order to reinstate it.

Becoming skilled as a listener to, and presenter of, such 'autonomous' discourse is clearly a difficult task. Indeed, it is one that many hearing adolescents (and, we suspect, adults too) have not mastered (Brown et al. 1984). Our own classroom recordings contain very few examples of deaf children even attempting to produce 'autonomous' discourse.

But isn't it unrealistic to expect such achievements of deaf children who have so much difficulty in understanding the 'basics' of language? At present given the general character of school discourse involving deaf children, it probably is unrealistic to expect children to develop into 'autonomous' communicators. Indeed, as we shall see, many deaf children do not become effective partners in conversation. However, we will be arguing that not all the reasons for this state of affairs reside 'in' the child. Rather, the way in which teachers 'manage' conversations often provides little or no opportunity for children to learn how to become good conversationalists. Whether this is a direct and inevitable consequence of children's deafness remains to be seen. We suspect, however, that it is not. It is possible to create productive, coherent conversations with deaf children, but doing so demands hard work and considerable skill on the part of teachers.

However, we move on too fast. For the moment, we hope that this short essay on the importance of conversation explains and justifies our emphasis on its value, not simply as a way of encouraging a child to watch, listen and verbalize but also as a source of opportunities for him to learn many other features of what it is to become a competent listener, talker and thinker. But, as we shall see, it is hard to hold productive conversations with deaf children. There are, in fact, several sources of difficulty considered in this and other chapters. Some of these, such as speech that is often difficult to understand, arise 'directly' out of the handicap. In the last chapter, for example, we presented a few extracts of conversation between a teacher and her children. In one sense, such transcripts give a misleading impression of what is taking place. Having the luxury of a videotaped recording enables researchers to go over a child's utterances many times, to consult colleagues or the child's teacher to help work out what is being said as fully as possible. This, of course, is far removed from the 'reality' of the interaction and a poor reflection of the teacher's task. He or she must respond in 'real time' to what a child says, with only 'mental' re-runs of the interaction for consultation. Though their knowledge of the child should provide them with a better basis for understanding than an 'outsider' (without a recording), they may still find it difficult to comprehend what is said to them.

However, there are two other dimensions of difficulty involved in the promotion of productive and 'egalitarian' conversations with deaf children that have different sources and are, potentially, under the teacher's control. One arises as an 'indirect' product of comprehension problems. Generally speaking, in everyday conversations, when we do not understand what is said to us, we are likely to take *control* of the interaction to seek clarification, a paraphrase or explication of what has been said. Deaf children offer many opportunities for such episodes of 'listener control', which, exploited in excess, can have marked negative effects on a child's desire to communicate.

A second cause of problems stems from the nature of teaching and schooling itself. When we have considered our formal analysis of conversation between teachers and children in the classroom, we will argue that they resemble not conversations so much as 'pedagogical' discourse. Such 'teaching talk' is not designed to fulfil the roles played by conversation. It does not encourage talk from children nor facilitate their attempts to discover how to make themselves comprehensible. If anything, it achieves the reverse, as we now see.

TEACHING AND CONVERSING

When we began to consider ways of trying to describe the structure of conversation, we were working both in schools for deaf children and in nursery schools and playgroups for preschool hearing children. Most of the teachers in both these settings considered talking to and with children an important part of their work. The general climate of opinion in early childhood education includes a stress on the importance of communication and language in helping children to become competent individuals and effective learners. In recent years, research into the processes of language development and the study of individual differences in children's acquisition and use of language have reached almost epidemic proportions (e.g. Tough, 1977; Blank, Rose and Berlin, 1978; Wells, 1979; Tizard and Hughes, 1984; to mention a few). The emphasis on the importance of language in education is commonplace in many countries.

Working in twenty-four different preschool settings for hearing children and in six schools for the deaf over a period of a year or so, we were struck both by marked similarities between and revealing differences across the various settings. In some classrooms, children seemed relatively active, loquacious and responsive. They talked a good deal, asked questions and contributed to discussions. In others, children seemed rather reticient and unforthcoming. They spoke little and often in short phrases or even monosyllables. Although the deaf children were considerably older than the hearing preschoolers, they were, as one might expect, far less verbal. Most of the deaf children in our studies had better-ear hearing losses of at least 80 dB, but we were still struck by marked variations in the language of deaf children with similar hearing losses but in different classrooms. We accepted that, in part, such variations might reflect 'intrinsic' differences between children but we also felt that they were influenced by the ways in which teachers communi cated with them.

The basic idea behind the system we eventually devised to try to capture the essence of differences and similarities across settings suggested itself when one of us was listening to a conversation between a teacher and a group of children from outside the room in which they were talking. Although not able to see the participants, he was struck by the fact that each time the teacher talked, there was little doubt about what sort of response the children were likely to make next. Anticipating how the teacher would react after the children had spoken was a little more uncertain, but still usually possible. The structure of the interaction was so predictable, we felt, because the teacher's different verbal 'moves' towards the children exerted so much *control* over the children's part in 'conversation'. Unless they were to ignore her or strike up a topic of conversation outside the one she had initiated—which, as we shall see, children are unlikely to do—then their pattern of response was usually preordained.

This led us to the notion of 'control' in conversation. Subsequently, we were to find (as one usually does in research) that several other students of classroom discourse had come up with very similar ideas (e.g. French and MacLure, 1981; Dillon, 1982). In fact, a number of quite detailed and elaborate systems exist for describing and analysing such discourse. Our aim, however, unlike that of most researchers in this area, was not to develop a comprehensive linguistically sophisticated analysis of discourse. Rather, we wanted to find a way of describing the interactions that would explain why children seemed more or less active and loquacious in different interactions. The main categories of the system we developed are shown in Table 4.1. Other, less common, categories, together with 'response' categories (i.e. used to code what the children did in response to their teachers' moves), are provided in full in the Appendix.

Table 4.1 Levels of control in conversation

Level of control	Examples
1. Enforced repetitions	Say 'I have one at home'.
2. Two-choice questions	Did you have a good time? Did you go with Jim or Pete?
3. Wh-type questions	What happened? Where did she go? Tell me about Sunday.
4. Personal contributions, comments, statements	That must have been awful! They call it a zoom lens. I love the lakes in Scotland.
5. Phatics	Oh lovely! Super! I see. Hmm.

Imagine overhearing a conversation in which each of these different 'moves' occurs in turn. The person or people *listening* to these moves are being cooperative and compliant, attempting to meet the 'force' of any requirements laid down by the current speaker. After the first, most controlling move (an enforced repetition) the response of our compliant listener is fully predetermined. Within the limits of his receptive and expressive language ability, what he says next is fixed. The next move, 'two-choice' questions, specify at least one word that the listener should respond with. Should he so wish, he can meet the 'force' of this move with a single word (which, as we shall see, children usually do). The next category, 'Wh-type questions' also dictates the nature of the ensuing response. If the listener understands the move, the 'semantic focus' of his response (e.g. where—a place or location; when—a time; who—a person) is predetermined. The current speaker still controls the direction and content of the conversation.

After a 'contribution', however, the listener is left with a number of alternatives. He may simply acknowledge what is said in some way (perhaps saying nothing, just nodding), he might ask a question, continue with the theme or make a contribution of his own. The speaker tacitly offers the listener a chance to take over the control and direction of the subsequent conversation. The final category, 'phatics', includes any move that fills a 'turn' without offering any substance or direction to the *content* of discourse (unless, of course, it involves irony, sarcasm or some other 'hidden' meaning). It may signify reception and comprehension of what is said, but leaves the next person to speak with control of the conversational floor. If *he* then responds with a phatic move of his own, this may be a signal that the current focus or topic of conversation has been exhausted (e.g. John: 'I went home then'; Mary: 'Oh really'; John: 'Yup'), in which case someone may introduce another topic, ask a question or they may part conversational company.

In the study of children in nursery schools and playgroups already mentioned, we found that preschool hearing children acted like compliant listeners most of the time when in conversation with the teacher. In other words, they responded to different types of teacher moves in the manner described above. This led us to some very specific measures of child *initiative* in conversation that we need to consider before discussing conversations with deaf children. What does it mean to be 'active and forthcoming' in a conversation? Well, for us, it involves the following ingredients. An active participant will sometimes take *control* of the interaction by asking questions. They will also *contribute* readily and frequently after a contribution or phatic from their partner. They will extend the theme being discussed and occasionally introduce new topics of talk. Finally, when they answer questions addressed to them (particularly two-choice ones) they will characteristically not do so with a single word but will go on to add further information (i.e. make a 'double move' by answering *and* contributing to the topic).

As we shall see, whether or not children are active and forthcoming in conversation depends mainly upon the ways in which teachers manage the interaction. What about older deaf children? Do they understand enough of what is going on even to be 'compliant' listeners?

When we first posed this question (see Wood *et al.*, 1982) we were unsure of the answer we would get. For deaf children to be influenced by different structures of conversation in the same way as hearing children, they must be 'aware' of the basic force of different moves from the teacher. They would have to be able to discriminate questions from statements and phatics, for example. They would also have to be able and ready to follow the less controlling moves from the teacher (e.g. contributions) by saying something themselves. If they do not readily take initiative in conversation (by saying something or asking questions after a contribution or phatic) then it may be the case that teachers have to *question* deaf children in order to encourage them to play any role in conversation at all. We were not sure what the answer would be.

In fact, we found that deaf children's patterns of response to different teacher 'moves' were almost identical to those of hearing children. They did, as one might expect, tend to confuse different 'Wh-questions' more frequently (but see Chapter 5); otherwise, their reactions were the same (see the Appendix).

Having established this level of competence in children, the next question we asked was whether different teaching styles had similar effects on the two groups of children. Did the way the teacher controlled the conversation influence how much children said and how much initiative they showed? It did.

TEACHER POWER, CHILD INITIATIVE AND LOQUACITY

The conversations that we analysed were based on audiotaped (hearing groups) and videotaped (deaf groups) interactions between teachers and children in their own classrooms. With the deaf groups, these involved 'news sessions' in which teacher and children talked about what had happened, say, over the weekend at home. Having transcribed the interactions 'verbatim' we classified teachers' and children's turns into the move categories shown in Table 4.1. These also include a number of 'hybrid' moves such as 'tag contributions' ('Strawberries are delicious, aren't they?') that are not illustrated in the table, but which are available in the Appendix.

The principle measure of teaching style, 'teacher power', is simply the proportion of each teacher's conversational turns that end in a controlling move (questions and enforced or requested repetitions). A second measure (more sensitive with preschool children) also includes all 'tag' moves since young children tend to respond to these as two-choice questions. A teacher who asks questions and/or demands repetitions frequently at the expense of other moves, thus gains a 'high power ratio'; one who asks relatively few gains a low ratio.

We measure children's responses in two main ways. One is an assessment of how much 'initiative' they show, the other estimates how talkative or loquacious they are. The most general measure of child initiative takes into account a number of features of children's talk. How often does a child not only answer a question but go on to elaborate on his answer by making an unsolicited contribution? How likely is he to make a contribution after the teacher has made either a contribution or has simply acknowledged what he has already said? How often does he ask questions?

Broadly speaking, what we find is that this measure of child initiative in conversation is related *negatively* to teacher power. Consequently, teachers who ask the most questions are least likely to gain elaborated answers from children, receive spontaneous contributions or be asked questions by them. Thus, children become increasingly passive as a teacher increases control via questioning.

Another way of examining the child's involvement in the conversation is to see how *much* he says. On average the deaf children in our studies produce responses of between two and three words (or word-like sounds) in length, but how much they say in each turn depends upon what the teacher has just said. They offer short responses after two-choice questions (they only elaborate on them about 25 per cent of the time) and relatively long ones after contributions and phatics. Thus, where controlling moves are frequent, children's turns tend to be short. In sessions where teacher control starts high and stays high, children become progressively less likely to show any signs of verbal initiative and their responses become more and more terse. Thus, if we want to understand why some children say a lot in conversation and others very little, it is not enough to consider the relative talkativeness or linguistic competence of the children. What they say and how much they talk is also strongly influenced by the conversational style of the teacher.

Teaching style also influences the readiness with which children talk to (and hence listen to) each other. When teacher control is high, children seldom address comments or questions to their peers. However, when control is low, children are more likely not only to contribute comments and questions to the teacher but also to converse with each other. Thus, the whole 'tenor' of a group conversation is directly influenced by very specific, and very simple, features of teaching style. In the next chapter, we offer some examples of conversations to illustrate these general principles.

If a teacher wants to get children talking and showing initiative, she should be prepared not only to question but also to inform, react, listen and acknowledge. Rather than directing the conversation by questions or trying to use it to 'improve' language (we shall return to this topic later) she needs to become more contingent upon and accepting of what the children have to offer. Of course, if the goal is *not* to get children showing initiative and being talkative, all this goes by the board.

WHY ARE CHILDREN SO PREDICTABLE AND WHY DO TEACHERS ASK SO MANY QUESTIONS?

Children are not generally noted for their predictability. Teachers, however, are widely known for their questions! Usually, when we compare the activities of children of very different ages we find marked differences in their performances. Yet we have found that the way in which children of very different ages and even cultural backgrounds respond both to different types of teacher move and to the overall structure of discourse is remarkably similar (Wood and Wood, 1985). *What* is talked about varies with age, as does the complexity of the language involved (see Chapter 8). But the 'typical' style of teacher talk is independent of the age of the children involved, and the ways in which children respond to each type of teacher move and different styles of management are remarkably consistent. Why? What implications might the answer to this question have for attempts to help deaf children acquire language?

One of the main reasons why patterns of children's responses to teachers are so similar despite great variations in age and background stems from the fact that, unlike teachers, they seldom make more than one 'move' in *their* conversational turn. Teachers typically utter a string of moves ('Oh, that's nice. I went to town on Saturday and I bought some new shoes. You've got some new shoes, haven't you? Did Mummy buy them for you?'; and so on). Young children, deaf or hearing, rarely act in this way. Thus, if you ask children questions you tend to get what you ask for but little else. They can be encouraged to show more initiative and make multiple moves, but only if questions and enforced repetitions are relatively infrequent. The reason why multiple moves are so important is that they almost invariably introduce new topics, themes or information into the conversation. They are a source of 'surprise' and offer new conversational avenues for exploration. Responses to teacher questions, on the other hand, usually help to fill conversational 'gaps' that she has opened up. They can, of course, lead to new lines of thought but tend not to do so if they are used in excess (as we see in the next chapter).

Although children are 'compliant listeners' (most of the time) it is important to realize that compliance, as we have defined it, is *not* the only option available to competent listeners if they have equal 'status' in the conversation.

For example, in everyday conversations questions are sometimes followed not by answers but further questions. Imagine, for instance, a woman asking her colleague 'What time are you going into town?' and getting back 'Why do you want to know?', then responding 'Oh, I need a lift', to which is said 'Well, I could get away by noon'. When a question meets another question as a response it is usually a signal that 'negotiation' is taking place and that there is a degree of equality in the interaction. If answering a question may lead to important and potentially undesirable implications, we usually ask another before answering it to ascertain what the implications are.

The 'rules of engagement' in classroom conversations are relatively specific and limited. Children seldom 'negotiate' with teachers through questioning because of the asymmetry of power in their interactions. Classroom discourse does *not* normally provide children with opportunities to explore a range of functions served by language, for these often rest upon particular personal relationships. Indeed, we suggest that children's responses to classroom discourse are deeply rooted in and symptomatic of their *relationships* with the teacher and in the relative 'status' of teacher and pupil.

WHY DO TEACHERS ASK SO MANY QUESTIONS?

The teaching role, as we argued in Chapter 3, has not 'evolved' to foster language development in young children (though it may fulfil other linguistic roles, as we shall see in Chapter 8). Where a teacher is faced with the task of imparting knowledge to large groups of children, then one obligation may be to keep 'all minds trained on the same topic'. Attempts to gain and maintain control over the attention and thought of a group of learners is often sought through questioning. Indeed, the use of questions and the expectation of appropriate responses to them are 'sanctioned', even demanded, by the school as an institution. Reflect, for example, on the very different relationships and interactions that tend to take place between teachers and children *outside* school, on visits, after-school activities and the like. The 'ground rules' that underlie discourse in the classroom are 'special' and often different in a variety of ways from those implicated in most everyday interactions (e.g. French and MacLure, 1981; Mercer and Edwards, 1981). She who can question and remain more or less confident of getting a predictable answer is in absolute conversational control. She is likely to be teaching, interrogating, interviewing, cross-examining or in some other position of authority over the other participants in dialogue. She is also the one upon whom all others must be contingent.

We have already mentioned that when hearing children are learning to converse at home it is usually they themselves who initiate the majority of verbal interactions (Wells, 1979). What is talked about is usually contingent on their interests and uncertainties. In school, however, it is more often the case that children must take the lead from and be contingent upon the plans and direction of the teacher. This 'reversal of contingency' offers one explanation for children's apparent 'compliance' in classroom discourse.

There is currently a good deal of debate about the importance, quality and functions of question–answer exchanges in classrooms (Dillon, 1982). One obvious function served by questions is to keep the minds of a group of learners (hopefully!) focused on the same theme or topic. Whether or not such questions 'work' in facilitating subject learning is not at issue here, but their role in facilitating language development is. When a teacher is confronted with thirty or forty pupils, it is perhaps inevitable that he or she must lead classroom discourse through questions. Although the teachers in our studies were *not* confronted with thirty children, but between two and eight, they still seemed to manage the interactions *as though* they were working with large groups and attempting to 'teach'. We question the wisdom and value of this 'carryover' of the teaching register *if and when* the aim is to help children benefit from conversation.

But, one might argue, preschool hearing and deaf school children do not or cannot sustain interactions with their teacher if they are not managed through questions. Perhaps they lack the linguistic or intellectual resources to do otherwise. For example, do children know how to respond to questions with a question of their own? Are they insensitive to the fact that answering questions may have implications for what may happen subsequently and, in consequence, do not think before they answer? Perhaps they are not intellectually advanced enough to participate in such complex interactions, and that is why they are so predictable in discourse.

We suspect this is not the reason for their compliance. We have already said that our system of analysis has been used with much older pupils, and others have used it to study tutorial discussions involving university undergraduates and found similar results (Kingdon, 1983). The 'typical' structure of teaching behaviour was remarkably similar across these different contexts, as were the patterns of pupil responses to them. Unless we are to assume that university undergraduates also have limited linguistic resources, cannot anticipate and so on, we must conclude that the relationships between teaching style and pupil response are most likely to be a product of the asymmetry of power implicit in the teacher/learner relationship. Whether young hearing children and deaf children also have a wider range of linguistic resources is a question explored in the next chapter. It is worth noting, however, that Wells (1983), discussing our speculations about hearing preschoolers, argues that their performance in contexts other than school (when they are embedded in different personal relationships) displays a much wider and less 'predictable' range of verbal responses.

So far, we have emphasized the basic similarities between the structure of conversations involving deaf and hearing children and the commonalities across teacher behaviour in the two contexts. But there are some important differences too. These, however, revolve more around the *purposes* being pursued by teachers rather than in the exercise of control.

WHAT DO TEACHERS USE CONVERSATIONS FOR?

Teachers of the deaf are specially trained to 'teach' or, perhaps, to help children acquire language. How do they go about it? There are, as we shall see, 'special' features of teachers' talk to deaf children. Are these a product of training and of benefit to the child? Perhaps the differences we found are a reflection of the expertise of teachers. Before addressing these possibilities, however, we need to outline the system of analysis we developed to explore such differences (Table 4.2).

REPAIR

When a conversation is running smoothly, most of the 'moves' made by speakers will be 'substantive' in nature. Contributions that develop, elaborate and extend the topic at hand and questions designed to solicit additional

Table 4.2 The function of teacher moves

Function	Examples
Substantive	Tell me about your dog. What happened on Sunday? I like cream cakes too.
Continuity	How nice. Oh, it was red, was it? Yes, I see.
Repair	What? Say that again. Say 'I have one at home'. I don't understand. Wait a minute, you saw a *train* or a *crane*?

information or elaboration will usually be serving *substantive* functions. The listener, meanwhile, when not asking questions designed to solicit substantive replies, will be showing non-verbal and verbal signs of attention, interest and understanding. If the conversationalists are achieving mutual understanding, then 'continuity' moves from the current listener (such as 'Mm', 'Really!', 'You don't say!') help to fulfil their obligations to the speaker.

Occasionally, however, the listener may be distracted or not hear what is said. Or they may lose the thread of conversation, finding something ambiguous or unintelligible. In these circumstances, the listener is likely to take control over the interaction, 'stop' the flow of conversation and try to 'repair' the breakdown in understanding. They may do so by asking a repairing question 'Did you just say . . . ?', a repairing phatic (e.g. 'Sorry?', 'Pardon?') or with a repairing contribution such as 'I didn't understand what you just said'.

When we examined a series of conversations involving teachers with hearing children and compared these to classroom conversations with deaf children, we found, perhaps unsurprisingly, that the greatest difference between the two lay in the incidence of 'repair'. However, less obviously, most of the repairing moves came from the teachers and not the children. Although the children involved were very deaf, they seldom exercised 'listener control'. Either they were understanding everything said to them (which seems rather doubtful) or they did not know 'how' to seek clarification; or the asymmetry of power between teachers and children inhibited them from taking control of the conversation. We shall show in the next chapter that the latter explanation is most likely to be the case.

A lot of teacher repair with deaf children arose as a 'natural' product of unintelligible speech and ambiguous utterances from children. Other repair sequences, however, seemed more 'pedagogically' inspired to help children 'improve' their utterances. When we measured the frequency of repair by teachers of hearing children in classroom talk, we found between 6 and 10 per cent of their moves were repairing. Although repair of deaf children by their teachers was more frequent, we found very marked individual differences between teachers of the deaf in their readiness to repair children's utterances. For example, one teacher with a group of children with average hearing losses of 83 dB displayed 14 per cent repair. Another teacher, whose group had average losses of 87 dB, made 68 per cent repairing moves. Whilst some teachers seized almost every opportunity to clear up ambiguity or to check the meaning of an unintelligible utterance, others did not. Also, some teachers made more frequent demands for 'enforced repetitions' which, by their nature, always go 'backwards' and serve a repairing function.

Enforced repetitions are extremely rare in interactions between hearing children and teachers. They may occur occasionally in play (e.g. the teacher says to a child 'Say goodbye to Uncle Fred for me'), in 'lessons in etiquette' (e.g. 'Say please') or in teaching songs or nursery rhymes. Some teachers of the deaf (though by no means all) use such moves relatively frequently when talking to deaf children. One teacher, in our initial study, employed them in 43 per cent of her turns. For example, one child having said 'Yesday—Mother Day', his teacher responded with 'Say, "Yesterday was Mothers' Day"'. We presume that the purpose or function underlying such tactics is to 'teach language', but syntactically motivated repair is uncommon in the speech addressed to hearing children. As Roger Brown (1977) observes somewhat wryly, we often repair children's meaning but almost never their grammar, yet they grow up to tell lies (violate meaning) but with a capacity to speak in well-formed utterances!

Our notion of 'repair' thus covers two main activities: the deliberate modelling or teaching of 'better English' and also natural reactions to the handicap. In all cases, however, it is a hallmark of repair that it goes 'backwards' into previous conversational territory rather than moving it, or permitting it to move, on.

REPAIR AND DIFFERENT MOVE TYPES

One important feature of the relationship between repair and 'move type' needs to be underlined because it highlights specific problems that many deaf children face. When a listener does not fully understand what a speaker has said or there is some 'mis-match' between what the listener was tacitly expecting and what was said, repair may be achieved *with any move type*.

Herein, we believe, lie many pitfalls in talking to deaf children. Our 'natural' response when we do not understand is to stop the proceedings and repair the break in mutual understanding before proceeding further. Where this is done speedily and effortlessly (on both sides) it prevents the accumulation or perpetuation of ambiguity and misunderstanding. It is also the case, however, as we shall see in the next chapter, that the *way* in which children are repaired influences the development of communicative competence. Deaf children provide so many potential opportunities for misunderstanding that, should we seek continually to clear up, check and disambiguate every ambiguous move from them, we are likely to find ourselves, as some teachers were on our recordings, not so much involved in conversation as embroiled in cross-questioning and cross-checking.

As we indicated above, repair (like other functions) can be achieved in many ways using any type of move (questions, contributions and so forth). In some classrooms we also found that teachers were most likely to repair the deafest children. In so doing, we argue, they were magnifying rather than overcoming the communication problems of these children. Not only does the child have to work out what *type* of move he is facing and strive to understand its force and content (e.g. is it a contribution or a wh-type question?), he must also, more often than his less deaf or hearing peers, work out whether that move is going *back* over previous territory or *forward* into new areas.

In such encounters (which we illustrate in the next chapter) children often appeared bewildered and baffled. They did not seem to know whether or not the teacher was really asking for the *same* thing again; whether she did not hear what he had just said or had misunderstood it; if he himself had misunderstood what was asked on the last occasion; or whether a completely new element had been introduced into the conversation that he had just missed.

Another counter-productive aspect of repair is the way in which it tends to be associated with increased levels of teacher control which, in turn, breed further repair. Some interactions with deaf children are characterized by ever-increasing spirals of control and repair. Although repair can (and we will argue in the next chapter usually *should*) be achieved by contributions ('I don't understand that') or repairing phatics ('Pardon?'), teachers are most likely, once in a repair sequence, to resort to questions. Thus, teacher power increases with the effects we have already outlined above.

CAUSES AND EFFECTS: WHO DOES WHAT TO WHOM?

Teaching styles, which we have described in terms of power and function, are highly correlated with a number of features of children's responsiveness and productivity in conversation. Certain aspects of teaching style, we have argued, stem from implicit or explicit theories about how language should be 'taught'. Others are responses to the *nature* of the handicap and the way in which it is likely to distort the structure of interactions by evoking *natural* but often counter-productive responses from the hearing adult. The fact that teachers vary substantially in the way they control conversations and in their levels of tolerance for ambiguity in children's language suggests that high power and frequent control are not, however, *inevitable* outcomes of conversations with deaf children. But, you might well ask, are teachers different simply because their *children* are different? In our analyses of interactions, we found that the hearing loss, age and intelligence of children did *not* explain differences in the amount of teacher control. But it is still possible that factors located 'in' the child—such as native linguistic ability, natural loquacity or desire for initiative—explain why teachers vary in style. Perhaps they are simply responding to such differences between children?

One way to investigate this possibility is to examine the effects of very different styles of teacher conversation on the *same* children. If the arguments we have been putting forward here have any substance, then it should follow that as teachers decrease control, for example, children should start to show more initiative and become more talkative. We turn to a test of this hypothesis in the next chapter. We also take up the thorny questions—'What is a "good" conversation?' and 'How is it achieved?'.

CHAPTER 5

To Question, or Not to Question . . . ?

Can teachers *change* the way in which they 'normally' talk to deaf children? If so, do their pupils reciprocate in any systematic way to become more or less talkative? In this chapter we look at two studies where teachers did try to change their styles of talking. We examine the effects of different styles on the same children and begin to etch out the 'role' and place of different types of conversational move towards children. 'When is a question fruitful; when is it stultifying?' is one issue we address. Our comments on such issues leads us on to one of our major concerns: what does a 'good' conversation look like?

Another question we explore has already been considered to some extent in Chapter 4. If high teacher control inhibits children from talking when the goal of the teacher is to *encourage* them to talk, why do the majority of teachers ask so many questions? We have already suggested that problems arising from the nature of deaf children's speech and language provide one possible explanation and that the 'teaching role' is another. In this chapter, we will explore other reasons.

CHANGING STYLES OF CONVERSATION

When we were beginning our studies of conversation with deaf children, we outlined our plans for research and the ideas behind them to a conference for teachers of the deaf. We were approached by one of the teachers, Jean Lees, who was already beginning to study her own style of talking to children and exploring ways of modifying that style to explore the effects of change on children's responses. She had already attended a course based on the work of Joan Tough (e.g. Tough, 1977) which focused on aspects of children's language development and the role played by teachers in facilitating it.

Having recorded examples of her classroom conversation, she decided that she was asking too many questions and doing rather a lot of 'checking' of what children said to her. She eventually joined the team and undertook a systematic study in which she modified her style of talking to children in a number of ways, maintaining each style for several weeks and recording and analysing interactions with children en route. Basically, she found that as she questioned children less and made more contributions of her own, children displayed greater initiative in conversation, said more and were much more interesting to listen to.

Lees' (1981) research inspired some confidence that children will respond predictably to changes in teacher style, but she was already more or less convinced that they would do so. Perhaps children sensed her enthusiasm for her own preferred approach and responded accordingly. Was it her style of talk *per se* that was instrumental in bringing about change? Further, was Lees unusual in being *able* to change her style? A second consideration in trying to evaluate what happened as she changed style was the time scale involved. Lees employed different styles over periods of three weeks or so, providing children with ample opportunities to discover the rules of each new linguistic 'game'. How long does it take for children to respond to changes in a teacher's style? As we shall see, it takes a lot less than three weeks.

In parallel with Lees' research, we were beginning to undertake similar studies with both hearing and deaf children. We recruited teachers and illustrated five different 'strategies' of conversation. These were modelled on the five main categories of level of control described in the last chapter. We asked the teachers to try to bring about ten-minute conversations (that we videotaped) in which they biased the interactions towards each different move type in turn. Thus, with each teacher, we recorded *enforced repetition*, *two-choice question* and *Wh-type question* sessions, together with one loaded with *contributions* and a fifth high in *phatics*. These sessions, recorded on different days over a period of about four weeks, were 'sandwiched' between two 'normal' conversations in which the teacher did what came 'naturally', albeit in front of a camera.

We have done this study with a total of five teachers: one with six hearing children (four of whom were learning English as a second language), the remainder with deaf children aged between three and eleven years. The original studies, outlined in Chapter 4, were concerned with deaf children aged six years and upwards, and we will focus in this chapter on sessions recorded by two teachers, Mrs. Smith and Mrs. Jones, both with eleven-year-olds. Each teacher selected two of her most deaf (but otherwise 'normal' children) who had better-ear losses between 92 and 104 dB and WISC-R non-verbal IQs ranging from 81 to 121.

The details of procedure and statistical analyses used in these studies have been presented in detail elsewhere (Wood and Wood, 1983, 1984). We will concentrate here on describing and discussing the main results.

Could the teachers change their style at will? Yes. Although, as one might expect, they varied in the degree to which they managed to bias their language into one move type or another, all showed marked changes in style along the lines requested.

The teachers changed; did the children? They did. Although the sessions analysed were only of ten minutes' duration, children responded quite differently to them. Were the changes along the lines we had predicted? They were. The more control a teacher exerted over the conversation, the less initiative children displayed and the shorter their responses became. When, at the end of the experimental sessions, teachers returned to their 'normal' style, using a level of questioning midway between low and high control sessions, their children 'followed' them, with lower measures of initiative and loquacity than they had displayed in contribution and phatic sessions. The same pattern of results was found with the six hearing preschoolers too.

The main results of these studies reinforce all the various implications drawn from the analyses of teacher power and its effects in the last chapter. Teachers must accept a large measure of responsibility for the way in which children play their part in conversation with them.

In the remainder of this chapter, we move away from discussions of averages and common patterns to look in more detail at the 'texture' of various sessions. We look in some depth at episodes from interactions high in each move type to seek insights into the way in which each linguistic move influences the structure, coherence, intelligibility and productivity of discourse. We try to highlight the pros and cons of various ways of involving children in discourse and speculate about the structure of productive teacher–child conversations.

Session 1: Enforced Repetitions

In their initial and final sessions, where they adopted their normal styles, neither of the teachers demanded many enforced repetitions. They found the strategy *easy* to adopt: Mrs. Smith increased the proportion of these moves tenfold over her initial, normal session figures; Mrs. Jones managed a sixfold increase.

One important result worth underlining is that these children's mean lengths of turn were no longer (overall) in this session than in normal sessions. Research with young hearing children has produced analogous results (e.g. McNeill, 1966). Attempts to encourage children to imitate utterances that are longer and structurally more complex than those produced as part of their spontaneous language usually fail. Although the teachers did manage, on occasion, to 'build up' a relatively long utterance from children, as in the following example, more often than not children's imitations would include a new word or an added inflexion (for instance, adding an '-ing' to a verb), but, at the same time, some other element present in an earlier attempt at the same utterance would 'drop out'. Although we have not used spectrographic analyses or any formal measures of children's voice quality or intelligibility we had no sense that the solicited utterances were any more rhythmic (indeed, if anything, they seemed less so) or more intelligible. Furthermore, we were often unsure, as in the following excerpt, whether or not what the child was asked to repeat was what he had really *meant* to say in the first place.

Mummy is fed up with working—or does she work? (Mrs. Smith)

T.   How's your Mummy?
C2. Ah poorly.
T.   Mummy's poorly? Can you say 'she's poorly'?
C2. She's poorly --- --- --- --- ⟨gestures and waves round⟩ --- --- headache.
T.   She's got a headache.
C2. ?Fed ?up work ⟨?shovelling⟩ --- ?heavy --- work.
T.   Oh dear, she's fed up with working. Can you say that? 'She's fed up with working.'
C2. She (then quietly) ?fed ?up ?with working.
T.   Yes. (to C1) What's the matter with his Mummy?
C1. Fed up of work.
T.   Yes, she's fed up with working. Can you say that?
C1. He, he fed up working.
T.   Not he . . . *she's* fed up with working.
C1. She's fed up.
C2. (interrupting) Doesn't work!
T.   Oh, that's rude. Let him finish.
C1. She =febbe . . . She fed up.
T.   She's fed up . . .
C1. (shadows T) She's fed up.
T.   With working.
C1. She =febbe with working.

Key: ---:   A word-like utterance.
         ?word: Our guess at the word.
         =word: The sound pattern we can hear.
         ⟨gestures⟩:   Angle brackets enclose our description of the child's gestures.

We cannot draw any definitive conclusions on the basis of a few ten-minute sessions about the extent to which long-term 'language lessons' along these lines might facilitate the development of speech. It could be argued that this strategy—which continually stopped these eleven-year-olds in their tracks—might be of more value down the age scale, where children are only just on the point of putting words together. For instance, when Margaret Tait tried out this strategy with a pair of three- to four-year-olds, the children gave every sign of enjoying telling a 'naughty' doll to 'Stop it!' and calling it a 'Naughty girl!', offering two word utterances rather than their usual one. Interestingly enough, however, Tait had 'abused' our instructions by making the enforced repetitions part of a game (which, as we said in Chapter 4, is one of the few contexts in which we found teachers using enforced repetitions with hearing preschoolers).

Nonetheless, in view of the fact that child initiative is always very low in such sessions, we would argue that they have no starring part to play in *conversation*, whatever value they might or might not have in more formal 'speech' sessions or games. As we argued in the last chapter, sustained high control tends to exert an effect over the whole 'tenor' of the interaction so that even children's responses to less controlling moves are affected.

Another problem in these sessions was that children sometimes did not recognize the 'force' behind enforced repetitions. In conversation, particularly with young children, a listener might repeat part or all of what the child has just said in a 'phatic' way (e.g. 'I went to town yesterday'—'Oh, you went to town!'). Such moves, we have argued, signal that the message has been received and understood, and children in these sessions sometimes nodded happily in response to an attempted enforced repetition, not realizing that they were expected to improve on what they had just said!

A dangerous nail on the bath (Mrs. Jones)

T. The nail was sticking out?
C1. ⟨nods⟩
T. Yes, and . . . .
C1. Ow!
T. You stood on it?
C1. ⟨nods⟩
T. Say 'I stood on the nail!'
C1. Yes.
T. 'I stood on the nail.'
C1. (mouthes in unison with T) I stood = ni.
T. No, 'I stood on the nail'.
C1. (in unison with T) I stood on the = ni.
T. 'On the nail'.
C1. On the ---.
T. Yes, and so you didn't come to school.
C1. Daddy ⟨knocks on edge of desk⟩.
T. Ah!
C1. Daddy, alright.
T. 'Daddy knocked it in. Daddy knocked it in.'
C1. Daddy knocked in.
T. 'Knocked it in'.
C1. Knocked it in.
T. And what did he use?
  . . .

(over several turns they establish that a 'hammer' was used, then):
  . . .

T. A hammer, right. So Carol's Dad, right? Saw the nail . . . and he thought, 'Ah, that's dangerous.'
C1. (shadows T, mouthes 'nail') . . . ?danger.
T. Your Daddy saw the nail . . . sticking out . . . .
C1. Nail ⟨disagrees, points to self⟩.
T. 'That's dangerous.' He got out his hammer, right?
C1. Daddy what? Me ⟨points to foot⟩ Me cry . . . .
T. Yes, Daddy said, 'What's the matter?'
C1. ?Said 'What'. (She starts to add what *she* had said.)

T. 'What's the matter?'
C1. Me say ?floor. Where? ⟨seeing it⟩ Ah!
    ⟨getting tools⟩ ?Find (i.e. hammer) ⟨hammers nail in⟩.
    Right ⟨pats hammered-in nail⟩.
T. Right . . .
C1. Mummy ⟨points to foot⟩ right ⟨puts plaster on⟩. Mummy not better.
T. Daddy said, 'What's the matter?'
C1. Daddy?
T. 'What's the matter?'
C1. ?Daddy alright ⟨knocks 'nail'⟩.
T. It's alright, is it, now?
C1. Yes.
T. 'It's alright. It's alright.'
C1. Yes . . . .
T. 'It's alright', you say that!
C1. I alright.
T. 'It's alright.'
C1. ?You're alright.
T. Yes. (to C2) What did her Dad say?
C2. (no response)
T. He said, 'It's alright.'
C2. Alright ⟨nodding to C1⟩.

So, whilst children will usually repeat when requested they are sometimes unsure whether or not they *have* been asked to do so. When repetitions remain frequent, children also tend to stop talking and displaying initiative. Indeed, if the cost of trying to say something is confusion and a probable failure to 'get it right', it seems perfectly understandable that children should want to keep a low conversational profile.

Session 2: Two-Choice Questions

Although the two teachers managed to increase their use of these questions considerably (from 30 to 75 per cent and 9 to 20 per cent) they found these sessions heavy going, as did the children. The children's verbal responses were shorter in this session than in any other. Note, in the following extracts, how children's early loquacity gives way to monosyllabic responses and non-verbal reactions as high control is established and maintained.

Schools and doctors (Mrs. Smith)

T. Are you happy or are you fed up this morning?
C1. I'm fed up.
T. You're fed up this morning!
C1. ⟨nods⟩
T. You're both fed up. Oh dear, now I'm fed up. Are you fed up because you had to come to school?
C2. I ?hate school, I like Senior school. I like it.
T. You like Senior school. Which school do you like, Senior school or Junior school?
C2. Senior school.

T.   Senior school. (to C1) Which school do you like?
C1.   Senior.
T.   Senior school. Oh dear! So, do you like Junior school?
C2.   No.
T.   No, he doesn't like Junior school. Well, you're both fed up!
C2.   I like Susie. Hello! Susie –––.
T.   You like Susie Bates.
C2.   Yes.
T.   Can you remember Susie Bates?
C1.   Yes.
T.   Can you remember Anthony Roberts?
C1.   Anthony Roberts ⟨nods⟩.
          . . .

(and, a few minutes later):
          . . .

T.   Oh! You went to the doctor's yesterday, didn't you?
C1.   ⟨nods⟩
T.   (to C2) Tom went to the doctor's yesterday.
      (to C1) Was he a nice doctor?
C1.   ?Better (puzzled).
T.   Was he a nice doctor or a horrible doctor?
C1.   Nice.
T.   He was a nice doctor. Was he a man or a lady?
C1.   Man.
T.   (to C2) Is your doctor a man or a lady?
C2.   Nicholson, lady.
T.   A lady?
C2.   Yes.
T.   Is your doctor a nice lady or a horrible lady?
C2.   Lady nice ⟨nodding⟩.
T.   A nice lady?
C2.   Yes.
T.   (to C1) Was she, was he, an old man or a young man?
C1.   ––– (probably 'young') man.
T.   A young man.
C1.   ⟨nods slightly⟩
T.   Mm. And you liked him, did you?
C1.   ⟨nods⟩

As we argued in Chapter 4, when control is high, children tend to give single-word responses or non-verbal reactions (e.g. nods and shakes of the head) to two-choice questions. Such responses are 'legitimate' in that they fulfil the force of the question, but it is the 'ease' with which they can be answered that underlies the difficulty both parties face in knowing whether or not mutual understanding *has* occurred. Unless children are making thematically related contributions of their own or answering more 'informative' questions appropriately they provide no evidence of actually having understood two-choice questions at all. And if the teacher does not *react to* or *build upon* a child's answer then the child, too, is given no basis for determining whether his answer was appropriate or intelligible.

Another problem that emerged in this session was the effect of strings of two-choice questions on the child who was not immediately being questioned. For example, after asking a series of questions of one child, Tom, about whether he liked hospitals and would like to work in one, the teacher turned to the other child, Harry, to ask him what preference Tom had expressed. Harry made no response and showed no signs of having understood any of the preceding discourse. Asked about his own future interests, he 'agreed' on four separate occasions (all single-word or non-verbal responses to two-choice questions) that he would like to work in a hospital. Three minutes later, he said that he would hate to work in a hospital. We doubt that such confusions emerged as a product of any change in Harry's vocational aspirations over the intervening period! He, like other children, answered some questions without really understanding them.

Although two-choice questions might *seem* easy to answer and generate responses that seem intelligible, they are, used in excess, a frequent basis for misunderstanding. This is not to say that the occasional 'Oo, did you enjoy it?' or 'Was he very angry?' might not be effective in inviting children to expand on their theme; rather it is the 'abuse' of these moves when they occur in 'strings' that exerts such a stultifying effect on conversation. As Mrs. Smith complained when we discussed the sessions: 'The ball kept coming straight back into my court.' As her session progressed, children became increasingly passive and gave her nothing to work out from. So she found it progressively more difficult to think of things to ask about. Whilst, in a 'contrived' session such as this one, we get an exaggerated and perhaps distorted picture of the way such moves normally function in discourse, the inhibiting effect of these questions on children's initiative (and the teacher-directed course of conversation) are not totally dissimilar to some normal 'bouts' of conversations we have observed in classrooms.

Session 3: Wh-Type Questions

There is an extensive literature on the educational value of Wh-type questions. They are often put forward as important tools for extending children's understanding, encouraging them to reflect and helping them to 'decontextualize' their thinking (see Dillon, 1982, for a critical overview of research in this area). However, as we have already argued, they are also likely, in excess, to inhibit children from playing an active role and taking initiative in conversations (only around 6 per cent receiving elaborated replies). As we had predicted, children's initiative was lower in this high control session than in the lower control ones. However, the effect of frequent Wh-type questions was not quite so stultifying as we had expected; initiative and talkativeness were no lower than they were in the normal sessions. In part, this was because Wh-type questions occasionally led to arguments. Since answers to such questions, when they are given, can be evaluated by listeners, they offer an opportunity for disagreement and debate, as we shall see later. From a teacher's point of view, Wh-type questions, unlike two-choice ones, are unlikely to receive an appropriate response without the child having understood the force of the question. They may thus be an important 'diagnostic' tool for monitoring comprehension. But they are also often difficult for children.

Instances of incomprehension and misunderstanding were higher in this than any other session. In Mrs. Smith's sessions, the frequency of no responses or inappropriate answers from children rose from 8 per cent in the initial 'natural' conversation to 10 per cent in this session. For Mrs Jones, the comparable figures were 14 to 27 per cent.

In Chapter 4 we reported that teacher power and frequency of repair were highly correlated and suggested that one led to the other. This suggestion was borne out by the results of these experimental sessions. Here, too, sessions high in power were also high in repair which was highest in the Wh-type question sessions (this was the case for the hearing children too). When questions are numerous and difficult, the ensuing misunderstandings and ambiguities in children's responses 'pulled' teachers into repair sequences. As illustrated in the transcript given below, children's failure to understand a question often led the teacher to ask yet more questions in an attempt to reinstate mutual understanding.

Before looking at the transcript, however, we need to consider what it is about some questions that make them so difficult for children. What kinds of questions *do* children answer? There are at least three possible answers to these questions. First, questions may be more or less demanding intellectually. Marion Blank (Blank, Rose and Berlin, 1978), for example, has provided a classification of teacher language in terms of the 'level of cognitive demand' it embodies for young children. This system enables questions (and other request utterances) to be 'scaled' for the degree of difficulty they present. Low level demands include questions on topics such as the names of objects and their attributes—size, shape, colour and so forth. More demanding discourse involves attention to attributes that enable objects to be related, classified, grouped and distinguished. Such questions draw attention to more abstract relationships *between* objects and events—to things that are not directly perceived but stem from linguistic and intellectual structures that serve to organize experience. The most cognitively demanding language in Blank's scheme involves reasoning, speculating, planning and so on. Thus, the level of cognitive demand increases as the topic of discourse becomes less focused on the 'here and now', and moves on to explanations, logical inference and abstract reasoning.

Most of the talk in the experimental conversations, like 'news sessions', concerned events outside the current context and involved questions of different levels of demand. Some questions were concerned with labelling attributes ('What colour is . . . ?') or asked for information about things in context. Others demanded reasons and justifications. Mrs. Smith's session started off with just such a mixture. In examining the transcript note not only the questions that children answer or fail to answer but also the incidence of repair. We also draw attention to what happens after the odd phatic move is allowed to creep in (e.g. 'You like Senior School'), when a child immediately introduces a new element to the conversation.

Schools again and ties

T.   How are you?
C1. Alright thank you.
T.   You're alright, that's good. Are you fed up?
C1. No ⟨shakes head⟩.
T.   (to C1) Let's see, shall we ask him (C2)
    'Why are you fed up?' . . . you ask him.
C1. (?to C2) Why are you fed up?
C2. (no response—laughs)
T.   (to C2) Why are you fed up? Why are you fed up?
C2. Don't want school.
T.   You don't want to come to school. Why?
C2. I like Senior school.
T.   You like Senior school.
C2. I like Susie Bates.
T.   Pardon?
C2. Susie Bates.
T.   Oh, you're always talking about Susie Bates.
    (to C1) Do you like Susie Bates?
C1. Yes.
T.   Why, why do you like Susie Bates?
C1. ?As ?a friend, friend.
T.   You think she's your friend. Well, that's very nice.
C2. Friend.
T.   (to C2) Is she your friend?
C2. Yes.
T.   Lovely. And do you like school?
C1. No.
T.   No. Why?
C1. I like Senior.
T.   You like Senior school. Well, I'm very sorry. You don't like Junior school?
C2. ⟨shakes head⟩ No, I like Senior school.
T.   (laughs) Well, why don't you like Junior school?
C1. I like Senior . . . Work hard.
C2. ?I ?know Richard, friend, Richard, Richard.
T.   You like Richard?
C1. Yes ⟨nods⟩.
C2. Friend, Richard.
T.   Yes, well, you'll see Richard again soon. You've got some friends here, haven't you? Why don't you like Junior school?
C1. Too hard.
T.   (laughs) It's too hard. You don't work very hard here, not all the time anyway. Do you think when you go to Senior school that will be easy?
C1. No.
T.   Or will that be hard?
C1. Easy.
T.   Easy, mmm. Who told you it was easy?
C1. Richard.
T.   Richard did, did he?

C2. ⟨gestures where tie should be⟩ Senior school green, yellow, green.
T. That's the tie is it?
C2. ?You ?wear shirts ⟨fingers his shirt⟩.
T. Yes. Where's your tie?
C2. – – – change, change ⟨fingers sweater⟩
(still appears to be talking about Senior school).
T. *Where* is your tie this morning? Where is it?
C2. At home, green, yellow, . . . (i.e. still Senior school tie!).
T. Have you got one now?
C2. ⟨nods⟩ Senior.
T. Very nice.
C2. ?With ?my father's money ⟨counts money⟩.
T. Mmm. What colour is Tom's tie?
C2. Green and yellow.
T. No. What colour's Tom's tie?
C2. Brown.
T. Yes. (to C1) Where is his tie? Where is it?
C1. Red.
T. Yes, but where is it?
C1. Pocket.
T. It's in his pocket.
C2. ⟨points⟩ There it is . . . on the desk.
T. (looks) It's on the desk, is it? Why is it on the desk? Why haven't you got it on?
C2. It's red ⟨touches where tie should be⟩.
T. Yes, I didn't say what colour was it . . . .
C2. (tries again to give colour?) – – –.
T. I said, 'Why haven't you got it on?' What's the matter with it?
C2. It's over there (points to desk).
T. I know it's on the desk. Why?
C1. (to C2) ⟨questioning gesture⟩ Why?
C2. I ah . . . small.
T. (to C1) You ask him.
C2. I – – – small.
T. (to C1) What did he say?
C1. Small.
T. It's too small. It's too small.

There were no obvious relationships between the level of abstraction implicit in a question and the likelihood that children would or would not answer it. Some 'Why?' questions demanding justifications were answered in a sensible and intelligible way when requests for colour names and locations were not. We are not claiming that cognitive demand is not a factor influencing a question's difficulty, but it did not explain most of the comprehension problems children evidenced in these sessions. Put more positively: although, as many people have noted, deaf children find talk about things outside their immediate experience difficult, they are not totally unable to do so. They are not incompetent in recalling and recollecting, reasoning and justifying. The problem lies in the difficulty of *communicating* about such things.

A second potential source of difficulty with questions, especially for deaf children, lies in perceptual and linguistic confusions. 'Where', 'what', 'why' and 'when' may be confused because they look similar on the lips. We cannot rule this factor out as an explanation, but did not find many instances where the children definitely confused different Wh-type questions.

A third factor that influences a question's difficulty is subtle and hard to define but important in its influence on understanding and misunderstanding. It revolves around the notion of contingency. We have already cited examples of seemingly simple questions that were misunderstood and more demanding ones that were answered appropriately. The questions that failed to get answers often seemed, so to speak, to 'come out of the blue' and 'cut across the child's conversational bows'. We have not developed a formal description of this feature of discourse but, broadly speaking, what seems to be important is the extent to which a question relates to an ongoing theme and in particular to a contribution or response that a child has already made. If, as in the 'school tie' example, answering a teacher's question involves thinking about a different time, place and object than that established in the preceding move, children seem likely to misunderstand. The child has to reorientate several aspects of his thinking following a single move. Where a question arises more directly out of what he says and extends the theme he is exploring, he seems much more likely to understand it. Sudden changes in the 'direction' of talk and a breakdown in shared expectations may thus be an important element in accounting for incomprehension in addition to cognitive or linguistic complexity. We return to a discussion of 'contingency' in questioning in the final section of the chapter.

Another important but, as yet, neglected aspect of the communicative situation is the way in which verbal and non-verbal 'cues' interact in the child's attempt to achieve comprehension. Even when talk is 'decontextualized' children rely on a variety of situational and paralinguistic clues to supplement their understanding. Indeed, the same is true of communication between hearing people (e.g. McNeill, 1979). Not surprisingly, deaf children often seem very reliant on such information. In the following excerpt, for example, the child misinterprets a relatively simple question from the teacher because her non-verbal cues are at variance with what she is saying.

Wedding dress—or the ring? (Mrs. Smith)

T.   What colour does the *lady* wear when she gets married? What colour? ⟨points to ring finger⟩
C1. White.
T.   White, yes.
C2. ⟨points to ring finger⟩ ?No, yellow.
T.   Oh Harry!
C1. Gold, gold.
T.   Yes, that was the gold ring.
C2. Oh.
T.   ⟨points to ring⟩ But I said to Tom, 'What colour does the lady, what colour is the lady's dress?' *What colour?* ⟨indicates dress⟩ When she gets married in church? What colour?
C2. White.

Here the child gets the message that the teacher is asking about colours, but because she touches her ring he assumes that that is what she is asking about. The question itself is not a difficult one structurally and this child answered much more 'demanding' questions within the session. Such problems illustrate the range of cues that children are attending to in their efforts to make sense out of the interaction. There were many failures of mutual understanding on the recordings that sometimes lasted over several minutes of talk. For example, the same child said that his father had worn a black tie to his own wedding and that he himself had attended in a blue suit. He persisted with this story over three and a half minutes of discourse, despite all the arguments from the teacher and the other child (who suggested that he must have been a baby in his mother's tummy!). Eventually the argument ended when the first child capitulated. He had not been there; he'd been sent home! Or had he?

The wedding suit

C2. Blue, blue coat. Blue.
T. You did?
C2. And a white shirt.
T. And a white shirt, when you went to somebody's wedding?
C2. Yes.
T. Who was the lady? What was her name, can you remember?
C2. Mummy.
T. Oh, Mummy. But not when Mummy got married you didn't go to church.
C1. ?Harry a baby . . . a baby.
C2. Not married, married, yes married.
T. Yes. I know she's married.
C1. A baby (points to C2) ?a . . . ⟨rocks a baby⟩.
T. Yes, perhaps when he was a baby, when he was christened, when he was baptized, mmm.
C2. ⟨indicates arm⟩ Mummy ---.
T. Were you a little baby?
C2. No baby.
T. You tell me about it. What happened?
C2. What you say?
T. When you went to church in your blue suit—What for?
C2. Mummy white.
T. Your Mummy had a white dress, did she?
C2. Yes.
T. I think we're a little bit muddled up. When your Mummy was married in church . . . ⟨ring finger⟩ your Mummy and Daddy . . . I don't think you were . . .
C2. Mummy Daddy two.
T. Yes, but you weren't there, I know, but you weren't there.
C1. Me married ⟨shaking head⟩.
C2. No, I watch ?on, watch.
T. You were watching?
C2. ⟨nods⟩
C1. I --- watch . . . .
T. (to C1) No, that's right. You weren't there, were you?
C1. Inside! ⟨points to tummy⟩
T. That's right, that's right! (laughs)

C2. No! (not what he meant)
(C1 explains situation to C2.)
(C2: 'Ah', and smiles.)
(T, aside: 'They were getting slightly muddled!')
T. (to C1) What does he say? You ask him, you try to sort it out.
C1. He was a baby.
T. (to C2) Yes, you weren't at your Mummy's wedding.
C2. ?Married, Daddy he there me there (still seems to be convinced he was there).
T. Well, you bring me some photographs tomorrow. Have you got some pictures you can show me?
C2. Yeah.
T. Your Mummy and Daddy—
C2. Not me ⟨shaking head⟩.
T. —and you. No, you're not there.
C2. ?No, ⟨shakes head, points to self⟩ before home—finish, go home ⟨being sent away⟩.
T. You went home. I think you're muddled up Harry. Never mind (pats C2's knee), it doesn't matter. What did you have for breakfast this morning?

The question that led to this argument and to subsequent questions designed to check its plausibility or accuracy led to uncertainties that were never fully resolved—another general feature of the Wh-type question sessions. Questions following unanswered questions, seemingly designed to 'get to the bottom of things', often met this fate. In a more formal teaching situation, where it is important to 'get the answer right', it may be necessary to pursue inadequate responses to the bitter end. However, if the goal of the session is to encourage conversation and a relatively free exchange of ideas (and if the question is not an important one), it is worth asking whether the uncertainty and ambiguity that often follow on from strings of questions and repair are worth either the effort or the price they demand in terms of lower initiative and shorter responses from children. It might be argued that only by making sure the child 'gets it right' can we provide him with effective 'feedback' about the quality of his efforts and the nature of his communication problems. The difficulty is that when question piles on question, ambiguity on ambiguity, puzzle on puzzle, it is seldom clear what any feedback feeds back to.

Session 4: Personal Contributions

In this session, we asked teachers to try, as far as possible, to avoid questions and concentrate on telling children about their own experiences or commenting on what the children had to offer. As we had expected, children showed more initiative and were more talkative in this session than in either the normal chat sessions or the high control ones. Sometimes children said more in contribution sessions than in the phatic ones; at other times, the pattern was reversed. Some reasons why sessions might vary in effectiveness are explored below.

Although we analysed only ten minutes of each session with each group, the effects of low control were measurable. Initially, however, in both contribution and phatic sessions, teachers and children often suffered a rather uncomfortable period when the children seemed somewhat bemused by the rather unusual behaviour of their teachers. Mrs. Smith started off by trying to comment on C2's answer that he was tired, and then agreed that she too liked to stay in bed and had to travel a long way to school. As the following extracts show, the children were slow to 'take over', but rather seemed to be waiting for her to 'get on with it', i.e. to establish the theme or topic of conversation by asking a question. Eventually, however, the 'fear of silence' seemed to gain the upper hand and children began to make contributions of their own, becoming increasingly active and loquacious as the session proceeded.

Hard beginnings

T.	(to C2) Oh Harry, you do look fed up. What's the matter?
C2.	Tired.
T.	Are you tired? (to C1) I think he looks very tired.
C1.	(no response)
T.	Do you think he looks tired?
C1.	No.
T.	Do you think he *looks* very tired?
C1.	⟨nods half-heartedly⟩
T.	Look, look at him.
C1.	Yes.
C2.	I like ?stay ?to home.
T.	Pardon?
C2.	I ––– go home, sleep.
T.	Oh dear, I like sleeping as well in the morning. I like to stay in bed.
C2.	I ––– wake up. ⟨sleeping⟩ Mummy, wake up. Shut up! (?to Mummy)
T.	(and C1) (laugh)
C2.	––– ⟨pulling at shoulder⟩ Wake up ⟨prods⟩.
T.	Yes, I like it in bed.
C2.	––– ––– ?too late ⟨points to watch⟩.
T.	Dear me, poor Harry!
C2.	Yes –––.
C1.	I ?have dream.
T.	(to C1) Did you?
C2.	––– ?driver ––– ⟨looks at watch⟩ forget . . . car ––– see, waiting. ?Here long time, long way house.
T.	I know, poor Harry!
C2.	–––
T.	I come a long way to school in the mornings, in my car.
C2.	(no response)
T.	I live a long way away.
C1.	(no response, yawns, looks at hands)
T.	(laughs)
C1.	Breakfast? (Does Tom think it's time they talked about it or is he asking 'did you have . . . ?')
T.	Have breakfast? I had some breakfast this morning. I had some orange juice and . . . brown bread and cheese.
C1.	(smiles)
C2.	I ah, I like swimming, Senior.

The observation that it *does* take children time to settle in to the role of initiator and controller of conversation illustrates an important, general point. The teacher has to 'hold back' from a normal tempo or rhythm of interaction, leaving longer pauses after her move than she would in normal conversations. There is, in fact, a fair amount of evidence suggesting that teachers generally leave rather short 'silences' between their moves. One study of forty science lessons with hearing children (Swift and Gooding, 1983), for example, revealed that teachers usually gave children just over a second to respond after their questions. Teachers were helped to extend their pauses to three seconds (an electronic buzzer sounded if children had not responded after this time to let the teacher know when to go on). The extended pauses led to longer and more thoughtful responses from children.

Children need more time than teachers normally give them to think about what they are going to say. Perhaps we judge the time they need by the speed of our own thought processes and speech rates. Or it could be that long pauses simply heightens the fear of silence effect. Whatever the origins of the phenomenon we suspect it must be particularly important in relation to deaf children who need even more time both to comprehend what is said to them and to formulate a response. It is obviously difficult to 'manipulate' very basic aspects of one's spontaneous behaviour such as pausing. Furthermore, it takes time for children to understand and/or to accept the fact that they are being offered an active, controlling role if they are not used to it. The hard going experienced by teachers and children in getting the low control sessions off the ground is thus, we argue, symptomatic of the rather unusual demands being made on both.

Mrs. Smith increased the proportion of personal contributions in this session over her initial one from 10 to 44 per cent. After the first, rather awkward minute, outlined above, one child finally asked her a question: 'Breakfast?' Whether he was offering this as a safe, familiar topic of conversation (it had been a focus for questions in previous sessions) or was really interested in finding out how she had broken her fast that morning, we could not tell. However, the teacher treated it as a genuine question and answered it. The child met the answer with a smile and nod, and then the second child took over the floor and changed the subject completely to talk about swimming. The ice was then broken, and the conversation progressed from the cost of swimming to swimming in the sea and being bitten by crabs, to fathers eating crabs and one of the children seeing a 'fish' which may or may not have been the film monster 'Jaws'.

Swimming with Jaws

C1. I like freeze --- cold, cold outside.
C2. (pulls C1's chin round) S'alright, s'alright outside, strong.
T. It's horrible (i.e. swimming) outside, horrible.
C2. I --- brave, --- brave.
T. Horrible, it's much too cold.
C1. Mrs. . . . ?on ?the holiday . . . .

C2.   No! I ---.
C1.   (interrupts) Mrs. Smith, at ?the holday --- --- boys, big boys swimming, raining!
T.   In the rain?
C1.   Yeah.
T.   Oh, they're barmy, they're barmy boys.
C2.   ?Before ... long time ago ... --- --- --- ?bus on ?your ?way holidays, ?shining.
T.   Did she? Was it ... ?
C2.   ?Goose ?fair, ?dusty ?fair ...
T.   It was sunny, was it? I like, I like swimming in the sunshine. But I don't like the sea.
C1.   ⟨shakes head⟩
T.   I like the swimming pool, not the sea.
C1.   Jaws! (sounds like 'rough')
T.   Yes, it's too rough.
C1.   Jaws! ⟨grabbing, roughly⟩
T.   Mm, and it's too rough in the sea.
C2.   I like it --- --- ?way. =Eee! ⟨something small⟩ Ah! ⟨pain in foot⟩
C1.   A =boo Mrs. Smith.
T.   I don't like crabs.
C2.   =Eee =eee ⟨beating them to death!⟩
T.   Oh! Do you kill them?
C2.   --- ?blood dead.
T.   Oo ... how horrible!
C1.   Mrs., my father, ?shop holiday ?shop eat it.
T.   Crab?
      (C2. 'Ah!')
C1.   Open ⟨scooping out⟩.
T.   They're lovely, they're lovely to eat.
C2.   I saw, I saw ?swimming holiday, I saw --- I saw fish, =ages ⟨long, jaws closing, swims⟩.
T.   A real one?
C2.   ⟨draws J in air⟩
C1.   No! ?not ?real, long, long way ... Africa.
T.   Yes.
C2.   (gets C1 by chin) ⟨prints JAWS on shelf⟩
C1.   Jaw.
T.   That's a film. Did you see a real one? A real whale?
C2.   Yeah ⟨points aghast⟩ --- ?scared swimming, no ?walk =ages.
T.   I think I would be frightened swimming where there were whales.
C1.   Mrs. Smith, holiday, picture, film, Jaws =hee.
      ⟨'jaws' open wide⟩ Man inside ⟨points inside mouth⟩.
T.   I haven't seen Jaws. I didn't see the film.

Maintaining the role of contributor was not an easy one for the teachers. Indeed, at one point in the interaction the teacher was trying so hard to merely comment on what the children were saying that she 'found herself' saying things that weren't true. When one child mentioned that his sister had been in hospital she said 'I haven't been in hospital', and then, off camera as it were, complained: 'What am I saying, of course I have. What absolute rubbish. I'm telling fibs just to keep this conversation going. I'm trying so hard not to ask him a question. Oh dear Harry, is she alright now?—I'm sorry, I *have* to ask *that*!'

Clearly, asking questions is a normal part of conversation and can be a way of showing genuine interest in what another person has to say. The 'abnormal' nature of the conversations inspired by our instructions provides some insights into the issue of *when* a question is 'legitimate'. In this session, what the children had to say was almost entirely of their own choosing and, as such, came as a 'surprise' to the teacher. Since she had not dictated what they would talk about, what she heard was often informative. Once the conversation was underway there were many things that the child offered which could have formed a perfectly natural basis for questions. Indeed, we suspect that the points at which the teacher felt most uncomfortable were just those points at which a question occurred to her 'naturally'. Setting out to converse with a child and not asking questions is as unnatural as continually interrogating him (though the latter seems to come far more easily and 'naturally' in schools). Once the child is cast in an active role, by the strategic use of low control moves, any questions that arise are likely to refer to what the child has said or is saying and, hence, will be contingent upon his thinking. Questions asked at such points are likely to be 'invisible', non-stressful and enabling of further elaboration rather than simply controlling and dictating the course of discourse, as is more often the case.

Mrs. Jones' contribution session proceeded less smoothly. She managed to increase her use of contributions from 27 per cent in her initial session to 35 per cent in this one. Although her children were more forthcoming and verbal in this session than either the normal ones or the high control conversations, they were generally less active both than the children in the other group and than they proved to be in the 'phatic' session. Mrs. Jones asked many more questions than Mrs. Smith in this session and this was reflected in much lower initiative being shown by her group. Another related difference, perhaps attributable to the fact that the second group were less verbally able than the others, was a very different pattern of responses by the two groups to teacher contributions. Once they got started, Mrs. Smith's children almost always took up an opening to make a contribution, responding to the teacher's comments with phatics alone very rarely (2 per cent of all occasions). Mrs. Jones' children, however, were far less likely to take up their opportunites— in part because she was exerting more control—and simply acknowledged what the teacher said a good deal of the time (23 per cent phatics). Here we find the 'classic' problem of cause and effect. Because children are initially unwilling to take up an opening to speak and simply give a phatic response, the teacher is more likely to 'fill the gap' with a question. In so doing, she *decreases* the probability that children will take up later openings to contribute. This, in turn, leads her to be more likely to question. Thus, the downward spiral of increasing control begins and expands.

A major difference in the two sessions, in consequence, was the amount of 'warm up' time children needed to take initiative. Mrs. Jones started out the conversation with a question, which was answered, but ensuing contributions were met with nods from children and few contributions. Eventually, after several minutes of hard going, a dramatic change in the 'tenor' of the interaction occurred. She picked up on a child's comment about the kind of toaster he had at home, to say that she herself did not own one, but had to use a grill to toast bread and 'many times it gets burnt and I have to throw it away'. The children finally got 'with her' and took over control. One child observed 'black . . . black' with a fair degree of mime. Then both children talked about sandwich-makers, and went on to other domestic chores like cleaning out bedrooms. The teacher took up the cleaning theme to talk about clearing out desk drawers at school. This topic extended for some time, and one child, en route, produced conversational turns 17 and 23 words long (early in the session, her average had been 5.8).

Once conversation was initiated, the teacher was able to steer and elaborate on the topic without excessive questioning. Children occasionally picked up on her contributions and pursued them, asking questions or reacting to them in some other way. Though one cannot always be confident that children understand contributions (they can be ignored legitimately or not responded to because they were not heard or understood) these responses showed that, some of the time at least, children did both understand and were prepared to respond to what the teacher contributed. These were the beginnings, then, of a more equal and (certainly for us as observers) more interesting 'shared construction' of stories which both the teacher and children created. Helping children to converse in this way is not easy, but can bear fruit. Although we would not recommend that teachers try to avoid questions all the time (more later) it might be a useful rule of thumb to start out with the *intention* not to question children. One will fail, since questions will come 'naturally', but, in so doing, one might well avoid the 'dydactic traps' that talking to deaf children usually open up.

Session 5: Phatics

In this session, we asked teachers to sit back and, as far as possible, say nothing substantive. They were simply to acknowledge what children said— 'Yes' or 'really!', 'Ah-ha' and so on—or make vague comments like 'Good gracious!' or 'That's nice'. We asked them to avoid all questions as far as they could, including 'tag' utterances like 'Oh, did you?', since children sometimes react to these as 'genuine' two-choice questions.

Here, as in the contribution sessions, the opening sequences were some-what tense and heavy going. The teacher's silence ultimately forced children to 'take over', but it took a minute or so to establish the fact that it was to be 'their' conversation. But, once children began to converse, the effect was dramatic, particularly on the second, less 'verbal' group of children. In every other session their MLT was less than 2 words; here it rose to 4.1 words per turn. One girl produced turns 17, 16, 25 and 50 words long. She went into considerable detail about an episode in which, somewhat reminiscent of Poor Orphan Annie, she had been forced out into wet and cold streets to help her older sister, Alison, to deliver newspapers.

Delivering newspapers

C1. Mummy, Mummy ⟨shaking ?chips⟩. Tea finish. ?Alison --- ⟨writing⟩ ?Alison ?poorly, poor. ---! ⟨shaking head⟩ Me, ?before ⟨poorly⟩. Me ?make finish (i.e. the 'beautiful' paper creation she has already mentioned) me --- paper ⟨taking it somewhere?⟩, --- ?newspaper ⟨opens newspaper⟩. Alison 'Help me'. ⟨she thinks about it⟩ ⟨I⟩ ?Help ?Mummy; Mummy 'Alright, leave it.' ⟨she goes off to do it⟩ ---? ⟨?asking where they go, searches for right house, comparing ?numbers on papers with house numbers⟩ Ah! ⟨as finds right one and posts it. Is given another, asks⟩ There? ⟨points⟩ That in. ⟨pushes it in. She looks around for next and posts it⟩. ?Alison ⟨hands out things⟩. ?Heavy ⟨heavy bag over shoulder⟩ Heavy, heavy ⟨trudges along with it⟩ --- ⟨hands over something⟩ --- ⟨gives something⟩ --- ⟨reads ?address and gives ⟩ ⟨me⟩ ?don't ?know, ?don't ?know house, me ⟨hands out⟩ --- ⟨me post⟩. ?Me home, home. Cold, cold, wet, wet ⟨pulls 'wet' hair⟩. ?Dry, finish. ?Eat dinner, --- ?finish watch ⟨TV⟩. ?Lots ?Daddy --- car ⟨hand to head—?police⟩ ?play, finish, ⟨me⟩ bed. ?All (i.e. that's all folks!).

One striking feature of children's responses to the low control sessions, and of this child's performance in particular, was that once they began to tell stories, they became not only verbally but also physically active. They would sometimes stand up, mime and gesture fluently. Indeed, we were led to wonder if the freedom of movement engendered in these sessions might not be one reason why teachers usually exert so much control. It is more difficult to 'manage' active children, and the mime and gesture they produced might well be anathema to a teacher who is looking for 'speech'. Our own view is that, whilst teachers do have to maintain order and discipline in order to ensure the smooth running of group discussion, children can only be encouraged to communicate freely, readily and productively if they are allowed to do so, as far as practicable, in their own way. Any attempt to make them stop their physical activity is likely to depress their desire to communicate. As we argued at the start of chapter 4, various aspects of linguistic competence are facilitated by attempts to tell 'stories'. If a child is only encouraged to make short communicative responses within a tightly controlled framework established by the teacher, then he has little opportunity to discover how to *construct* such frameworks for himself. Lacking these skills, he will have little facility in organizing his thoughts and experiences in such a way that they can be communicated to others, either *en face* or in print.

It was often difficult to follow what children were communicating in this session. In questioning sessions, the framework supplied by the teacher makes even short and often poorly articulated vocalizations by the child interpretable most of the time. But the child's role is minimal. In the contribution session, the teacher was able to help direct and even clarify aspects of what children were saying to ensure some degree of coherence in the discourse. In the phatic session, where teachers played a minimal role, the children's offerings were often difficult to decipher not only because they used a good deal of gesture and mime but also because they would leap from topic to topic without establishing any intelligible connections between them. It was as if they were painting a series of pictures rather than relating stories. This lack of coherence in their organization of discourse also, we feel, explains why teachers usually exert so much control. But if a child is never given an *opportunity* to try to produce a coherent story, how is he ever to learn what this involves? It is unlikely that repeated and extended 'phatic' sessions would provide him with enough guidance and feedback ever to discover how to make himself worth listening to. At some point, contributions, questions and requests for clarification are called for. The issue is how we integrate low and high control moves into a pattern which enables children to contribute and elaborate but also to discover how to take their listener's needs into account. How do we balance control and initiative with children who are very difficult to converse with?

CONVERSATION: INITIATIVE VERSUS CONTROL

By encouraging teachers to change the way in which they talk to children, we have been able to show that the effects of numerous teacher questions and frequent repair go hand in hand and inhibit children from playing an active, productive part in conversation. When teachers question less, become more receptive to what children have to say and talk more about their own views, ideas and so forth, children reciprocate by making more frequent and longer contributions to the discourse. They are more likely to elaborate on their answers to teacher questions when these are relatively infrequent and they become generally more involved in the interaction.

However, at the other extreme, we found that exposure to a 'laissez-faire' style was equally unsatisfying, though in different ways to high control sessions. When the teachers abdicated their role as managers and orchestrators of interaction, children became more active and loquacious but were also often incomprehensible. Too much control stifles the child, but too little robs the teacher of any opportunities to help the child discover how to make himself understood. How is it possible to steer a productive 'middle course' between the extremes of over-control and self-defeating attempts to repair children's understanding on the one hand and an approach that provides no opportunities for teaching on the other?

The first point to make is that there is no 'rule book' or 'script' that can be written to dictate how one achieves productive conversations. We have emphasized the 'contingent' nature of effective teaching which demands an opportunistic and responsive attitude towards a child's ongoing activities and utterances. When children tell us interesting and surprising things, then, by definition, we are not able to *anticipate* their offerings. Indeed, we do not *want* to anticipate them. The essence of conversation is the transmission and sharing of *new* ideas. If the child's role is not to be predetermined by teacher questions, then the teacher will have to react as the moment dictates and, since we cannot anticipate what that moment will bring forth, we cannot write down any scripts.

However, whilst there are no such scripts to guide the achievement of productive conversations, we can highlight ways in which teaching styles are often self-defeating and explore possible tactics for helping to avoid the pitfalls that classroom conversationalists often fall into.

Obviously, we would recommend that, in general, teachers ask fewer questions than they usually do and that they give children more time to think and communicate after they have addressed them. They should also become more attentive, accepting and responsive to what children have to say. However, any slackening of control should not imply that teachers will never ask questions to extend, develop or in some other way raise children's awareness. Nor should it imply that the teacher will not be giving the child clear signals about the clarity, coherence or accessibility of what he is saying. Given that we can encourage talk from children, which, we have argued, we can, two specific issues arise. When is a question likely to facilitate and extend the child's understanding without depressing his desire to communicate? When and how should repair occur?

EFFECTIVE QUESTIONS

In an extensive and detailed (but not easily available) study of teacher questions and children's responses to them, Robinson and Rackstraw (1975) draw attention to several features of the uses and abuses of questions. Generally speaking, attempts to encourage children to entertain a line of thought or to engender curiosity about a topic of discourse by starting an interaction through questions are usually unsuccessful. Even when (hearing) children respond to such opening questions, their replies are likely to be inappropriate or irrelevant. They seem to respond more to 'please the teacher' and to assume that all of her questions have a single 'right' answer. Rarely do they seem to think about the import or implications of questions.

When, however, questions arise *after* a shared 'realm of discourse' (our term) or verbal 'text' has been established, questions which relate to it are more likely to meet with appropriate and thoughtful responses from children (Prosser, 1974). Indeed, we suspect that this is one of the main reasons why children are more likely to produce relatively long and elaborated answers to teacher questions in low control sessions. Sessions in which both teachers and children have made a variety of contributions are more likely to provide such a realm of discourse for questions to arise out of and refer to.

The implications of our results and the study of questioning with hearing children are that teachers are more likely to receive considered answers to their questions if they first 'set the scene' to establish a background against which these can be interpreted. There are many different tactics which might achieve such a state of affairs. For example, a teacher might begin a conversation by telling a 'story', describing a scene, speculating about the future, or recalling a past shared experience. Put another way, narrative should precede inquiry. Alternatively, children might be encouraged to introduce and develop their *own* themes. This can be achieved through 'chairing' moves like 'You tell us about your weekend'. Although such moves determine who will talk, they do not necessarily exert control over what is *said*.

Establishing a shared realm of discourse before asking questions is not easy, as we saw in the contribution sessions. It is likely to take time, will require patience and all concerned may need to tolerate the 'fear of silence'. However, we found that within a few minutes of conversation, children usually began to take the lead. Similarly, Lees (1981) discovered that after a few weeks of offering frequent contributions to children she found it very difficult to return to her 'traditional' style which involved more questioning and repair because the children were reluctant to *let* her do so. They were likely to 'ignore' her attempts to control them. They interrupted her, went beyond the force of her questions and so on. We can only speculate about any longer-term effects of such an approach, but we suspect that they would be significant. Once any new 'rules' of the conversational game have been established and children realize that their options in talk are relatively open, we believe they will begin to 'expect' to play a more active and egalitarian role in talking to teachers and that this will improve both their confidence and competence as communicators.

Once a topic has been introduced and developed, then, we believe, questions are more likely to be comprehensible to children, particularly when they are given time to think and respond. Answers to two-choice questions may well be elaborated upon if they build on an extant topic and are not too numerous. Similarly, more demanding Wh-type questions, such as those encountered in our experimental sessions, may lead to argument, discussion and genuinely informative responses from children if they relate in some sensible way to an established line of thought. Furthermore, if, following a child's response to a question, the teacher either makes a contribution that develops or extends the theme or simply acknowledges what the child has just said, then she gives the child an opportunity to think further and, if he has anything left to say, to make additional comments.

In general, then, a productive conversation will be characterized, to use a nautical metaphor, by an 'ebb and flow' of control. Questions following narrative may help to explore and extend a child's thinking. Question following question in an unbroken sequence of teacher control are counter-productive and inhibit children's initiative, but, embedded within lower control moves, they lead children into new lines of thought and greater understanding of the topic at hand. Thus, we suggest that questions should be used more sparingly and selectively to extend, develop and explore themes and topics which are first established through teacher or child narrative.

REPAIR—WHEN AND HOW?

Children must discover 'how to mean'. They not only have to learn how to make intelligible sounds and acquire the 'rules' of syntax, but, to be meaningful, they also have to discover how to work out the needs of a listener, monitor his understanding, diagnose the nature of any misunderstandings and find ways of reestablishing mutual comprehension. The study of these aspects of children's developing linguistic competence have been neglected until recently, most attention having been paid to the acquisition of 'syntactic' rules (see Romaine, 1984). However, evidence is beginning to emerge about everyday experiences that may underlie the development of these wider aspects of communicative competence in hearing children. One series of studies in particular is important to our discussions of repair and its place in productive discourse. For example, Robinson (1976) observed what parents did in talking to their preschool hearing children when their child said something unintelligible or ambiguous. One common repair strategy (as in schools for the deaf) was to ask children questions designed to clear up uncertainty or to check an interpretation of what they said (e.g. 'Do you mean . . .?'). Another, less common approach was to respond to children's utterances with a repairing contribution of the form 'I don't understand what you mean' or 'I don't know whether you mean *x* or *y*'.

Children whose parents repaired through contributions were more knowledgeable about how communications between *other* people break down. They were better than others, for example, at detecting when misunderstandings arose because a speaker gave an inadequate 'message' or because his listener had not understood adequate ones. They knew who to 'blame' for a breakdown in mutual understanding. In a follow-up study, Robinson and Robinson (1982) showed that preschool hearing children who were exposed to interactions in which their inadequate utterances were repaired through contributions learned how to interpret communication breakdown whereas those exposed to a questioning style of repair did not.

The implications of these observations and experiments for repair with deaf children are relatively easy to summarize but, we suspect, are rather more difficult to put into practice. Basically, attempts to repair children should take place in the 'declarative' rather than the 'interrogative' voice. In other words, teachers should draw children's attention to breakdowns in comprehension *not* by *asking* what they said or meant (e.g. 'What did you say?', 'What do you mean?') nor by *guessing* with two-choice questions such as 'Do you mean yesterday or tomorrow?', 'Did you go with Mummy or Daddy?'. Rather, they should be as explicit as possible in *telling* children about the source of their own uncertainty. If a child's offering is totally incomprehensible, then a general, repairing contribution such as 'I don't know what you mean' or 'I didn't understand that' may be all that is possible (but read on). However, if the child's message is simply *ambiguous* and permits more than one interpretation, then the teacher should be as explicit as possible about her state of uncertainty: 'I don't know whether you mean you went with Mummy or with Daddy.' In other words, repairing Wh-type moves should give way to general statements of incomprehension, and two-choice repairing questions should be replaced by contributions which specify the possible interpretations of what a child has said.

In response to the 'how' of repair, then, we suggest the use of contributions rather than questions. These are preferable in three ways. They do not increase teacher power and, hence, are less likely to inhibit children from active responses. Second, they give the child a chance to *understand* another person's state of mind in response to what they have tried to say. Finally, in our view, they mark the fact that any breakdown in communication is the *shared* responsibility of both the speaker and the listener. As we see in the transcripts below, for example, when teacher repair is achieved mainly through contributions, children begin to 'reciprocate' by trying to help the teacher understand what they mean. Thus, they are not only encouraged to be active partners in conversation but are also provided with opportunities to develop skill and confidence in helping other people to understand them.

What about the 'when' of repair? In general, we suggest that teachers need to tolerate greater levels of uncertainty than many of them (in our studies) currently do in conversations with deaf children. In practice, this will mean that a teacher will not repair each and every ambiguous or unintelligible move from children. If and when a child learns how to 'stay on topic' and to signal the fact that he is changing topics (which some of the children in our study were starting to do), then, by letting the child take a few more moves in conversation, the teacher may get further insights into what he means. Then, if and when the 'penny drops' a checking phatic move like 'Oh, I see, you mean . . .' can provide the child with an opportunity to see if the teacher has indeed understood the message. Another approach, which is even more demanding, is for the teacher to interpret what she *thinks* a child has said and respond appropriately. For instance, if she formulates a contribution that only makes sense if the child actually *meant* what she thought he had tried to say, then the child is given information which might help him to check her understanding.

If such 'rules' of conversation were to become a *familiar* part of classroom interactions, we are reasonably sure that deaf children would begin to appreciate them and start to reciprocate by paying more attention to what the teacher says and by helping her to understand them.

We turn now to three transcripts. In the first, a teacher responds to a child's utterance that is intelligible but employs descriptive phrases (round and round, sit down) for which a name (musical bumps) exists. She responds with a move that involves 'invisible' repair through phatics ('Oh yes, musical bumps'). The child is five years old and very deaf (102 dB). He is managing, however, to monitor the teacher's utterances and take elements from them.

Musical bumps

T.   Did you go out to play?
C.   (pause) Not out play ⟨shakes head⟩. ?I ––– the music.
T.   You played with the music!
C.   ––– ––– ?games.
T.   You played games!
C.   Yeah.
T.   What sort of games did you play?
C.   Um?
T.   What sort of games did you play?
C.   Round and round, sit down.
T.   Oh yes, musical bumps.
C.   = Mu, musical bumps.
T.   ⟨nods⟩ That's right. Any more games?
C.   ––– ––– ?did that ⟨poses⟩.
T.   Musical statues.
C.   Statues.

The next, more extensive examples, show two very different styles of repair. The first involves repairing *questions* and the second more repairing *contributions*. Note how, in the latter, children react to the generally low control of the teacher by actively trying to make her understand. They do *not* let her explicit statements of uncertainty and lack of understanding go by.

Whose birthday was it?

T.   No. (to C6) Graham, whose birthday was it?
C6. Graham, he.
T.   Whose birthday?
C6. Graham.
T.   No. Ah, yes, it was Graham's birthday. But what about Tom? (C5) Was it Tom's Mummy or Daddy?
C6. (no response)
T.   (after pause) Don't know. Right Tom, you come here. I want you to tell them whose birthday it was, whose birthday.
C5. Daddy's, Daddy's.
T.   Tell them all.
C5. My Daddy's.
T.   'My Daddy's birthday.'
C5. My Daddy's birthday.
T.   Good lad. Whose birthday?
C6. Daddy, your Daddy.
     (C1. Card, was a nice card) (?question)
T.   (to C6) Your Daddy's birthday?
C6. No. Tom's.
T.   Tom . . . .
C6. Daddy, Daddy, Tom's Daddy . . . .
T.   Tom's Daddy's . . . .
C6. Birthday.
T.   Birthday. Whose birthday was it?
C1. Send a birthday card (points to C5).
T.   Your Daddy's birthday?

C1. Card, card.
T. Who? Whose birthday?
C1. Daddy.
T. Your Daddy?
C1. No, Tom's.
T. Tom's birthday?
C1. Yes.
T. Tom's birthday?
C1. Yes.
T. No. Wasn't Tom's birthday.
(C2 to C1: 'No!')
C4. Tom's Daddy's birthday.
T. (to C2) Terry!
C2. Mummy birthday.
T. Mummy's birthday?
C2. ⟨nods⟩
T. No.
C2. No! Me!
T. Your birthday?
C2. –––
T. No. We're talking about Tom.
C4. Tom.
C1. Daddy.
T. Just a minute, Pam (C1).
C4. Tom Daddy's birthday.
T. 'Tom's Daddy's birthday.'
C4. Tom's Daddy's birthday.
T. Good boy. Right.

Star Wars—Cars and mammoths together?!

T. Er, David! David! I don't understand that bit. David, I don't understand this bit.
What are you hitting your cheek for? What do you mean?
C3. ?A ?mammoth elephant.
T. An elephant? Elephant?
C3. No, no, er, different kind of horns. ⟨tusks⟩
T. A different kind of helmet.
C2. No! No! (picks up book)
C3. Yes! ⟨points to C2's book⟩
C1. A thing ––– horns ––– elephant.
C2. Look, look! (shows book)
T. What's this, let's have a look. (goes over to look at book)
C2. Mammoth. (points to book)
T. Oh! A mammoth. A different kind of elephant. An old-fashioned kind of
elephant with big tusks.
C3. I see one –––.
T. Oh. Where did you see that?
C3. I see in a picture.
T. In a picture, yes.
C3. ––– –––, ––– two.
C2. Tell them about ––– ––– story.
C3. Er . . . R2, R2 went hide in a cave ⟨gestures ???⟩ –––.
(NB. R2-D2 was one of the robots in *Star Wars*.)

C2.   R2 ––– ?find ?a ?cave, ?go ⟨round and round⟩ and a little man hit him, that man fell down, a man with a beard . . . man with a beard.

T.   A man with a beard, yes.

C3.   ––– –––, ––– see him.

T.   He saw the mammoth in the cave.

C3.   And sit in car, no wheels, no ?road.

T.   You don't have cars and mammoths together.

C3.   No! No, ––– wheels ?float car.

T.   There were mammoths long before there were cars.

C3.   No, two man, two man –––.

T.   You're getting it all mixed up, all mixed up David.
(David gets up and goes to blackboard.)

C2.   No! No!

T.   There were mammoths a long time before there were any ––– –––.

C2.   ––– ––– ––– story.

T.   Funny story!

C2.   They ?only ?lived in the story then ?the ?cameraman ––– see. Then ––– ––– –––.

T.   And what, was he dreaming about the film or something?

C2.   No, ––– ––– cameraman on film.

T.   It was a made-up film.

C2.   No. (Gets up and joins David at blackboard—they draw mammoth and hover-craft.)

CONCLUSIONS

The children who took part in this study were eleven years of age. Shortly after taking part they left the junior school to move on to a senior school where, in the normal course of events, they would be exposed to more 'formal' education and to lessons in which teachers try to transmit information and knowledge. Some of the problems they face in communicating with their teachers have been illustrated in this and the preceding chapter. If they find formal instruction difficult, and if their progress through the curriculum turns out to be much slower than that of hearing children, we should not, perhaps, be surprised. Similarly, given the problems they face in trying to provide 'narrative' accounts of their own experiences and ideas, it is also unsurprising that they are unlikely to be able to write or read very well (even if they had no other problems in this direction).

Whilst changes in teaching styles towards lower control of conversations resulted in longer, more animated and interesting contributions from children, they also revealed the tremendous difficulties children face in trying to present a coherent, intelligible narrative. Although we do not know how often deaf children are given opportunities in the classroom to tell stories or narrate accounts of their experiences, such chances, in our experience, are very rare. Even when teachers do attempt to do so, the characteristic 'register' of the classroom, the question–answer exchange, effectively inhibits children from trying to produce coherent, lengthy accounts.

When we consider the enormous problems facing both children and teachers in trying to lay the foundations of receptive and expressive linguistic competence in conversation, we can, perhaps, understand why so many years of experience in school result in what seem like 'depressing' outcomes. Some will conclude, no doubt, that the communication problems facing children that we have been illustrating are an inevitable and largely inescapable consequence of severe or profound deafness. We are not so sure. We believe that the child's problems are often exacerbated by styles of teacher control. Possibly, if the 'balance of control' in interactions can be adjusted, so that low rather than high control becomes more typical of children's experiences in discourse, then their powers as conversational partners and, eventually, as narrators will improve. Any such improvement, however, will demand not simply a laissez-faire policy from teachers but an approach that achieves contingent control of interactions and the strategic use of repair and feedback. We have illustrated the great skill that would be needed to achieve this state of affairs. It is obviously not going to be easy to find or train teachers to whom contingent control of interactions will become 'second nature'. We have gone only a short way in trying to understand the complexities of discourse with deaf children and made a very few preliminary suggestions about how improvements might be sought. We suggest that teachers and schools— whatever methods of communication they are using—can measure the efficacy and value of their attempts to facilitate the development of their children's linguistic competence by examining and analysing their own techniques for *conversing* with them.

CHAPTER 6

The Assessment and Teaching of Reading

This is our gloomiest chapter. How marvellous it would be to be able to write a treatise outlining an approach to teaching reading to deaf children that would guarantee them reading levels at least on a par with hearing eleven-year-olds when they leave school. Sadly, we are not able to write such a treatise. Rather, we have to be content with an attempt to gain greater understanding of why, despite years of effort by teachers to teach them how to read, the vast majority of severely and profoundly deaf children leave school essentially incapable of doing so. First, we will look at attempts to assess deaf children's reading ability and ask what various tests have to tell us about what they do and do not know about written English. We move on to outline some of the explanations that have been put forward for deaf children's poor levels of literacy and explore their educational implications. We take a brief look at attempts to teach children how to read and get some ideas about where all the time goes and why so much effort in teaching reading usually bears so little fruit. Finally, we consider some of the relationships between language and literacy.

Why do the majority of deaf children leave their classrooms illiterate? This is a vast and complex question. Although many years of study have gone into the investigation of reading in both deaf and hearing people, the many processes involved in skilled reading and the relationship between these processes are still not fully (or even largely) understood. When we add our uncertainties about the nature of linguistic competence in deaf children to our ignorance about the precise nature of reading processes we are confronted with a problem of quite staggering complexity.

We would be prepared to demand a Nobel Prize for anyone who could provide a compelling solution to this problem. However, since we have not come across a suitable candidate, we will have to be content with an exploration of some potential contributing causes to deaf children's problems in trying to read.

It is clear—and not an over-statement—that we do not know how to teach deaf, or even partially-hearing children to read (Conrad, 1979, p. 175).

This bold, challenging and pessimistic statement was based on a review of the now-extensive research literature on the reading achievements of deaf children and Conrad's own findings from a large-scale survey of deaf and partially hearing children about to leave English and Welsh schools in the mid-1970s. As Conrad and others (e.g. Quigley and Kretschmer, 1982) point out, studies in many parts of the world over a number of years, involving children from very different educational backgrounds, have yielded consistent results. Since Conrad's investigations also included a study of the relationships between literacy and several other aspects of linguistic competence, we will concentrate on his findings here.

Conrad's fifteen- to sixteen-year-old sample included 468 deaf and partially hearing children who were tested using the Brimer Wide-span Reading Test (Brimer, 1972). In this test the child reads a cue sentence and selects one word from this sentence to fill in a gap in another. For example:

Pack the eggs in the box.	Hens lay . . . .
Brush up the leaves and burn them.	When logs . . . , smoke rises.

The 468 children achieved an average reading age of nine years on this test. Conrad not only tested reading but also measured lip-reading skills and speech intelligibility; he administered tests of 'internal speech' designed to show how far they read using a phonemically based approach (i.e. 'translating' printed symbols into speech sounds), and collected teacher assessments of oral language levels. He also measured non-verbal intelligence and obtained better-ear hearing losses. Broadly speaking, he found that these measures were interrelated. Children displaying more 'internal speech' (we discuss this more fully later) were more likely to read and lip-read relatively well, to speak more intelligibly and be rated higher on language ability by their teachers. All these measures correlated with degree of hearing loss and, less powerfully, with non-verbal intelligence. Thus children with losses in excess of 85 dB in this study were unlikely to evidence internal speech and produced mean reading ages of about eight years. However, those children with losses greater than 85 dB who *did* evidence 'internal speech' also read relatively well, suggesting that the capacity to read and memorize words in terms of their sounds, rather than degree of deafness *as such*, was what differentiated good and poor deaf readers.

The pattern of associations between these measures implies that children without internal speech read using a visually based strategy in which the orthographic 'shapes' of printed words are associated 'directly' with meaning (e.g. Hung, Tzeng and Warren, 1981). In other words, they do not access the meaning of what they read by first converting the visual symbols into speech sounds, but rely instead on memorized associations between printed word shapes and the things to which they refer.

WHAT DO TESTS OF READING TEST?

In a series of studies (Webster, Wood and Griffiths, 1981; Wood, Griffiths and Webster, 1981; Beggs and Breslaw, 1983) we have compared the scoring patterns of deaf and hearing children with nominally similar reading ages on three tests of reading. One was the Southgate Sentence Completion Reading Test (Southgate, 1962). In performing this test, the reader is required to complete a sentence with a word drawn from a set of five alternatives. For example:

Ducks can . . . .
pond/swim/water/farm/sing

I drink . . . .
cake/hens/milk/picture/man

Birds are covered with . . . .
trees/skirts/sky/nests/feathers

We gave the Southgate test to sixty deaf children (with a mean hearing loss of 87 dB and mean age of eleven) who achieved a mean reading age of seven years nine months. They were matched with sixty hearing children who achieved similar mean scores on the test. We found that deaf children attempted far more of the test items than hearing children did. In scoring the Southgate and other tests, when a child gets a string of wrong answers, no further items are analysed since to do so would increase the number of correct scores by 'chance', thus artificially inflating the reading age estimate. In this study, however, deaf children usually got enough right answers scattered throughout the test to keep scoring. Indeed, many of them reached the end of the test in the allotted time span. The test starts with easy items and gets progressively more difficult. The hearing children tended to do those items that were consistent with their reading age, try one or two more beyond this 'ceiling' and then give up. The deaf children, however, did not; they tended to persevere to the end. Thus, they made more errors in achieving their reading ages than the hearing children.

THE ANALYSIS OF ERRORS

The analysis of errors is a most revealing process and one of the most useful things one can do with the results of formal tests. An examination of children's errors often reveals patterns that can be used to obtain some insights into what they know and how they interpret the test itself. We also use error analysis in Chapter 9 when we explore deaf and hearing children's mathematical abilities. When we examined the errors of deaf and hearing children on the Southgate test, we found some marked and informative differences. The test is designed to offer children a number of plausible bases for error. Some of the 'distractor' words look rather like the right answer (e.g. A pig has a curly . . . . tall/tail/stale/tell/stile), some sound rather like it (e.g. A sheep's babies are called . . . . lame/calves/look/lambs/lamps) and others mean similar things (e.g. The alphabet has twenty-six . . . . words/figures/letters/ laces/books). These distractors work because children are likely to confuse words that look the same, sound the same or mean similar things when their knowledge of written language is tenuous. This limited understanding is revealed by their choice of plausible distractors.

When we examined the errors made by hearing children we found, as we would expect, a relatively even distribution across the distractors. Put another way, knowing what mistakes one hearing child with a reading age of nine made on a given item does not generate any good predictions about the errors made by other hearing children of the same reading age.

This was not the case with the deaf children. In fact, when we looked at their performance on all items we found that, by and large, they made the *same* errors. This implies that they were adopting a systematic strategy for handling the test but not one that was very sensitive to the orthographic or grapheme–phoneme cues that mislead hearing children. Below we list some examples of these common errors (popular answers in capitals).

Birds are covered with . . . .
trees/skirts/sky/NESTS/feathers

Careless driving leads to . . . .
happiness/CARS/tractors/accidents/improvements

Rich men can afford to live in . . . .
luscious/poverty/luxurious/luxury/WEALTHY

Ducks can . . . .
POND/swim/water/farm/sing

These examples suggest that deaf children are capitalizing on word associations. In fact, we need attribute to the deaf reader no more than a sight vocabulary for isolated words and a sense of the real-world associations between those words to get such a score. We are not saying, however, that this is all that they do have (read on). Although word association does not help explain errors on all tests, on the Southgate it is consistent both with many errors and some rather sophisticated-looking correct answers to later items, where the right answer happens to be the only highly associated word in the list of possibilities. For example:

> There was a bridge over the . . . .
> rain/running/RIVER/rest/ruler
>
> I drink . . . .
> cake/hens/MILK/picture/man
>
> A dog's babies are called . . . .
> chickens/papers/PUPPIES/calves/potatoes

These results, we argue, lead to the conclusion that the reading ages given by the Southgate test for hearing-impaired children are not simply reflecting delayed reading development. Most hearing-impaired children are doing something quite different from hearing children to gain their reading score.

Although some tests, such as Brimer's (see below), do not permit extensive use of a word association strategy, others do. A recent analysis of reading tests completed by a large sample of deaf and hearing children in the United States found similar 'test-taking strategies' being used by deaf children to those identified in our research (Wolk and Schildroth, in press).

On the Brimer Wide-span Test (Brimer, 1972), used by Conrad, we found many errors which were more 'inscrutable' than those made on the Southgate test. Here we used a technique for classifying errors designed to estimate the degree of linguistic sophistication involved (see Webster, Wood and Griffiths, 1981, for details). Basically, hearing-impaired children made more 'non-linguistic' errors than their hearing controls (again, of similar nominal reading ages). On some items, for example, they inserted into the test sentence a word from the cue sentence that occupied the same spatial position (e.g. the fifth word in each sentence). On the basis of our examination of these and other analyses we concluded that the reading tests we have used do not measure the same things in deaf and hearing children.

If one accepts this conclusion, then we must reconsider the status of the 'reading plateau' found in many studies of deaf children's reading and the various implications that may be drawn from it. Furthermore, if deaf children are using special, non-syntactically based strategies on reading tests, does it follow that they are *not* developing a productive grammar for spoken and/or written English at all? We shall now turn to a consideration of the first of these two questions. The second question provides the focus for the next chapter.

ASPECTS OF SYNTACTIC COMPETENCE IN DEAF CHILDREN

The most comprehensive attempt (that we know of) to look at *how* deaf children interpret different aspects of written English, rather than concentrating simply on their scores and the errors they make on hearing-referenced reading tests, is a series of detailed studies by Quigley and his colleagues from Illinois in the United States. Their research culminated in a 'Test of Syntactic

Abilities' (or TSA) which, as the authors explicitly point out, is not a test of reading in the normal sense but investigates how children handle a wide range of syntactic devices in print. Like all research, it has its limitations; the main constraint on this work (which is acknowledged by its authors) is that it looks mainly at children's performance with 'isolated' written sentences and does not examine the factors involved in reading extended text. However, notwithstanding this limitation, the test provides some valuable insights into children's levels of performance and developmental progress on a range of features of written language.

For example, one technique they used to explore deaf children's knowledge of various complex syntactic structures was to present a series of pairs of simple sentences such as 'I saw the man. The man hit the dog' and then to ask children to judge whether more complex constructions, such as 'I saw the man who the man hit the dog', represent an acceptable combination of the simple ones. If the child judges that it is not, then he is asked to write a correct version. Another strategy was to provide children with a number of candidate complex sentences and ask them to choose the one that looked correct.

One important feature of the test which grew out of these studies is that the 'distractor' sentences it uses are derived from empirical studies of *deaf* children. Thus, the test gives valuable information not only about what deaf children cannot read and the syntactic structures they find most difficult, but also provides insights into how they think acceptable written English is structured. Since the various different distractors also embody a developmental sequence, it is possible to chart progress in children even before they get correct answers. In short, the error patterns are revealing.

It is not our aim here to go into detail about the items in the test, nor the developmental sequences it suggests. Rather, we wish to address a number of general features of the research that serve both to address the 'ceiling of reading achievement' issue and to give some insights into the grammatical knowledge of deaf children. The research involved deaf children aged from ten to eighteen years of age and a smaller age range of hearing controls. In relation to almost every aspect of syntax tested, the deaf children showed consistent if very slow progress throughout the age range tested. Although, by eighteen, their performance was still rather poor in comparison to ten-year-old hearing children, there was no evidence that the process of learning to read actually stopped at any specific age, which implies that any improvements in techniques for teaching reading might be useful over a wide age range.

More important, perhaps, are the insights that the test gives into what children think the structure of English (at least as written) is like. We want to draw attention to two general features of the children's scoring patterns. These, we suggest, reveal aspects of deaf children's performance that are not specific to particular features of grammar (e.g. auxiliary verb systems, pronominalization, determiners and so on) but have the status of general 'rules'. First, is the 'subject–verb–object' rule (or S-V-O). Many constructions in

English, particularly in the speech addressed to young children and encountered by them in early reading books, are consistent with this syntactic rule (although some linguists prefer to use the 'semantic' terms 'Agent–Action–Patient'). If a child assumes that the elements in the surface structure (the physical arrangement of sounds in speech and graphemes in print) are always organized such that the first noun encountered is the subject (or agent) of the sentence, followed by a verb (action) and then the object (patient), he or she will have few problems in understanding the meaning of structurally simple sentences such as 'Fred is eating ice-cream'. Similarly, if simple sentences are conjoined with no 'deletions' of subjects or objects as in 'Mary likes ice-cream and Peter likes cakes', then the child (who can read the main words) following the S-V-O rule will have no difficulty understanding what is meant.

However, English is not nearly as simple as this. There are no foolproof, simple or direct relationships between semantic and syntactic features of meaning. In passive constructions, for example, such as 'Mary was hit by John', the 'deep' subject (agent) is not Mary but John. The relationships between word order and 'deep' underlying meanings are not simple nor limited to a single set of 'mapping' rules between meaning and expression or, more technically, between semantic relations and grammatical roles (e.g. Brown, 1973, p. 149ff; Wanner and Gleitman, 1982, p. 29ff). Similarly, when we come to look at complex and compound sentences we find that subjects are often deleted as in 'Mary fed the dog and went out'. Here the deleted subject of the verb 'went' has to be 'retrieved' from the first clause. In sentences such as these, presented in isolation at least, young hearing children (aged up to eight or nine) and deaf children (as late as eighteen years) seem to work on what has been called the 'Minimum Distance Principle' (Chomsky, 1969). They tend to choose a noun in the sentence that is closest to the verb with a deleted subject. Thus, the errors produced by deaf children in Quigley's test are all consistent with either S-V-O or MDP.

The boy was helped by the girl.	(boy helps girl)
The boy who kissed the girl ran away.	(girl runs away)
The opening of the door surprised the cat.	(door surprised cat)

Before going on to consider the implications of these findings, let us outline some caveats about using such evidence to talk about children's general linguistic abilities. First, we have to bear in mind the fact that the data come from studies of reading rather than speaking or speech comprehension. As we will argue more fully in Chapter 8, written text is not simply speech written down. The written word involves features that are not present in spoken discourse, and vice versa. So, we have to be cautious when making any general statements about linguistic competence on the basis of tests of reading. In speech, for example, there are often pragmatic cues arising from situational factors, non-verbal and paralinguistic information, as well as from the structure of discourse, that supplement meaning and may help children to understand (or ignore) syntactic structures. In print, robbed of such cues, children may fail. Furthermore, there are syntactic structures in print that are rarely found in speech (for instance, 'Harry's leaving surprised the girl').

A second caveat is that the origins and processes involved in the development of S-V-O and MDP strategies by hearing children are still the subject of debate (Bowerman, 1979; Romaine, 1984). Uncertainties about the factors that lead hearing children to understand complex structures in the way they do make it difficult to predict how and why deaf children show similar patterns. We explore this question more fully in Chapter 8 when we consider environmental factors that might limit children's development of complex linguistic structures. A third, and final, caveat is that statistical generalizations based on large numbers of subjects do not tell us very much about the processes that go on inside an individual child's mind as he reads. However, bearing these reservations in mind, let us explore some possible implications, both theoretical and educational, of these findings.

The first point we want to underline is that the statistical patterns found in the analyses of language comprehension of hearing and (older) deaf children are similar in some important respects. Despite the problems of drawing inferences about the abilities of individual children from group data, the fact remains that such data generate common *patterns* that have to be explained and which suggest some parallels in the development of deaf and hearing children.

If one accepts the argument that deaf children make use of rules like S-V-O and MDP, then it follows that these children possess a generative, if limited, linguistic system. Further evidence of this fact is presented in the next chapter. If this is true, how is it implicated in reading?

BARRIERS TO LITERACY

The problems faced by poor (hearing) readers and the development of reading schemes designed to help them overcome their problems have been the subject of a great deal of research and theory. Contemporary debates between different theorists and between teachers with different views on reading are heated and, in relation to the concept of dyslexia in particular, have reached temperatures usually reserved for arguments about the education of deaf children. Having braved the fires of one debate we have no intention of entering that relating to 'poor' readers (see Bryant and Bradley, 1985; Underwood, 1979). However, since there are some similar issues involved in discussions of deaf and poor (hearing) readers that have been explored in studies of the latter, it is worth attempting a brief overview of such work.

Theories of reading and explanations for the problems of poor readers traditionally fall into two camps. One concentrates on the 'basics' of reading, namely the nature of 'grapheme–phoneme correspondence (GPC) rules'.

These rules specify how the sound system of speech relates to the graphemic elements of writing (and involve many complex irregularities in English). Advocates of this approach provide so-called 'bottom-up' explanations of the reading process. They argue that the first stages of learning to read and the principal source of problems for poor readers is achieving mastery of such rules. Good readers, the argument proceeds, have 'automated' GPC rules that enable them to read text quickly and without any conscious effort at 'decoding' words into sound. The poor reader and beginning reader do not possess this automated system for 'encoding' print. Rather, if they do not immediately recognize the shape of a written word, they have to deliberately sound out each element of it and 'build up' a spoken version of it. This, a slow and laborious process, limits not only how fast they can read but the number of words that they can 'hold in mind' long enough to relate them and achieve comprehension. Thus, the poor reader is not only slow but also understands less of what he reads than a better reader because the effort of working out each word takes up the time and mental capacity that the good reader uses for achieving comprehension of sequences of words and text.

The opposing view is that GPC rules are less central both to the reading process and the explanation of poor readers' problems. Advocates of this view point out that good readers 'interact' with what they read. They do not read each word in a text, as studies of eye movements in reading illustrate. Indeed, since skilled readers may read at 200 to 300 words per minute it is clear that they do not read every word. Rather, they tend to look selectively at specific words or structures in text (although no one has yet managed to explain why they look at what they do look at nor what they do with it!). The skilled reader, the argument proceeds, formulates and tests hypotheses about what the text means, exploiting knowledge not only of GPC rules but grammar, general knowledge, and so on. Poor readers, the argument concludes, do not make use of these higher level resources (hence, the term 'top-down' explanations of reading problems). They limit their attention by looking at each word in turn, rather than trying to interact intelligently with the text.

Conrad's research into 'internal speech' may be used to provide a 'bottom-up' explanation for the reading levels of the deaf. The deaf reader, like the poor (hearing) one, does not possess automated GPC rules. Indeed, unlike the hearing reader, very deaf children may have no *basis* for developing such rules because they lack the phonemic knowledge to map graphemic information onto (although Dodd and Hermelin, 1977, argue that this is not the case). Such a child, from a 'bottom-up' perspective, *cannot* become a good reader. But how did Conrad find out that such deaf readers lacked 'internal speech'?

If hearing people are given a list of words to read which sound similar (e.g. blue, zoo, true, etc.) they find it more difficult to memorize them than they do a list of words which sound different (but are otherwise similar in length, familiarity, etc., e.g. home, farm, bare). The explanation for this phenomenon, which is reflected in other aspects of learning, is that similar things are more likely to cause mental 'interference' and, hence, are more difficult to memorize. When Conrad asked deaf school leavers to read and memorize such lists he found that many of them, and the vast majority with hearing losses over 85 dB, showed no such interference effect. They found a list of similarly *sounding* words no more difficult to memorize than a dissimilar list. From this, Conrad concludes that when these deaf children read words they do not convert them into 'internal speech'. If they did convert what they read into sounds, then they would have shown the interference effect (which less deaf children who read better tended to do).

This evidence, in the hands of a 'bottom-up' theorist, would mean that such children cannot become good readers; they lack the 'basics' out of which reading grows. If one accepts this view, then only by developing a child's auditory awareness and auditory memory could he ever be expected to improve his reading. If this proves impossible, he will not improve.

Conrad's test, however, only used lists of isolated words. The evidence we reviewed in the last section shows that deaf readers possess and use some knowledge of the *structure* of written language and can read some sentences at least. For a radical 'top-down' theorist, this would imply that the child might be able to read well but only within the limits of his 'higher-order knowledge'. Put another way, perhaps deaf children do not have a specific *reading* problem at all but can read anything that they possess the requisite linguistic knowledge of. What limits their reading is an impoverished understanding of the structures of *language*. If so, any improvements in their understanding of English (with or without phonemic awareness) could lead to improved standards of reading. Furthermore, if the child does not invent or is not taught strategies for *interacting* with text, but learns or is taught that reading involves a word-by-word approach, then he may lack effective 'top-down' skills which, if developed, might also improve reading comprehension.

These issues are not resolved and cannot be resolved here. We will give our *opinions* later. However, a more recent theory of reading development and reading problems attempts to integrate 'bottom-up' and 'top-down' approaches in an account that, in company with our study of deaf children's reading lessons presented in the next section, puts reading problems into a somewhat new light and may suggest new strategies for approaching the teaching of reading. Briefly, Stanovich and West (1979) have provided evidence for a model of the reading process based on the general idea that poor readers, who, they argue, lack automated GPC rules, try to enrich the information they have to work with when they read by making *more* use of 'top-down' information than good readers do. Thus, poor readers rely more on cues and clues derived from their general knowledge and knowledge of language to 'fill in' gaps left by poor reading. Because this strategy is prone to error, takes longer and demands a good deal of conscious effort, the poor reader reads slowly and understands less of what he reads than the good reader.

Deaf children, we shall argue, are in an analogous situation but are doubly handicapped as readers. They, too, as we shall see, use information from the immediate context and their general knowledge to supplement what they read. But they also have available fewer linguistic resources (e.g. less knowledge of grammatical aspects of language and word meanings) than the poor hearing reader does. So, we suggest, the deaf reader is likely to put his or her intelligence to work in using paralinguistic, non-verbal and contextual cues to help understand what is being 'read'. If this process turns out to be slow, laborious and error prone, we should not be too surprised.

TEACHING READING TO DEAF CHILDREN

There are a bewildering number of different 'schemes' for teaching reading. Some are specially written for groups like deaf children; many are designed to teach any child. So far as we are aware, however, few attempts have been made to look systematically at *how* children are *actually* taught to read in the classroom. Nor, to our knowledge, are there any well-designed evaluations demonstrating the effectiveness of any reading scheme being used with deaf children. The field abounds in opinion but is noticeably lacking in evidence.

We have undertaken one small-scale but detailed study of reading lessons with deaf children aged between six and ten years. The aim of this research was to provide some insights into the experience of deaf and hearing children being taught to read (Howarth *et al.*, 1981). We do not claim, of course, that such a study is representative of all teaching practice, but we will argue that the processes and problems we observe are likely to be common ones for many deaf children and their teachers.

While we do not intend to go into details of statistical analysis here, we need to say a little about the procedure used. We wanted to compare the experiences of deaf and hearing children being taught to read. But one problem facing us was who should we compare with whom? Chronological age is not, as we know, a suitable basis for comparing the linguistic abilities or literary skills of deaf and hearing children. We also rejected the use of standard reading tests since any estimates of reading ages were likely to suffer from the difficulties outlined above.

It is often said, and has been demonstrated by Quigley and his colleagues, that the relationships between language abilities and the demands of reading are quite different for deaf and hearing children. The deaf child is likely to be exposed in print to both vocabulary and syntax that are not part of his existing linguistic competence. Indeed, Quigley *et al.* (1978) have argued that it is through reading that deaf children may first be exposed to many aspects of language, a point we take up in Chapter 8. Whilst the structures encountered by young hearing readers, by and large, will have been present in their speech for some time (though, as we have said, reading is likely to introduce new structures and to make rather different uses of existing ones) this will not be true for most deaf children.

In sum, the relationship between the reader and what he is reading is likely to be fundamentally and quantitatively different for deaf and hearing children. We wanted a research strategy that would enable us to test this hypothesis.

Eventually, Patricia Howarth invented a simple but ingenious technique for matching children—one that, we feel, gives insights into the very different demands placed on hearing and deaf children when they are being taught to read. She filmed deaf children (from a number of schools) being taught to read in the normal course of classroom activities, recording a lesson that would have taken place had she not been there. Then she hunted around local primary schools for hearing children, to discover schools that were using the same reading books as those in the deaf sample. Having matched schools in this way, she waited until a teacher came to teach the same pages of the same book used with one of the deaf children. Thus, children were matched in terms of what they were being asked to read in the normal course of schooling.

The videotaped reading lessons were transcribed and several features were analysed. First, we determined how often reading 'stopped' and who initiated the stop. Did the teacher stop the child or did he stop spontaneously? Second, we looked at the reasons for stopping. How did the teacher react to and interpret each breakdown in reading? Third, we examined the children's reading rates. Together, these analyses suggested that both the experience of reading and the structure of the reading lesson were quite different for hearing and deaf children.

On average, deaf children both stopped reading spontaneously and were stopped more often by their teachers than the hearing children were. Furthermore, many more stops with hearing children included an element of praise from the teacher. There were also clear differences in the reasons for stopping. Teachers of hearing children usually interpreted stops as signalling a breakdown in a child's knowledge of grapheme–phoneme correspondence rules. In other words, they seemed to assume both that the children already knew the words and syntactic structures within the text, and that they were able to articulate the speech sounds appropriately. They simply could not *read* very well, having yet to develop adequate 'word attack' skills.

In contrast, although deaf children were also stopped because teachers decided they did not know these rules, they were more likely to be stopped because they did not *pronounce* a word properly (even though, at times, it seemed the child knew the word he was stopped on). The most marked difference, however, was that teachers of the deaf stopped their children much more often in order to teach the *meanings* of words. They also interpreted many of the child's own stops as evidence that he had met a word he did not know. In consequence, deaf children were stopped not only more frequently but for a greater *variety* of reasons than the hearing readers. Teachers of the deaf interpreted their children as having a greater range of difficulties and therefore pursued more complex and varied goals than the teachers of hearing did with their children. Thus, for most deaf children, the experience of reading and the structure of the reading lesson were quite different from that of hearing children reading the same pages of a book.

The third feature of the reading lessons we analysed—reading rate—was also revealing. In order to get a rough measure of reading fluency, we counted the number of words read between stops and divided this by the time taken to read them. In addition to differences between deaf and hearing children we found some marked differences between deaf children from different schools. Children from one school for the deaf were reading much more fluently and faster than other children.

If, for the moment, we ignore children from the 'successful' deaf school, the reading rates for the remaining deaf children were around twenty words per minute. For the hearing children, reading the same material, the average was sixty-four words per minute.

Experimental studies have shown that when we are exposed to speech rates of less than forty words per minute our comprehension starts to break down. It therefore appears highly unlikely that a deaf child with poor expressive and spoken language can make much sense out of text read at half this rate.

For a deaf child whose knowledge of language was well below that demanded in the text, reading lessons became a language lesson and speech-training exercise. The overall result was a slow, disjointed lesson punctuated by long periods of questioning, story telling and demonstration as the teacher attempted not only to get the child to read but also to learn language. We were left in considerable doubt about how such a lesson could leave the child with a sense of any 'story' or even of phrases and sentences in reading. What exactly, we wondered, does the deaf child think reading *is*?

Clearly, the behaviour of the teachers in this situation is an understandable response to a child with underdeveloped language, poor articulation and, perhaps, with little understanding of what 'stories' are all about. But, is the child 'ready' to read?

Returning now to the issue of 'top-down' processing and the gap between the demands of the text and the level of ability of the child, we can put forward some more specific hypotheses about why reading lessons are so difficult and, arguably, often counter-productive for both teacher and child. First, because deaf children read so slowly, stop so frequently, and, like young hearing children, tend to 'bark at print', it is unlikely that they are exploiting any knowledge they might have about speech rhythm, intonation or stress. Even if they have enough low frequency hearing to hear and understand such cues to linguistic structure, they are unlikely to be producing or hearing them in lessons typified by long stops and slow, deliberate articulation. Further-more, teachers never actually *read* to a child whilst he looked at print. Whereas, with a young hearing child, we can read to them, 'mapping' our fingers onto words read whilst he looks on, there was none of this with deaf children. The problem of divided attention discussed in Chapter 3 emerges to further exacerbate the child's reading problems and the teacher's difficulties in teaching him. If the teacher wants to get the child to listen to a word or lip-read it, then she attracts his attention to her before doing so, presumably on the basis of the not unreasonable assumption that he will not hear the sounds well enough nor understand what she says without the help of lip-reading and other paralinguistic cues to meaning. This means that the child now has to *remember* the word, phrase or whatever and go back to the text in order to relate it to the written form. Thus, the process of reading for the child is disrupted by the problem of divided attention and limited by his intelligence and powers of memory.

Next comes the question of the gap between what he is trying to read and his likely level of linguistic ability. On our recordings, deaf children usually stopped reading, presumably because they could not read a word, did not recognize it, did not know it, could not pronounce it or could not understand its connection with other words (grammar). If they stopped on a noun or verb, teachers would usually try to define the word or remind them of it if they thought the children knew it. In the following examples, we illustrate some of the ploys used by teachers either to teach or prompt the child to recall a word.

C. (reads) The waves will take it on the rocks.
T. (interrupts) What are they? (pointing to the word 'waves')
C. Waves ⟨waves 'goodbye'⟩.
T. Waves, yes, not that kind of wave. What wave . . . ? Can you show me the wave?
C. (Child picks up a bookmark and starts to wave it.)
T. No, not that kind of wave.
C. ⟨Undulating, 'sea waves'⟩.
T. Those waves. Yes.

Even more difficulty was encountered with 'function' words such as demonstratives and pronouns. For example, consider what happened a little later in the 'wave' session.

T. The waves will take it. (Points to boat and to rocks in picture. Looks questioningly at the child.) . . . It? What's 'it'?
C. It.
T. What's 'it'?
C. It.
T. What will they take? What's 'it'?
C. (Child points to a rock and squeals.)
T. No, not the rock. They're the rocks, look (pointing to 'rock' in text). Can they get it on the rocks? Can they get what? . . . It's the boat.
C. The boat.

In Chapter 8, we will illustrate the complex 'pluri-functional' nature of many so-called function words. Pronouns, for example, serve more than one purpose in language. They take their meaning from the role they play in grammar and cannot be defined 'ostensibly' as can some nouns, verbs and adjectives. The child's problem in *reading and understanding* such words often lies not in his inability to *recognize* the word but in an inadequate knowledge of its function and the grammatical structures within which it is embedded.

Research by Quigley and his colleagues has illustrated the problems that deaf readers face with many aspects of written syntax. They have also shown that the gap between deaf children's comprehension of syntactic structures and the demands of texts written to teach children how to read is so wide that it presents enormous if not insuperable demands on the deaf reader (Quigley and Kretschmer, 1982, p. 69ff). In our study, too, children were often expected to read text containing grammatical structures that were not a part of their linguistic knowledge. If the deaf child has a potential to read, we suggest that the sorts of reading lessons we have just considered are hardly likely to achieve it.

We have already mentioned that seven children from one school (average hearing loss 92 dB) were much more successful than the other deaf children. They were reading at an average seventy-seven words per minute and, in some cases, were articulating at a faster rate than their (younger) hearing matches. One deaf child, for example, was reading at 142 words per minute. The fastest hearing child read at 130. There were stops for reflection on linguistic meanings but usually of a quite different order to those considered above, as the following excerpt from a transcript illustrates. The child involved in the interaction below is ten years of age, has a hearing loss of 108 dB and a non-verbal IQ on the WISC-R of 129. She was one of the deafest but also one of the most intelligent children in the sample. She read at an average of almost eighty-eight words per minute from a text with an estimated reading age level of ten years.

C. (reading) . . . sitting on the edge of the rocks, waiting for the dragon to finish his forty winks (stops reading, laughs and looks at the teacher).
T. What are forty winks?
C. (Pupil laughs again and blinks her eyes rapidly) Meaning nap.
T. No, oh no, it doesn't mean it literally that he goes one (blinking . . .) two, three.
C. (Giggles.)
T. It doesn't mean it literally.
C. (Shakes head.)
T. If you don't mean something literally, like *catching* a cold . . . .
C. Oh, I see. It's an idiom.
T. Yes, he's not literally going to have forty winks.
C. (Giggles and starts to read again.)

Although we have no objective measures to determine how far these children *understood* what they read, their rate of articulation (much of which was intelligible) together with their responses to teacher questions and the occasional outbreak of mirth at funny bits persuaded us that they were understanding what they read.

It would obviously be unwise to try to make any general pronouncements about the 'causes' of success from such a small sample. However, in other studies of children drawn from this same school we found evidence that their linguistic abilities (and mathematical competence) were significantly better than those of children of similar age, sex, hearing loss and (in some studies) non-verbal intelligence but drawn from other schools. In addition to using and maintaining the most appropriate hearing aids available for each child, this school also places a great deal of emphasis on how language is *used* with children.

In relation to their reading, one factor that we believe is implicated in their success is that the school leaves formal reading lessons to a relatively late stage (this varies according to the child's linguistic development but is often around eight years or so) on the grounds that reading should only begin when the child's language meets the demands of text. They reject the notion that reading can or should be used to *teach* language. Rather, before this, every child experiences regular, intensive concentration on conversation and a great deal of emphasis on listening to story telling. Our evidence cannot be offered as conclusive support for this view, but the success of these children does show that severe or profound hearing loss is *not* an inevitable barrier to reading. We suspect that the quality of teaching contributed something to their success.

WHY CAN'T MOST DEAF CHILDREN READ?

Deaf children, taking a reading test, are likely to adopt special and often non-linguistic or non-syntactically based reading strategies. Where the demands of the test, or a reading text, are well beyond the child's levels of linguistic competence it seems inevitable that this must be the case. Deaf children are bound to put their intelligence to work to seek solutions to such demands, using their knowledge of the world and their pragmatic knowledge of language (e.g. word associations) in attempts to use general contextual cues to overcome their limited linguistic resources.

When we looked at reading lessons we found analogous and complementary features in the teaching and learning process. Often the child's attention was concentrated on the meanings and 'sounds' associated with words isolated from their syntactic and story context. Furthermore, the process often took place at such a slow pace that it seems inconceivable that children could be discovering much, if anything, about the structural properties of text or language. Indeed, when, in another study, we examined the eye movements of deaf children reading and compared them with those of hearing children with similar reading age scores (Beggs, Breslaw and Wilkinson, 1982), we found that the deaf (but not the hearing) children were reading using a word-by-word strategy, their eyes alighting on each word in turn. The eyes of their hearing 'matches' ranged more widely and less predictably over the text, bypassing words or word sequences, as happens in more skilled reading. One deaf child in this study not only displayed word–word fixations in reading but actually read from left to right on one line and then dropped his eyes to the word at the right-hand side of the line below and proceeded to read that line *backwards*!

Our analyses of reading assessment and teaching of reading must surely show that for a group of deaf children, who we have no reason to believe are atypical, the experience, purpose and significance of reading were often fundamentally different in kind from that of hearing children. But these studies focused on linguistic structures that were often too far in advance of children's knowledge of language to make productive reading possible. Indeed, if there is any weight in the hypothesis explored in Chapter 3, that effective teaching and learning demands that a child is confronted with *manageable* and *intelligible* problems, then we must conclude that the activity of reading for the deaf child in many of the lessons we have observed is not only unlikely to be successful but may be counterproductive. Constant failure in the face of insuperable difficulty destroys the learner.

Conrad's research, in company with several more recent studies (e.g. Leybaert, Alegria and Fonck, 1983; Quigley and Paul, 1984), shows that deaf children read well to the extent that they display a knowledge of the phonemic structure of language. Children lacking such knowledge rely on visual features of text and, within the limits of known methods for teaching reading, there seems to be no way in which such children can achieve literacy. Rather, in reading lessons and tests of reading they must supplement their limited abilities to read by using their general knowledge and intelligence to develop strategies that guarantee only a limited degree of success. Similarly, when faced with complex grammatical structures, they display strategies for trying to understand what is on the page, often leading quite systematically to misunderstanding. Teachers, faced with trying to teach reading to children with these difficulties, often respond by converting what are designed to be reading lessons into sessions on language and speech. In so doing, we suggest, they are likely to help children 'learn' those special but limited strategies that they adopt to try to make sense of what they read.

More optimistically, the fact that some children were relatively fluent in reading lessons despite hearing losses in excess of 85 dB (the average was 92 dB) questions any absolute statements about the theoretical impossibility of deaf children learning to read. It may be that these children have something 'special'. Conrad found only five 'special' children in his group with losses over 85 dB whose reading ages were commensurate with their chronological ages. They evidenced good internal speech. However, beyond congratulating the child, his teachers and parents, Conrad was unable to give any insights into 'how' these children achieved their special status. We need to explore the possibility that this arises out of experience and education. This also means that the focus of research into reading must change from a concentration on tests and large-scale issues to detailed studies of different processes of instruction and evaluations of their effectiveness.

WHAT ABOUT TEACHERS OF READING?

Although our research into reading has been largely descriptive and was not designed to test any particular theory of if and how reading can be taught, we do have some practical suggestions that might help to improve the practice of teaching reading to deaf children.

First, we suggest that teachers of the deaf use their reading lessons more 'diagnostically'. By recording lessons (an audiorecording should suffice) it should be possible to estimate a child's reading rate and fluency. The number and purposes of any stops in reading can also be diagnosed. If the number of stops for 'teaching' language and articulation are in excess of those for *reading per se*, then it is a clear signal that the text is too difficult or that the child is not ready for formal reading lessons. Similarly, if the child's rate of articulation drops below forty words or so per minute, it is unlikely that he understands much of what is being read. If the teacher is having to recourse continually to models, drawings or interactions with a child, designed to give him more information to help understand a word or phrase, then the teacher might ask whether they are, in fact, helping to *create* problems for the child by building up or even teaching those inappropriate reading strategies that many children display.

Given the problems that many deaf children face in speech *articulation*, the possibilities offered by more frequent use of 'silent reading' might be explored. This might also direct teachers' (and perhaps children's) attention away from the meanings of 'words' to the comprehension of *text* as advocated by Ewoldt (1981).

More radically, we suggest that more attention should be paid to conversation and story telling as foundations for literacy, for reasons explored in Chapter 8.

There is quite clearly no known 'answer' to the reading problems of deaf children. Whether our own findings simply shed more gloom onto an already depressing scene or help to reinforce attempts at new approaches to teaching deaf children how to make sense of reading remains to be seen. The issue of 'internal speech' and phonemic awareness as 'inevitable' constraints on the potential for literacy in deaf children is still an open one. Conrad (1981), for example, has recently discussed possible strategies for teaching reading that are not based on a knowledge of GPC rules. As yet, however, his speculations, like those of all of us in this complex area, only provide promissory notes and, perhaps, the motivation to try to find some new approaches to the teaching of reading.

CHAPTER 7

Reading, Writing, Talking and Listening

In the last chapter, we used the results of tests of reading involving large groups of children to gain some insights into the deaf child's understanding of grammatical structure. However, as we admitted, using such evidence to make statements about what is going on in a particular child's mind when he reads or communicates is hazardous. Now, however, we begin to explore the linguistic abilities of severely and profoundly deaf children in more depth in order to test some of our ideas about linguistic competence.

The obvious strategy for exploring what a particular child knows about and does with language is to study that child in depth. Using this approach, for example, Ivimey (1976) was able to show that the one very deaf child he studied did develop a productive linguistic system, although it displayed a number of unusual characteristics in comparison with what we know about hearing children's language. Hearing children, however, also display very marked individual differences in how they develop and use language (e.g. Bowerman, 1982). Tests of language, based on group averages which overlook such individual differences, may present a misleading picture of a 'normal child'; one who does not, in fact, exist, except in numerical form! On the other hand, case studies may tempt us into false overgeneralizations if we assume that the study of one child necessarily tells us much about any other.

We need both types of research. When the outcomes of case studies can be integrated with the general picture derived from larger-scale ones, they reinforce each other's conclusions. Since this ideal state of affairs has not yet been achieved in studies of hearing children's linguistic development, we should not be too surprised to find that it is far from being achieved with the

112

deaf, who are rarer, more difficult to study and present so many other challenges when we try to interpret what they know.

In this study, we steer something of a 'middle course' between these two approaches. We look in some detail at several aspects of fifty severely and profoundly deaf children's (mean hearing loss 93 dB, average age ten years eight months) experience and use of language but achieve nothing like sufficient depth to enable us to say in any detail what each child's 'theory' of language is, although we will test ideas about aspects of such theories. However, our main motivation in undertaking this work was to explore the relationships between children's receptive and expressive abilities with spoken and written English.

There are many different opinions about and attitudes towards the nature of linguistic competence in the deaf. In the last chapter we saw, for example, that their reading abilities can be conceptualized as a rag-bag of special 'tricks' involving little more than a limited sight vocabulary, some knowledge of word associations derived from everyday experience and certain special strategies for meeting the demands of tests. On the other hand, we also cited evidence favouring the view that deaf children possess a limited but productive understanding of linguistic structure. However, it might be argued that very deaf children, such as those we are studying, only possess knowledge of a few stereotypical or 'baked' sentence forms (Van Uden, 1970) which they have learned by rote memory. The hallmark of linguistic competence is a remarkable degree of 'generativity' and creativity (Chomsky, 1980). Young hearing children produce spontaneously a vast number of 'original' utterances that they have never heard. They use linguistic 'rules' to create novel acts of speech. Are deaf children also 'generative' in their language, as we argued in the last chapter, or are they simply using rigid and well-learned 'formulae' for producing and understanding the written word?

Another related issue concerns the relationship between talk and text for children with hearing losses greater than 85 dB. Conrad, recall, produced evidence indicating both that internal speech was important for reading and that most children with losses greater than 85 dB did not possess that competence. Does this mean that *reading* processes in such children, being visually based, show no connection with their powers of speech or their receptive ability in understanding speech? This question, amongst other things, is what our study of fifty deaf children was designed to answer.

The investigation includes observations of children's performance in classroom conversations and their scores on a reading test. We also asked each child who took part to play a communication game with one of his peers (communicating both through verbal and written messages). We videorecorded the interactions and developed a system for scoring children's utterances for degree of syntactic accuracy. Non-verbal IQs, teacher ratings and audiograms were also collected.

For each child, then, we had a number of indicators of his receptive and expressive language. We outline each of these indicators and explore the relationships between them below. For fuller details see Griffiths (1983). We have used several of these measures of linguistic performance in previous studies, but with different groups of children, so were not able to explore the relationships between them. This investigation also provided an opportunity to test the robustness of some of our previous findings. Could we repeat our previous results with another set of children and teachers?

PERFORMANCE IN THE CLASSROOM

By filming each child in normal classroom conversation sessions we were able to check our previous results of the relationships between teacher moves and child responses and those between teacher power and child initiative and loquacity. Would we find the same pattern of relationships? We did. In fact, the results of this investigation were almost identical to those found in the initial analyses, described in Chapter 4 (see the Appendix for a comparison of the results).

More important for our present purposes, however, was the study of individual children. The main measure we obtained from the classroom sessions was each child's average length of turn, but we also used a number of more specific and, we hoped, revealing measures. How often did the child respond to his teacher's questions with appropriate answers? How lengthy were these? Did he take up options to speak after a teacher made a contribution or phatic or did he simply respond non-verbally with a nod or whatever?

THE COMMUNICATION GAME

In a previous investigation we had adapted a widely used technique from the study of hearing children's communicative competence. In this task, two children sit or stand facing each other across a table. Interposed between them is a screen which hides two sets of materials. In the situation used here, that material consisted of two identical books containing a series of pictures which depict the same set of characters in somewhat similar settings. Thus it was possible for a child to confuse one picture with others if a description given to him was incomplete or ambiguous. The children could see each other but not their partner's picture book. One child was asked to describe a given picture to his peer who then had to try to select the target picture from his copy of the book.

The interactions were videotaped for subsequent transcription and analysis. In previous studies using this technique, we compared deaf and hearing children's performances and found that when deaf children recognized and could identify the important elements of the task, their performance was comparable to hearing children's. We found, for example, no evidence that deaf children were any more 'egocentric' in providing appropriate messages than similarly aged hearing peers. As one might expect, however, when the linguistic content of the game becomes more complex, deaf children tend to fare less well. In this earlier study (Breslaw *et al.*, 1981) we were interested in the children's degree of success in getting messages across to each other. We found not only similarities and differences between deaf and hearing communicators but also some very marked differences between the performances of deaf children from different schools. Although they were matched for age, sex, hearing loss and non-verbal intelligence (and suffered no known additional handicap) the children from one school performed much better than their comparison groups (note that the successful children were drawn from the same school that produced relatively fluent readers described in Chapter 6).

Such marked differences in performance prompted us to look in more detail at the language used by the children and led us to develop a measure of 'syntactic accuracy' of verbal communication; this was employed in the present study of fifty children. Even without a formal system of measurement it was clear to us that the deaf children who produced good scores on this task were also producing more grammatically well-formed utterances. But how might we produce a more formal measure of accuracy?

As anyone who has listened to very deaf children will testify, transcribing their language and 'glossing' what they say to give an account of what they are trying to *mean* is no simple affair. The situation we used confers two advantages over the use of 'spontaneous' utterances. First, knowing the material being described we have some sense of what the child is talking about. Second, if that child gets his message across successfully, then we could be reasonably confident that it contained the minimal units of information needed to make a selection. However, even with these constraints to guide us we were not confident in our ability to provide a good measure of syntactic accuracy. When we transcribed the interactions, we also coded any gestures that could help to interpret and augment what the children said.

How could we derive a numerical assessment from such utterances? Basically, what we did was to compare each (communicatively successful) utterance from every child with an 'idealized' version of it. This 'idealization' involved keeping as far as possible to the actual words and word order used by the child. We would *add 'missing' elements* such as pronouns, auxiliary verbs, tense endings and determiners where, we felt, these would normally be uttered in a well-formed version of what the child had said. We also *deleted* any 'incorrect' elements such as an irrelevant tense ending or an 'extra', redundant pronoun. Third, we *substituted* for wrong elements the correct ones (e.g. if a child used a pronoun that did not agree in number or case with the noun it referred to). Fourth, we *relocated* words where necessary. When we had completed this 'idealization' process we simply counted the number of elements in the original version and the number of additions, deletions, substitutions and relocations we had made. The 'accuracy' score was derived from these.

We accept that this is a rather crude procedure. However, we did find the measure reasonably reliable. Accuracy scores calculated by two independent scorers were highly correlated. However, were we to find that these measures did *not* relate to any others (e.g. reading scores) then we were prepared to accept that the measure was *insensitive* to children's grammatical competence and the issue of the relationships between spoken syntax and other measures would have to remain open. Conversely, if we *did* find some reasonable relationships between this attempt to assess linguistic competence and the others, it seemed reasonable to accept it as a crude but useful technique. In the event, as we shall see, it did show some interpretable connections with other aspects of linguistic competence.

We used the same idealization and calculation techniques to assess the accuracy of *written* messages derived for each child from the same task setting. These, of course, were somewhat easier to score since we did not have problems of speech intelligibility and non-verbal, gestural communication to deal with.

READING TEST ASSESSMENT

Given our scepticism about the use of hearing-referenced tests of reading with the deaf, it may seem surprising that we elected to employ one in this study. However, as we have already said, we do not suggest that reading tests measure *nothing* linguistic with deaf children; rather, they are likely to tap *different* processes in deaf and hearing readers. Indeed, this study was designed, in part, to see if reading test performances by deaf children *do* relate to other measures of their linguistic abilities.

The test we decided to use, the Edinburgh Reading Test (Stage 1, 1977) was chosen because it fulfilled a number of criteria. First, the test designers offer it as a test that teachers can use *diagnostically*. It includes a number of sub-scales concerned with vocabulary, syntax, comprehension and sequencing ability to provide a 'profile' for each child. The items within each sub-scale were also designed to test specific aspects of each area of reading. Second, the test designers had not only recently standardized the test on a hearing sample but had also kept detailed records of *error patterns* which we could use to make comparisons with those of our sample.

Each child was tested individually by the same member of the research team to help maintain consistency of administration.

RELATIONSHIPS BETWEEN MEASURES

Children who produced the longest turns in the classroom gained higher scores on the reading test. They also produced the most syntactically well-formed written messages. Those children who *wrote* relatively well-formed messages were also likely to show relatively accurate *spoken* messages. Although the measure of spoken accuracy was less highly correlated with all the other measures (perhaps because of the problems discussed above) it correlated significantly with the writing measure.

From this pattern of relationships, we suggest, it is reasonable to conclude that this group of very deaf but otherwise 'normal' children possess different levels of generative linguistic competence. This competence includes the creation of written and spoken messages, listening and talking in class, and reading. There were also some more detailed and specific relationships that strengthened and enriched this interpretation.

When we looked in more depth at the relationships between classroom language and the other indicators, we found that the strongest relationships involved the length of children's responses to a teacher's *Wh-type* questions, and, to a lesser extent, responses to her *contributions*. Responses to phatics and two-choice questions were much less 'predictive' of reading and syntax. We suggest that this finding is consistent with the view that the various measures are 'genuinely' linguistic in nature. Answering a teacher's Wh-type questions appropriately with relatively wordy responses demands competence in *both* receptive and expressive language. As we saw in Chapter 5, answering such Wh-type questions is demanding and, in consequence, we would expect longer, more appropriate answers from the linguistically more able child.

The fact that responses to *contributions* were also predictive of other aspects of linguistic functioning supports another observation made in Chapter 4. Generally speaking, children who gave long, appropriate answers to Wh-type questions also gave long responses to teacher contributions. This is consistent with our observation that the verbally more able children were 'understanding' their teachers' contributions and making relatively long comments in return (rather than simply nodding or making a phatic move). This, of course, is a speculative *interpretation* of the findings but one that is consistent with other features of our observations.

Responses to two-choice questions are usually terse and 'easy' (but recall the two-choice question sessions in Chapter 5). Perhaps this is why they do not discriminate between the relatively competent and less competent children. Similarly, as we said in Chapter 5, even verbally less able children can be encouraged to give long responses to phatic moves, but they also tended to become incoherent and difficult to understand when they did so. Perhaps this is why phatics, unlike Wh-type questions and contributions, do not help to sort out the relatively more able children.

However, it might still be argued that some other factor, such as intelligence, explains why some children do relatively well in different 'test' contexts. To see if this might be the case we examined the relationships between our linguistic measures and intelligence (amongst other things).

LINGUISTIC COMPETENCE AND INTELLIGENCE

As part of the investigation, we noted every child's age, sex, hearing loss and non-verbal intelligence score on Raven's Progressive Matrices (Raven, 1958).

By using a statistical procedure known as multiple linear regression (outlined in Chapter 9) it was possible to ascertain how far a given measure, such as reading test scores, was related to a set of other factors such as age, intelligence and hearing loss. One can ask, for example, if children who are relatively less deaf with high scores on the intelligence test fare better on our linguistic measures than those who are deafer and scored well on the IQ test. We found no evidence that intelligence or hearing loss contributed to success on the linguistic measures.

On first sight, this might seem counter-intuitive and at variance with the results of other studies. However, the reason is almost certainly due to the very different composition of our group compared with those in other studies such as Conrad's (1979), which involved a larger and more heterogeneous sample than ours. Conrad, for instance, tested children whose levels of hearing loss varied considerably. It would have been surprising if he had not found, for example, that partially hearing children did not read better, on average, than the profoundly deaf ones. Our group of children were all severely or profoundly deaf, and so were far more similar as a group. Conrad did find a relationship between measures of linguistic ability and non-verbal intelligence, however. But he too found that intelligence was *less* influential in its effects on the performances of very deaf children, such as those involved in our study.

We conclude, then, that neither differences in levels of measured intelligence nor differences in hearing loss accounted for variations in children's performance. Rather, the different measures, we suggest, were tapping variations in levels of *linguistic* competence.

BOYS AND GIRLS

We also investigated the effects of gender on our language measures. Although we found somewhat higher overall scores from the deaf girls, this was not statistically significant. However, we did discover a pattern in the scores that is consistent with our argument that the various tests measure linguistic competence.

As we have already said, the Edinburgh Test includes four different sub-scales (syntax, comprehension, sequencing ability and vocabulary). We found that girls who were relatively good on one sub-scale were also likely to do relatively well on others and on the other measures of linguistic competence. A similar pattern was found for the boys but the correlations between measures (though still significant) were significantly weaker than those for the girls.

Work with both hearing and deaf children (e.g. Norden, 1975) has produced similar findings. Basically, a given measure of *linguistic* ability in girls tends to be predictive of a *range* of other abilities. Such relationships are usually less marked in boys. The 'greater variability of the male' is characteristic of hearing children (Hutt, 1972). A similar finding in our deaf sample suggests that we were tapping differences that are linguistic in nature.

TEACHER PERCEPTIONS AND BEHAVIOUR

As part of the study, we asked teachers to rate their children's levels of verbal proficiency and general ability. Were the teachers' assessments of children's intellectual and linguistic competence consistent with our measures? They were. As Conrad also found, teachers' assessments of children's linguistic abilities correlate relatively well with scores on more formal tests. The fact that teachers agreed with our findings, particularly on assessments of verbal competence, suggests that both their perceptions and our tests are reasonably sensitive indicators of linguistic competence.

More interesting, however, was the pattern of relationships between teacher assessments, measures of children's competence and teacher's *behaviour* in the classroom.

We found that teachers were significantly more likely to *control and repair* children whom they perceived, and we measured, as being less competent linguistically. This strengthens and extends the observations made in Chapter 4. Children who are presumably less easy to understand and who find understanding more difficult are the *most* likely to encounter styles of teacher interaction that inhibit their active involvement in conversation. Such teaching styles, as we argued in Chapters 4 and 5, do not make the less able child's task in communication *easier*. Rather, an increase in teacher control and repair exacerbates his problems and is likely to depress his desire to communicate.

These results suggest that simply by listening to a *teacher's* utterances towards a child, one gets a reasonably good picture of his likely competence. If that child is continually subjected to high control and a good deal of repair, then he is *unlikely* to be verbally competent. Nor is he likely to be gaining much from the experience.

We are thus brought back to our notion of the 'spiral of control and repair', along with some new insights into why our classroom measures correlate so well with other indicators of verbal competence. Because teachers are controlling and repairing the less able child, we know, from the work outlined in Chapters 4 and 5, that the child is going to remain low in initiative and say little. Thus, the teacher, so to speak, 'emphasizes' individual differences in children's classroom performance by greater control and repair of the less able child, depressing his initiative and loquacity. Connections between children's classroom performance and our other test scores are *strengthened* by teaching styles.

THE EDINBURGH READING TEST AND MDP

In Chapter 6, we outlined our hypotheses about aspects of deaf children's grammatical knowledge of English. These, however, were formulated on the basis of other people's data and such *post hoc* analyses are always questionable. Only when one makes and tests predictions *before* seeing the evidence can one be confident that any hypothesis has been tested. One set of items on the Edinburgh Test examines comprehension of complex sentences that involve relative clauses. These provide an opportunity to see if children follow the Minimum Distance Principle outlined in the last chapter. We made predictions about children's answers by applying the MDP to each item and found that the majority of the group always gave the answer we expected. Sometimes, these produced a correct response. For example, one item is 'Janet kissed Philip, who ran away'. The reader then has to answer the question 'Did Janet run away? . . . yes/no'. Almost 80 per cent of the children circled the 'no'. The MDP would lead to the interpretation 'Philip ran away' and, thus, gives a 'correct' response. However, on another item: 'The policeman who chased Fred was angry', only 36 per cent gave the answer 'policeman', since the MDP would lead to the interpretation that 'Fred was angry'.

The fact that children's errors on this and many other items were predictable, illustrates both that they 'interact' with text in the way we expected and also that the test can be used diagnostically to gain some ideas about the strategies a child is using in reading.

SUMMARY AND IMPLICATIONS

Casual observation of deaf children in various language situations might lead one to believe that their linguistic competence was a selection of 'special tricks' (like those strategies used in reading tests) learnt to enable them to cope with the specific demands placed upon them at school. However, we have identified four measures of linguistic competence that show a high degree of intercorrelation. This led us to conclude that very deaf children *do* display a generative linguistic competence, albeit one limited in scope.

Having established that these measures are sensitive to differences in linguistic ability, we can consider the possibility of developing them into assessment tools. The Warnock Report (DES, 1978) on the education of children with special needs in England and Wales, and the ensuing Act of Parliament in 1981, made similar recommendations to those incorporated in legislation in other Western countries. It recommended that all children with special needs, including deaf children, should be educated in ordinary schools as far as possible. It is therefore becoming increasingly important for educational psychologists and the peripatetic teachers involved in specialist back-up services for deaf children to have access to reliable and valid tests of progress and achievement. These tests will be necessary not only to establish which children are likely to benefit by being educated in ordinary schools but also to monitor their progress once they get there.

Our work on the value of hearing-referenced reading tests with deaf children has pointed to several problems in interpreting the scores of deaf children. One possible route to improved assessment would be to undertake the development of a battery of assessment tools (based on measures like those used in this study and also those outlined in our discussions of the stages of pre-verbal development in Chapter 3) that have been specifically designed for, and could be standardized on, deaf children. Using such techniques, it should be possible to monitor the progress of children in their educational *context* with some reasonably 'direct' measures of communicative competence.

Since the several indicators of linguistic performance we have provided suggest a generative linguistic system, it may well be a useful exercise not only to use these measures for the purposes outlined above but also to identify exceptions to the rule and look more closely at children who do *not* follow the usual pattern. It is possible, for example, that a child who offers relatively long turns in conversation with his teacher (especially after teacher Wh-type questions and personal contributions) but who performs poorly on reading tests may have specific reading problems. There is no reason to suppose that such reading problems are any less rare amongst deaf than hearing children. The difficulty is to separate any specific reading problems from the effects of deafness itself. What we do once we have identified any such children is, of course, another matter! However, knowing who they are might be the first step in helping to improve their situation (particularly if their receptive and expressive language levels are relatively good).

A further issue concerns the extent to which teaching techniques and educational philosophy influence children's linguistic competence. We have provided some evidence of 'school effects' in this and other chapters and studies in the United States have also identified such effects (e.g. Quigley and Paul, 1984). Conrad has shown that intelligence and hearing loss are two determinants of linguistic abilities in the deaf. However, our data include the existence of other determinants which may be associated with home, school and/or teaching techniques. These demand further attention in research into the nature and origins of individual differences and their relationships to social, educational and demographic factors. We also need to establish whether helping teachers to avoid unprofitable strategies in conversation will lead to long-term changes in children's conversational and grammatical abilities. Would such improvements lead to progress in reading and writing? We return to the issue of *how* educational factors might be explored further in Chapters 8 and 10.

This leads us to consider the role of teaching style and teacher judgements of child ability. Conrad has shown that hearing loss and IQ are the variables that correlate most highly with reading. We have shown that these variables are also associated with a child's experience in the classroom. Children with less hearing and lower IQ scores are likely to be judged (and measured) as less verbally competent. These are the children who usually meet with most repair and control. This underlines our earlier suspicions that such children are more likely to meet with secondary consequences of their handicap. Our intervention studies have shown that such a relationship is not inevitable; teachers can change their style and children change their responses accordingly. Again, an exploration of the effects on children of long-term exposure to more contingent and enabling styles should help to determine the extent to which children's problems are 'made', or an inevitable consequence of their handicap.

One final note concerns the theoretical implications of this study for discussions of the *nature* of linguistic competence in deaf children. We have established connections between various measures of speech and literacy. Conrad used different measures and also found connections between these aspects of deaf children's linguistic competence, whilst the work of Dodd and Hermelin (1977) raises the possibility that lip-reading may form a basis for reading. Their hypothesis could provide an explanation for the relationships between the measures of spoken and written language of very deaf children found in this study. Another possibility is that the relationships between speech and text for such children may be mediated by vocal articulation. If a child's speech, even if it is largely unintelligible, is based on *systematic* patterns of articulation, then it is conceivable that when such a child reads he does so by recognizing words in terms of the vocal movements he has to make in pronouncing them. Thus vocal articulation (which some afford an important place in theories of reading, e.g. Baddeley, 1979) also provides a potential explanation for connections between talk and text in our group of children.

Whilst we cannot yet provide a compelling theoretical explanation for the data from this study, the fact remains that connections between the receptive and expressive speech abilities and reading and writing competence exist in very deaf primary school children. This conclusion implies that the development of spoken language influences reading and writing; that exposure to print facilitates the development of receptive and expressive speech—or both! What we cannot do, as yet, is to say how and why such connections originate and develop in a particular child. However, as we have said, we suspect that educational management and classroom experiences in discourse play a central role in influencing the child's abilities.

Finally, our studies revealed some interesting sex differences. Generally speaking, although there were no significant differences in overall levels of achievement by boys and girls, the girls' scores on each test tended to be more closely related to each other than was the case for boys. We will not be drawn here into arguments about *why* this should be the case (see Springer and Deutsch, 1981, for a short but succinct review of the question of neural organization in deaf and hearing people). Whether one subscribes to the view that such sex differences are attributable to biologically determined differences in the structure of the male and female brain and/or to the different social and linguistic experiences of boys and girls, it seems to be the case that the same influences act upon deaf children too. This could, then, be cited as one line of evidence favouring the view that linguistic development in deaf and hearing people displays some important similarities.

The final conclusion, though, is that however we eventually explain how very deaf children develop linguistic competence in spoken and written language and why their competence is often limited in characteristic ways, the findings of our research indicate strongly that there *is* such a competence to *be* explained.

CHAPTER 8

Teaching Talk to Children and Adolescents

In previous chapters we explored the manner in which teachers control and manage conversations with their pupils and examined some aspects of the implicit purposes or functions underlying their talk to children. Now we move on to look in more detail at the *structure* of teacher language. We will be comparing aspects of their language with some of the fundamental linguistic problems facing the deaf child to ask if and in what ways teachers provide children with communicative experiences that might help to promote linguistic progress beyond the 'simple' grammar outlined in Chapter 6. We will be analysing conversations involving deaf children ranging in age from five to fourteen years. How far does teachers' language in the classroom evidence 'progress' in structural complexity as a function of children's age? Before addressing these questions, however, we want to explore some explanations for deaf children's problems with words that serve grammatical functions and consider various interpretations of the origins and persistence of their problems.

The investigations of deaf children's reading problems undertaken by Quigley and his group (Chapter 6) illustrated the particular difficulties deaf readers face with so-called 'function words' or 'functors'. Pronouns, determiners (e.g. 'a' and 'the'), prepositions, auxiliary verbs (such as 'was') and modal verbs (like 'should'), together with verbal markers for tense and aspect (e.g. '-ing', '-ed'), all create problems for deaf children. Functors are 'forms that . . . mark grammatical structures and carry subtle modulatory meanings. The word classes or parts of speech involved . . . all have few members and do not readily admit new members' (Brown, 1973, p. 99). They are contrasted with 'contentives' which are nouns, verbs and adjectives and some, but not all, make concrete reference to 'persons, objects, actions and qualities'.

Deaf children's problems in using and understanding functors have also been revealed in studies of their writing. When they attempt to move beyond simple sentence structures such as those discussed in the previous chapter, to attempt more complex constructions that demand coordination or relativization of clauses and the appropriate use of functors, the intelligibility of what they write and its approximation to standard written English decline (e.g. Quigley and Paul, 1984; Myklebust, 1964; Vandenberg, 1971).

One aim of this chapter is to probe more deeply into the central questions being explored in the book. How do the specific problems faced by deaf children 'surface' and manifest themselves in the classroom and why do so many years of teaching and learning usually fail to overcome such problems?

WHY DO DEAF CHILDREN 'STICK' WITH 'SIMPLE' GRAMMAR?

Few, if any, students of language would deny that language is an intricate, complex and multifaceted phenomenon. There, however, agreement tends to stop. Although there has been a dramatic increase in theorizing about and studies of language and its acquisition, debates about the nature of the processes involved are widespread. Such disagreements are not restricted to linguists and psycholinguists. Implicit in the practices of different schools and teachers are very different assumptions about the nature of language and its 'teaching'. Our aim in this chapter is not to review the various theories of language acquisition being debated in current research. We shall, rather, attempt to spell out and illustrate some of the theoretical issues that are important in evaluating the implications of our own findings.

THE 'PERCEPTUAL SALIENCE' HYPOTHESIS

Deaf children have problems in learning spoken language and written representations of such language because they hear little or nothing of what people say. So much is self-evident. Should it not be equally self-evident, then, that the more specific problems they face, such as those with functors, are a simple and direct product of the relative difficulty that they encounter in *perceiving* such words or parts of words, which are often short, seldom phonemically stressed and, perhaps, hard to lip-read?

In one sense, the answer to this question is easily reached and defended. Deaf children, we shall argue, do 'know' many functors, can recognize them in print and do understand utterances that contain them in a limited range of discourse contexts. In another sense, however, the perceptual salience hypothesis is not easily dismissed. We will argue later that many functors in English are 'plurifunctional', serving several different, though related, linguistic purposes. Furthermore, some of these functions are easier for hearing children to understand than others and emerge earlier in language development. Deaf children can and do master the more obvious and 'primitive' functions of such words but not the more complex uses. Some functions are easier for a number of possible reasons, one of which is perceptual salience.

Research into the development of language in hearing children, referred to in Chapter 2, suggests that young hearing children are particularly sensitive to speech sounds that are stressed and to those that occur at the beginning of utterances. Stress may also be reflected in 'paralinguistic' features that accompany speech. For instance, it seems plausible to suppose that the word 'Who . . . ?' introducing a question may be intelligible to a deaf child because it is not pre-dated by other words and is accompanied by interpretable paralinguistic cues such as a 'questioning' posture. In Chapter 4, we provided evidence that deaf children meet such Wh-type questions frequently in the classroom and usually respond to them appropriately.

However, when the same word occurs in contexts such as 'What did the boy who came to tea say?' it is embedded within utterances and is unlikely to be stressed. It is also difficult to imagine any available paralinguistic cue to signal the significance of the relative 'who'. We know, from Quigley's research amongst others, that such complex question forms in written texts are likely to be misunderstood by deaf children. Similarly, in 'The girl went to town when the boy came back' the word 'when' seems likely to be less perceptually salient to a listener/watcher than in a question with a simpler structure like 'When did you go to town?'.

In short, the perceptual salience of the 'same' word varies as a function of the linguistic structure in which it is embedded. It is possible that some usages, but not others, are relatively accessible to the deaf child because of such differences in salience.

In relation to the deaf child's problems with tense endings like '-ing' and '-ed', the perceptual salience hypothesis provides an appealing explanation for their difficulties. However, the explanation for difficulties with other functors is more problematic. Complex uses of plurifunctional words seem likely to involve less acoustic stress but it is impossible to disentangle the 'purely' perceptual aspects of such words, such as stress and position, from their grammatical function.

ABSTRACT VERSUS CONCRETE WORDS

Another defining feature of what we have been calling functors is their 'abstract' or 'structure-dependent' meaning. Consider, for example, 'The boy who saw Mary was running'. The word 'who' is a 'co-referent' with 'boy'. Its presence and location in the sentence indicate that its co-referent is the subject of the clause 'was running'. Such complex constructions in English characteristically involve 'implicit' elements. As we saw in the last chapter, deaf children and young hearing children, given such an 'isolated' sentence, are likely to assume that it follows the patterns found in simple sentences and, thus, that 'Mary was running'. If, however, the child appreciates the fact that the presence of co-referential terms like 'who' serves as a signal for 'deleted' or 'implicit' elements, he may begin to understand such utterances in isolation.

The meanings of many 'contentive' words, defined above, can be exemplified, illustrated or in some way 'brought to life'. Although, as we argued in Chapter 2, the problem of divided attention may act as a barrier to the discovery of what words refer to (for children with little or no auditory awareness), they do develop a 'lexicon' or vocabulary of such words, though the growth of that vocabulary is very slow in comparison with that of hearing children (e.g. Gregory and Mogford, 1981). Abstract words refer not to things, attributes or actions/movements but to classes and categories of such words or to relationships between them, and the meanings of function words reside in the part they play within structured sequences of words. Take them out of the context of an utterance and the basis of their meaning is lost; meaning is structure dependent.

How one conceptualizes the actual *meaning* or significance of functors depends upon one's theory of the nature of linguistic structure. This, in turn, will constrain one's views of the ways in which children develop and may be helped to understand them. Our own approach (best exemplified amongst linguists by the writings of Romaine, 1984) places stress on the way in which these words function in discourse. Whilst we accept the power and value of the research outlined in Chapter 2, which demonstrates how the functioning of the auditory system constrains the early stages of development in hearing and speaking, we believe that the development of so-called 'complex' linguistic rules are the product of sustained interactions between the developing child and competent speakers.

In the next three sections, we try to provide some concrete examples of what this emphasis on the role of discourse has to offer. In so doing, we are not saying that participation in discourse is a 'sufficient' condition for the promotion of linguistic development. We have already accepted that the 'nature' of the deaf child plays an important and specific role in accounting for the pattern of linguistic development. However, we will explore the case that participation is a *necessary* condition for acquisition. We are not advocating a return to the view that the child is 'taught' language in any strict sense. Rather, to borrow a phrase from Lock (1980), we believe that conversation provides a context for the 'guided reinvention' of language by the child. The child is active and constructive in 'reinventing' the processes of producing and understanding language. But his creativity is constrained by interactions with others who have already mastered what it is he seeks to create.

The areas of language development we shall be considering are pronouns (and related systems of meanings), relativization and passive voice constructions. These areas were chosen both because we know that deaf children have problems with them and because recent studies of hearing children provide us with insights into relationships between discourse and their acquisition.

Though specific to these areas of language, we shall argue that the principles illustrated about relationships between conversation and language development are general ones.

DEIXIS—WORDS THAT 'POINT'

The study of 'deictic' processes in language is a relatively recent concern in psycholinguistics. Deixis, derived from the Greek verb 'to point' (Wales, 1979), refers to a range of processes in language which share in common the fact that they involve the use of non-verbal cues, words or longer utterances to 'point to' or 'co-refer with' other words.

The literal use of the word refers to non-verbal indicators of intended referents. Thus, when, in an interaction with another person, we point to an object or even, in some contexts, when we look at it, we may achieve communication and some degree of shared understanding if our partner can see and infer the 'object' of our pointing. The pre-verbal foundations of communication studied in Chapter 2 involved the development of such deictic processes. According to some theorists (e.g. Bruner, 1983), many words and verbal expressions also serve deictic functions. Some are verbal 'substitutes' for, or accompaniments of, the physical act of pointing. For example, 'Look at the slug', said in reference to a black, slimy object, involves the use of 'the' for (exophoric) deictic reference. Similarly, an exclamation involving demonstratives such as 'Look at that!' helps to 'point out' from utterance to context. Understanding the intended meaning and significance of such words demands participation in the physical context in which they are uttered (together with the capacity to infer what is likely to provoke such outbursts).

Other deictic processes involve 'implicit pointing', but not to extralinguistic situations, rather to elements of utterances within the discourse context itself. For example, if one says 'I saw a man yesterday . . . the man was running', the 'the' points not to some element of non-verbal context but to a word or idea in past discourse. Understanding such words demands a recognition of the fact that they *do* serve to refer back to other words, a capacity to remember what was said previously and knowledge of how to relate the 'old' and 'new' utterances. Unlike many 'content' words whose meanings have a (relatively) enduring and utterance-free meaning, deictic terms can only be understood with reference to the *discourse* within which they are embedded.

Another category of words that point to other words or expressions is pronouns.

PROBLEMS WITH PRONOUNS

Studies by Quigley and his colleagues (Chapter 6) have explored what deaf children can and cannot do with pronouns in isolated sentences or short sequences of text. The use of a pronoun to point to, replace or co-refer with a noun demands implicit knowledge of 'agreement' rules such as case (first, second, third person), number (singular, plural) and gender (male, female, neutral). Quigley's studies explored the development of deaf children's understanding of pronouns in terms of their ability to understand such rules of agreement. However, to understand how and why deaf children face difficulties with pronouns and other functional systems of English one also needs to consider the ways in which they are *used* in discourse. Far more than a knowledge of rules of agreement is demanded for an effective grasp of how people make pronominal reference. We present a few examples next to illustrate some of the complexity associated with pronoun usage, to explain why we think deaf children's difficulties with them reside in 'rules' of discourse and also to show that pronouns have to be conceptualized as part of complex and extensive *systems* of meanings.

When children first begin to refer to themselves verbally, they often do so by using their own first name or 'me' ('John do it', 'me do it', etc.). Use of the personal pronouns 'I' and 'you' appears at around the age of two and a half to three years (e.g. Clark, 1978). When one considers the complexity of personal pronoun usage, this achievement seems precocious.

Who is 'I'? Well, we might define it as a reference to the self by the person uttering the sound pattern 'I'. That individual remains 'I' throughout the speaking turn in which the sound is embedded. 'You' is the person being addressed by the current 'I', until turn-taking occurs, when 'I' becomes 'you' and 'you' becomes 'I'. Appreciating the 'meaning' of such pronouns, then, involves an understanding of the roles they play in discourse. Some children, on the verge of coming to employ these pronouns appropriately, seem to work on the assumption, for a short time, that 'I' is themselves. Others appear to think that 'I' is a significant other person like Mummy. Thus, one child was observed asking 'I carry you!' meaning 'You carry me', and another, 'I take you' meaning 'You take me'.

Where is 'here' and why do children seem to need to have understood aspects of personal pronoun usage before they master the meaning of 'here'? Well, in many usages, 'here' is that region of space occupied by the current 'I'. In a two-person, face-to-face exchange, 'there' may be where 'you' are. However, when 'I' becomes 'you', 'here' becomes 'there'. Of course, 'there' may be somewhere else; where 'it' is perhaps. Furthermore, if 'you' and 'I' are close together and talking about 'him' who is relatively far away, then 'here' is where 'we' are and 'there' is where 'he' resides. Should 'he' start to address 'us' (becoming 'I') then 'there' is where 'they' (meaning 'us' or 'we two') are. Having sorted out some of the discourse-based conventions for using and understanding where 'here' and 'there' are, the child may begin to understand 'this' and 'that'. In two-person, face-to-face encounters it is likely that 'this' is an object in the 'here' of the current 'I' and that 'that' is an object in the 'there' of the current 'you'. Of course, when turn-taking occurs, 'this' becomes 'that' and 'that' becomes 'this'. If 'we' are 'here' and 'they' are over 'there' then 'that' is likely to be where 'they' are and 'this' is in the 'here' of the current 'us' (i.e. it is 'ours' and not 'theirs', so to speak). If the speaker says to his listener 'go', he probably intends that the current 'you' should become mobile and cease being an object 'in' or close to 'here'. However, should the listener, who becomes 'I' on speaking, decide that both should move out of the current 'here' of 'us' then he might say 'You come too'. In which case, both of 'us' should cease being objects in the current 'here' to take up residence somewhere else—which, of course, will be 'here' when both of us start speaking 'there'. Unless, that is, we wish to renegotiate the field and establish 'here' and 'there' as separate spaces around 'I' and 'you'.

Since the meanings of such deictic terms rest on the roles they play in discourse, it seems reasonable to suppose that it is only by participating in discourse (and, perhaps, overhearing others converse) that a child can be expected to develop an understanding of their meanings. Detached from the context within which they are used, the meaning of such words is destroyed since, by definition, what they serve to point to will disappear—a point not lost on the poet (?!) Winnie-the-Pooh (Milne, 1926):

On Tuesday, when it hails and snows,
The feeling on me grows and grows
That hardly anybody knows
If those are these or these are those.

The interrelationships in the developing understanding of such functions of pronouns, adverbs of place and deictic verbs like 'come', 'go', 'bring' and 'take' have been studied by Clark (1978). One important finding was that hearing children aged up to twelve years of age still find it difficult to understand words like 'bring and take' when they are presented in 'isolated' contexts. Although children know such words and use them from an early age, they do not master all aspects of their use for several years. As we shall see, this is a familiar story.

Being able to use and understand such terms in everyday contexts where there is considerable pragmatic support to help determine their meaning (e.g. a mother holds out her hand to a toddler saying 'Come with me') and being able to understand their significance in 'isolated' utterances or in written sentences (where the only guide to their meaning is grammatical structure) are, developmentally, years apart. Being able to hear and recognize such words or, if you are deaf, being capable of lip-reading them or recognizing them in print, is a far cry from a mature understanding of what they mean. Access to their meanings, we suggest, comes about through participation in (or perhaps being able to overhear) discourse.

WORDS OF A PLURIFUNCTIONAL KIND

We have already referred to the fact that so-called function words are plurifunctional. The examples given above to illustrate the various deictic functions of 'the' are a case in point. Understanding the use of 'the' for exophoric, deictic functions (e.g. 'Look at the slug!') appears relatively early in language development, but the anaphoric function emerges later. As we have just argued, children often recognize and use words for several years before they understand and employ them for the full range of 'mature' functions.

At the risk of labouring the plurifunctional point, we shall consider a final 'set' of words to provide further illustrations and to explore the complex relationships between function words and linguistic structure.

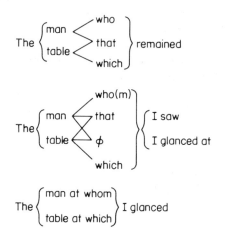

Figure 8.1 Choice of relative pronoun (Reproduced from R. Quirk and S. Greenbaum, *A University Grammar of English*, 1980, Longman, London)

In Figure 8.1, we reproduce a diagram taken from Quirk and Greenbaum (1980, p. 381) to illustrate processes of relativization in English. It indicates how words like 'when', 'that', 'who' and so on are used in the construction of complex sentences. Note how each of these words is used in speech to serve semantically related but distinct functions. For example, 'who', 'what', 'where' and 'when' all serve in both simple and complex questions. Although, in relative clauses, they continue to refer to similar semantic categories (e.g. a person, object, place or time) the linguistic demands they present are quite different. Grammatical words involved in the formation of complex sentences all serve other functions. On the basis of evidence from the analysis of conversations presented in Chapter 4, we argue that deaf children are able to comprehend utterances which involve these words but only when these involve certain more 'simple' or discernible functions. Where their meaning involves a considerable degree of structure dependency, as in relative constructions, deaf children often fail to understand them (at least, in written text). Again, being able to lip-read or read a given 'word' is but a short step towards understanding the 'meanings' and functions which it serves in written and spoken utterances.

Let us go back to the question of why deaf children have problems in mastering the more complex, structure-dependent meanings of function words. We have already explored the 'perceptual salience' hypothesis; other (not necessarily mutually exclusive) explanations are possible. The first rests on the concept of 'auditory memory' already introduced in Chapter 6 on reading. If skilled levels of lip-reading and reading of text demand a good auditory memory, then deaf children may be precluded from the acquisition of more complex structures in language, and, in consequence, from achieving any understanding of function words whose meanings relate to complex structures. If, as Conrad argues, most very deaf children do not and cannot develop auditory memories, if acquisition of complex (spoken or written) linguistic constructions can *only* be acquired by 'ear' and if it is impossible for deaf children to discover the meanings of function words and the structures within which they serve by any other means (e.g. through reading 'visually'), then it would follow that deaf children do not and cannot acquire knowledge of other than simple linguistic constructions and the less structure-dependent functions of plurifunctional words.

It is possible, then, to provide plausible explanations for deaf children's problems in terms of either or both acoustic salience and auditory memory. If either or both of these explanations are valid, then it seems reasonable to conclude that most deaf children will never learn to communicate in speech or writing at other than the most basic level.

However, there are other possible explanations for deaf children's problems with spoken and written language which hold out less 'terminal' implications. These are best explored before we accept the 'inevitability' of deaf children's problems. Whilst we cannot, given the state of our knowledge, rule out any explanation, the one we are about to consider has the advantage of providing possible accounts for individual differences in deaf children's achievements and testable implications for future educational practice.

LANGUAGE DEVELOPMENT AND DISCOURSE

Language development takes place over many years. Whilst students of child language have been justifiably impressed with the remarkable linguistic achievements that normally hearing children make in the years before they go to school, two things have emerged from studies of language development beyond early childhood. First, the development of linguistic competence extends (at least) into adolescence. Not only are children in school acquiring a more extensive and 'technical' vocabulary, they also continue to acquire knowledge of and the ability to use complex functions, structures and uses of language.

The second generalization we would draw from the study of language development is more controversial. In agreement with Romaine (1984) (and in fundamental disagreement with many other linguists) we suggest that the development of the understanding of syntactic structure in language continues into late childhood and adolescence. Many aspects of syntactic structure, though founded in discourse, are 'special' to specific contexts and purposes. Crudely, the process of learning to read and the experience of classroom-type (formal or 'autonomous') discourse is what leads children to new levels of linguistic competence. Perhaps a few examples will illustrate the value of these assertions and help to identify some of the *discourse-related* language problems facing the deaf child.

When two ideas or propositions are combined in a syntactically well-formed, single utterance, elegance and efficiency of communication are bought at the cost of increased structural complexity. For example, compare a relatively complex construction like 'The boy who was watching the girl picked flowers' with 'The boy was watching the girl. The boy picked flowers (at the same time)'. The complex construction handles the temporal aspects of the two propositions elegantly and demands fewer words. However, the cost of extra efficiency is an increase in complexity. To understand the complex utterance, a listener has to appreciate that the relative 'who' co-refers (with boy) to a 'deleted' subject in the final clause. The strategies employed by young hearing children and deaf children, as we have seen, would lead them to misunderstand such an utterance (at least if it is made in the absence of any other cues to meaning such as a picture or an ongoing event). Studies of both the capacity to *understand* and *produce* such complex utterances have revealed a number of important features of their development in children. First, the development of understanding and production occur at different rates. Answering the question 'When does a child "understand" a given structure?' is difficult (Romaine, 1984, p. 36ff). There is considerable evidence that being able to understand a complex utterance in isolation (as in psycholinguistic experiments) occurs quite late in development, but attempts to establish precise 'points' or 'stages' for the acquisition of different complex forms have proved inconclusive. Various factors influence the likelihood of their comprehension, not simply the 'syntax' of the construction. For example, children may understand a passive voice construction such as 'The patient was treated by the doctor' where everyday experiences (pragmatic knowledge) support the correct interpretation, yet fail to comprehend the sentence 'John was hit by Bill' where no such support from everyday knowledge (or from any preceding discourse) is forthcoming.

Basically, the ability to understand isolated utterances in terms of their *syntactic* structure 'alone' develops through late childhood and adolescence. Syntactic knowledge of complex linguistic structures, we suggest, is best viewed as the *culmination* of experiences in discourse.

Studies of children's linguistic productions have demonstrated the long developmental history of complex linguistic constructions. For example, one analysis of children's use of relative clauses, discussed by Romaine, has identified four stages in their production by children, which are illustrated below.

```
This guy he owns the hotel he went to B.
This guy that he owns the hotel he went to B.
This guy that owns the hotel he went to B.
This guy that owns the hotel went to B.
```

The final 'stage' of development marks the achievement of mature forms of expression—what Romaine (p. 55) calls the 'fully syntacticized pattern'. However, this is pre-dated by other stages or strategies. For example, in the first stage, the 'redundant' 'he' occurs as a co-referent with 'This guy'. The relative 'that' emerges and coexists alongside such 'redundant' (but interpretable) pronouns for some time prior to the eventual mastery of the mature form and the 'deletion' of redundant pronominal references. Note, in passing, the complex relationships between the use of pronouns and relatives like 'that'.

The apparent 'redundancy' in children's constructions and the dysfluency it introduces have also been noted in the development of mastery of other functions (such as anaphoric reference) in younger children (Karmiloff-Smith, 1979). Far from being a product of 'sloppy' speech or lack of precision in talk, such periods of dysfluency mark the child's progress as he works on, and solves, the problem of achieving mature speech forms. Complex linguistic structures do not appear 'full blown' early in life. Rather, they are the product of sustained periods of problem solving. For example, the 'redundant' use of pronouns in the examples given above illustrates how children come to realize strategies for producing 'efficient' complex constructions gradually. Interestingly, examples given in the handbook to the TSA, referred to in Chapter 6, illustrate somewhat similar features in deaf children's reading and writing (e.g. 'The boy who the boy hit the girl'). We suspect that although most deaf children fail to achieve understanding and use of complex constructions, they are 'working' on the problem and showing evidence of some knowledge of the fact that such complexities *exist* in written language.

But as we have said, such understanding in hearing children does not come quickly, readily or automatically. Rather, as Karmiloff-Smith (1979) argues, the use and understanding of language presents a 'problem space' for the child. He has to *work* at it. Further, we suggest, like all problem solvers, the child needs the appropriate *experiences* both as a listener and speaker if he is to solve his linguistic problems.

DISCOURSE DEMANDS

We have drawn attention to the fact that deaf children may experience specific problems in understanding 'functional' aspects of language such as tense markers, relatives and the like because they lack awareness of phonemic stress. Similarly, impoverished auditory awareness may entail a poor auditory memory, demand greater reliance on vision for purposes of communication and, in turn, lead to a limited command of complex linguistic constructions.

These 'organic' explanations for the deaf child's problems leave little room for optimism about their capacities to acquire spoken language or its written form. Unless improvements in hearing-aid technology, more effective techniques for facilitating the development of auditory awareness or, in relation to reading, the development of new and more successful instructional techniques prove possible, there is not much scope for hope. But we have also identified other ways of thinking about and looking at linguistic problems that may offer some hope for improvements in educational practice which might then help to overcome some of the problems children face.

We suggest, given the time taken by hearing children to master complex features of language, that we should be wary of any attempts to define when language learning 'stops' in the deaf child and recognize that the potential for language learning may be available throughout schooling (and beyond). Relatively poor performance at the end of schooling may be due to 'organic' features of deafness and/or to limited experience of language, together with a need for more time to master linguistic complexities. However, such time is obviously only likely to be used well if the child's linguistic experiences are relevant to his developmental needs.

As Quigley's studies have illustrated, deaf readers develop (slowly) their competence in handling structural aspects of language, at least to the age of eighteen years. Consequently, we should not assume that there is a relatively short, 'critical' period for language learning, nor base our educational provision on the assumption that children have 'failed' linguistically if they have not mastered aspects of linguistic understanding by some specific age.

We must also ask if the deaf child is actually provided with the *means* to solve his language learning problems. Is she or he actually *exposed* to forms of language use that they find difficult? We do not pose this question on the basis of any (naive) assumption that language development simply involves providing the right 'input' to the child. The children themselves bring their powers of perceiving, hypothesizing and problem solving to the language learning process, and any 'deficiencies' in one or more of these abilities may limit linguistic competence. But it is difficult to see how, in the absence of relevant experiences, a child could come to master language alone. We also believe that the importance of what is *said to* a child is far greater for the deaf child than a hearing one. Hearing children's linguistic development, we suspect, is less reliant upon the language addressed directly to them than is the case for deaf children. A hearing child can *overhear* conversation between others, deriving some understanding of how language functions by listening to others talking. Any such opportunities for overhearing speech by deaf children (depending, of course, on their degree of lip-reading skills and auditory awareness) seems likely to be limited.

Once a hearing child has mastered the 'rules' of *reading* it seems likely, even perhaps inevitable, that he or she will derive insights into, and gain a more explicit understanding of, their own language. Indeed, Romaine argues that the emergence of syntactic competence is facilitated by experiences such as reading and exposure to 'autonomous speech'. For example, when the child listens to a teacher talking about historical events or about life in other cultures, understanding of what is being said demands a capacity to create and manipulate some *representation* of the subject of discourse. In both text and autonomous speech, unlike conversation, there are relatively few extralinguistic cues to meaning, such as objects in the shared environment, the responses of one's partners in talk or appeals to common, shared experiences. A knowledge of syntax and grammar become increasingly important as the 'distance' between what is being said and what is being talked about increases.

If, as is the case with many deaf children, a child lacks a skilled, working knowledge of the rules that govern the translation of written symbols into spoken meanings and/or lacks the *knowledge* of spoken language to translate text *into*, then it seems unlikely that mere exposure to the printed word alone will facilitate the development of spoken language (or reading, for that matter). We have yet to see whether more carefully designed reading programmes such as that being developed out of the work of Quigley and his colleagues (Quigley and Paul, 1984) will help children to learn spoken language through reading. Our own view is that such an approach is only likely to succeed if children are also being exposed to *conversation* and *autonomous discourse* in interactions with their teachers. These lines of thinking, in company with more specific, discourse-related meanings of 'function words', explain our interest in and stress upon the importance of what we say and how we talk to deaf children.

But it is possible that deaf children are already *being* exposed to such experiences. If so, we will probably have to conclude that what constrains their development of more complex uses of language is not their *experience* of language but their inability to profit (except, perhaps, very slowly) from it. We turn now to our analyses of classroom conversations to find out in one context, at least, if this appears to be the case.

TEACHER LANGUAGE: FUNCTIONS AND STRUCTURES

Stored in our computer files are transcripts of recordings of conversations from twenty-seven different classrooms involving 196 hearing-impaired children. These involved children in oral educational programmes. The children are aged from five to fourteen years, with an average hearing loss of 92 dB. There is no relationship between age and hearing loss (i.e. on average, children in each age group have similar degrees of deafness). Children within each classroom group are of similar ages, reflecting the usual policy in English schools.

Given the power and flexibility of modern computing facilities, it is possible to 'search' such transcripts quickly to locate specific words. For example, we can instruct the machine to examine each transcript and print out any line containing the words 'when', 'what' and so on. By constructing a simple computer programme (what we term our 'Find' analysis) we were able to search and print out every line of transcript containing certain key words. The list of words we used is given in Table 8.1.

Table 8.1 Key words identified for 'Find' analysis

Key words	Examples of complex usage
AND	We saw the castle and then went home.
BUT	You can have the bat but not the ball.
OR	Did you go walking or swimming?
WHO(SE)	That's the lady who cooks your dinner.
WHICH	Show me the picture which you like best.
WHAT	I don't know what you mean.
WHERE	Do you remember where we went last week?
WHEN	What did you do when you got home?
THAT	I said the bus that you came to school in.

We have explored the relationships between the average age of children in each classroom group, on the one hand, and teachers' use of key words for 'complex' purposes, on the other. How often, for example, does a teacher's use of the word 'who' involve relativization? Does relativization in teacher speech increase as a function of the age of the children being addressed?

The first point to note is that the vast majority of teacher utterances were well-formed sentences that permitted reliable analysis. Children are exposed to syntactically 'accurate' speech. When we undertook similar analyses of teacher language to preschool hearing children and to sixteen-year-old hearing adolescents, we found the same result. Teachers use well-formed utterances.

The full results of our analysis, involving seventeen key words, are too complex to present in detail. However, the major findings are easily summarized. Overall, about 14 per cent of all uses of our key words by teachers of the deaf were involved in 'complex' constructions. Some (e.g. the use of 'when' in relative clauses) were relatively frequent; others (e.g. the use of 'which' in complex constructions) almost never occurred. There was *no* relationship between frequency of complex usage by teachers and children's ages. Indeed, a teacher with one of the youngest groups (six-year-olds) made the most frequent use of complex constructions. When we compared these results with those for hearing preschool children we found a very similar frequency of complex usage (though a somewhat different pattern of use of the seventeen words). However, when we analysed teacher talk to sixteen-year-old hearing adolescents we found massive differences in comparison to the deaf and preschool groups. Teachers employed complex functions some 27 per cent of the time.

Broadly speaking, then, we found no evidence for increased teacher usage of our seventeen words for complex purposes with older deaf children. Basically, on our measure, the 'register' of teacher speech to the deaf is similar to that experienced by three-year-old children in nursery schools and playgroups. This does not mean, of course, that there are *no* differences in the way teachers talk to fourteen-year-old deaf children and hearing three-year-olds. However, whatever any such differences might involve, they do not extend to the use of function words for complex purposes.

CONVERSATION AND 'AUTONOMOUS' DISCOURSE

Throughout this book we have laid considerable stress on the importance of conversation for both studying and facilitating the linguistic development of children. The analyses just referred to, however, can be viewed as evidence for the limitations of conversation in the later years of schooling as a basis for linguistic development. Whether one accepts this criticism, however, depends upon one's implicit or explicit theory of language and its development in deaf children. Let us consider some of the criticisms that can be made of our analyses.

First, it can be argued that the relative stability of our measures of teacher language occurs because children in each age group do not and cannot understand utterances that involve more complex language. Indeed, one might cite the very slow progress made in reading as evidence that children cannot understand complex structures, even at the age of eighteen years. What is the 'cause' of the rather static nature of teacher language? Our analyses simply do not permit firm conclusions on this question. The lack of development could be due to teacher factors, child factors or (as we suspect is the case) a combination of both. Although we cannot 'prove' any one causal interpretation of our findings, we can draw some hints from our data and make some recommendations about how teachers themselves might explore the issue further.

We have already noted that one of the teachers with the youngest groups of children made more frequent use of complex functions than others did. This was no 'accident', but part of her school's explicit philosophy for fostering language development. She was fully aware of the fact that she was attempting to talk to young deaf children in a way that exposed them to relatively complex purposes and functions in language. The performances of children from this school in our study of reading lessons, mentioned in Chapter 6, and in experimental studies of communicative competence, outlined in Chapter 7, were significantly superior to those of other deaf children even when, as in the latter study, they were of similar ages, non-verbal intelligence and deafness. Such 'coincidental' results do not constitute conclusive empirical evidence. However, given that it is now established that children from certain school environments do significantly better than those from others, it seems worth considering the importance of how and what teachers say to children as an ingredient of success.

Exploring this issue further, we examined the relationships between complexity in teacher speech and the incidence of repair in conversation. If the two were highly correlated this would provide plausible evidence for the view that children, rather than teachers, constrain what is said in the classroom. There was, however, no such relationship. Repair was no more prevalent in those sessions where teachers used relatively more complex functions than in others. Though not conclusive, this finding is not easily reconciled with the view that talking to children other than in simple structures invites automatic misunderstanding. As we said in Chapter 2, the view that language development is 'best' facilitated by exclusive use of simple structures is questionable. If so, we may wish to question the wisdom of maintaining a 'simple' register of speech with deaf children.

A second argument against drawing any general conclusions from our analyses concerns our exclusive attention to 'conversation'. We have already accepted that 'autonomous' language may be a vital ingredient for the development of more complex aspects of linguistic structure, yet we have not searched for examples of such language in the classroom. We accept this criticism. Classroom conversations are typified by relatively short and frequent turns, in which any utterance from a child is likely to be a direct response to the last move made by the teacher. Were we to look, say, at lessons in history, geography or mathematics, when teachers, perhaps, are more likely to be involved in more sustained, autonomous narrative, we might find a very different picture. In accepting this criticism we level another at common educational practices and 'theories' that govern what happens in classrooms. Generally speaking, we focused on conversational encounters because they are part of schools' approaches to 'teaching' or 'fostering' language development in deaf children. We are prepared to accept, even promote, the view that children aged up to ten years or so need informal conversation as an important basis for fostering communicative competence (providing, of course, that the pitfalls of overcontrol and frequent repair can be avoided). However, we question the wisdom and value of maintaining such interactions as a *mainstay* of language 'teaching' for older children. To be sure, conversation as a basis for socialization and for maintaining personal relationships continues to be important. However, in our view, the substitution of more 'formal' and demanding communicative situations and exposure to 'autonomous' speech (likely to be fostered in a broad curriculum) become increasingly important as children get older.

CONCLUSIONS AND SUGGESTIONS

The theoretical interpretations of deaf children's linguistic problems that we have been exploring are highly speculative. We have offered them in the hope that they will stimulate new lines of thought, research and classroom practices which might help to promote the social, intellectual and linguistic development of deaf school children. We have tried to identify some of the special problems that deaf children face in their efforts to understand and produce written and spoken language. We have asked why years of education so often lead to what look like 'depressing' levels of academic and linguistic achievement. In this chapter, we have stressed the importance of *time* in view of the tremendous complexities facing the teacher and child, and evidence suggesting that the potential for language development extends beyond the school years. One obvious implication of the time factor is the rationale it provides for continuing educational/vocational/training provision for deaf people beyond the 'traditional' years of formal schooling. Given more time and opportunity, there are some grounds for the hope that progress can continue. Perhaps, too, we might be a little less depressed at levels of literacy in deaf children, for example, when we recognize the tremendous task they face in learning to read. This observation is not designed to foster complacency but to engender better understanding of the situation educators and deaf children face.

We have pointed out and accepted the interplay between certain specific problems deaf children face and factors such as acoustic stress and auditory awareness. We do not yet know exactly how these factors are implicated in the problems deaf children face nor how general and pervasive such effects are. Nor can we ascertain the possibility that such effects can be overcome. We still do not know the extent to which a deaf child with little or no auditory awareness can acquire 'by eye' what is normally learnt largely through the ears. Any pessimism inspired by theories of the differences between the processes of language acquisition by ear and eye should not inhibit us from exploring and trying new approaches to the teaching, say, of reading. But we should recognize the magnitude of the problem we face with a child who has not been or cannot be helped to gain some useful measure of auditory awareness.

Finally, we return to the issue of 'simplified speech' which, we feel, is a common characteristic of teacher talk to deaf children. We have already stressed the limitations of such so-called simplifications as a basis of linguistic development. In addition to thinking about the 'language of the curriculum' we also suggest that teachers begin to consider the content and value of the topics and activities which feature in their discourse with older deaf children as well as the way in which they 'manage' interactions.

A recent book (which, unfortunately, arrived on our desks too late to receive greater attention in this book!) makes some important and relevant points about the development of linguistic competence (oracy) in hearing children. Brown *et al.* (1984) distinguish between 'chat' (what we have termed conversation) and 'informative speech'. They point out that children's participation in 'chat' usually involves exposure to shorter turns than is the case in informative speech which, as its label implies, is concerned with the deliberate (and more or less accurate and successful) transmission of knowledge or information. They write (p. 15):

We believe that simply practising listener-related 'chat' when information transfer is what is at issue, does not necessarily improve your ability to transfer information. Long turns which are used to transfer information—to recount an anecdote, justify a position, give instructions about how to take some medicine, describe a route—demand skill in construction and practice in execution.

The authors go on to suggest tasks and activities designed to foster the development of 'informative' speech in hearing adolescents that might also prove useful for use with older deaf children. They give some ideas for topics and activities that might lead teachers to use and encourage children to develop more complex and wide-ranging functions of language.

But, one might ask, is it possible or feasible to demand 'more' of deaf children when their existing problems seem so intractable? The response to this sort of question depends, of course, on one's views on the relationships between language, thinking and communication. We have yet to discover what happens in classrooms when teachers are involved in such activities. However, here are the sorts of things we will examine when we do so. If teachers can develop strategies for involving children in more 'demanding' communication situations and manage, at the same time, to avoid excessive use of specific questions and frequent repair, then there would be some indications of the feasibility of making more demands on the deaf child in communication. If children provide some evidence of comprehending what is going on then we will be motivated to look for *general* and *enduring* effects on children's communicative abilities. Brown and her colleagues have shown that such effects were forthcoming in their studies of hearing children.

On the other hand, if teachers find it impossible to develop techniques for achieving understanding with children without their interactions 'degenerating' into frequent, specific teacher questions and continual attempts to repair children's productions and comprehension, then we will be tempted to conclude that deaf children are not 'capable' of involvement in such interactions. Then two main possibilities remain. Either the foundations for conversation have not been achieved with such children because of their previous communicative experiences or it is theoretically *impossible* to involve deaf children successfully in such interactions.

Our analyses of conversations are now over. We realize that we have not provided the weight of evidence we would need to make a compelling case for the view that attention to the control, function and structure of teacher language will help to promote better levels of linguistic achievement in the deaf. However, such changes as we have recommended are, we feel, worth considering and trying out. If they do not lead children to a better command of spoken and written language, which we believe they will, they should at least reflect a more positive image back to the deaf child than that created by high control and frequent repair. If we decide that these things cannot be achieved with an oral/aural approach to the education of deaf children, then we will challenge advocates of other approaches to demonstrate that they can be achieved by other means. We return to the question of evaluating alternatives in the final chapter.

CHAPTER 9

Thinking, Talking and Mathematical Reasoning

A good deal of psychological research has been dedicated to the study of deaf children's thinking. The results of some studies indicate that deaf children's thinking is essentially similar to that of hearing children, though the deaf child is often delayed in the achievement of developmental 'milestones'. Other studies, however, suggest that deaf children's thinking is different or limited in some way. It has been argued, for instance, that deaf people are likely to be intellectually more 'rigid', 'literal' and 'concrete' than hearing people. In this chapter we offer a critical evaluation of these differing opinions with reference to mathematical achievement in deaf and hearing adolescents. We argue that, though delayed in their knowledge of mathematics, deaf children's mathematical reasoning is similar to that of hearing children. We also discuss the reasons for slower learning in deaf children and argue that the answer may lie, in part at least, in the teaching processes and curricula they experience.

One discovery that arose out of the development of the much-maligned intelligence test was the finding that on non-verbal or performance tests (involving little or no language) deaf and hearing people achieve similar distributions of test scores. The frequency of very high scores on such tests, for example, is not markedly different for the two groups. There is, however, evidence that the *average* of the scores for deaf people, even on the least linguistically biased tests, is a few points below that of the hearing. For instance, on the WISC-R performance test (Wechsler, 1974), Anderson and Sisco (1977) found that a sample of 1,228 deaf children obtained an average

IQ of 95 as against the hearing 'norm' of 100. The interpretation of such a relatively small difference is difficult (Wood, 1984). The sample of 2,200 hearing children on which the WISC-R was standardized was 'limited to "normal" children', i.e. it excluded 'institutionalized' children (Manual, 1974, p. 19). However, in Anderson and Sisco's deaf sample, all the children were in 'special education' (eighteen residential schools and four day school programmes). Thus although the norms so produced may be very useful when assessing children *within* special education, generalizations about 'the deaf' are hazardous when no deaf children who were mainstreamed into ordinary classrooms (and who might be of higher than average intelligence) were included in the standardization sample.

Furthermore, the assessment of intelligence in deaf children is made difficult by factors associated with causes of hearing loss. Children whose deafness is attributable to maternal rubella, for example, or to the effects of diseases (and their treatment) such as meningitis, are likely to suffer additional problems—some severe and obvious, others more subtle and less easily identified (e.g. Jensema and Trybus, 1978; Meadow, 1980, Quigley and Kretschmer, 1982). These additional problems are often associated with learning difficulties, behavioural and emotional disturbances. However, the cause of deafness in many deaf people is not known. Two large-scale studies, one in the European Community (CEC, 1979) and another in the United States (Jensema, 1975), found that the cause of deafness in 42 and 45 per cent (respectively) of deaf children was unknown. In a smaller survey of hearing-impaired children being educated in ordinary classrooms in England and Wales, we found a comparable figure of 46 per cent (Wood *et al.*, 1984). Given these uncertainties about both the cause of deafness and the effects of different causes on measured intelligence, it is clearly difficult to reach firm conclusions about the general significance of small variations in average measured intelligence across deaf and hearing samples.

We can, however, conclude from such studies that deafness *per se* does not necessarily lead to low levels of whatever it is such intelligence tests measure. If one is prepared to take high scores on these tests as indications of intellectual superiority or potential genius, then there are similar numbers of hearing and deaf people in these categories.

Intelligence tests, in company with experimental studies of reasoning and problem-solving abilities in deaf children, provide a firm basis for the conclusion that the deaf are as likely as the hearing to develop the capacity for rational thought—at least, when the use of linguistic symbols and literacy is not demanded. Furth's (e.g. 1971) widely known studies, involving Piagetian tests of pre-logical and logical thinking, demonstrated that deaf children do achieve logical thought, though they may be delayed in such achievements (more of this later).

Despite this evidence, however, there are many studies of thinking in deaf people that point to differences, if not in the capacity for rational thought, at least in how well they 'deploy' that capacity and in their characteristic styles of thinking. In fact, four general characteristics of 'deaf psychology' are often mentioned in the literature. The deaf are often characterized in relation to hearing people as being more rigid (less flexible), more concrete (less abstract), more egocentric (less aware of the perspectives of others) and more impulsive (less likely to take thought or consider alternative lines of action before acting). Before looking at some examples of the kinds of studies and observations that have given support for these generalizations, we will consider some of the theoretical explanations which have given credibility to them.

A 'SPECIAL PSYCHOLOGY' OF DEAFNESS?

The most explicit theoretical account of a special psychology of deafness was formulated by Myklebust (1964) on the basis of a number of empirical studies. He looked at several different aspects of deaf and hearing children's performance including linguistic abilities and literacy, motor activity and problem solving. His general theory, designed to explain different patterns of scoring by deaf and hearing subjects, hinges on the notion of what he called an 'organismic shift' (note the ring of biological inevitability) brought about by little or no functional hearing. Lacking access to sound, he argues, the intelligence and personality of the deaf develop in qualitatively different ways from that of hearing people. Though they may display similar levels of intellectual competence, the *nature* and the *deployment* of that intelligence is different. Let us reconstruct the main elements of the theory.

When we are attending visually to an activity or event, we are locked into our own, direct experience. The experience of sound in parallel with vision provides an avenue whereby happenings and events to which we are not paying close attention can intrude upon and relocate our sphere of attention. Sounds that are at variance with our tacit range of expectations within a situation (e.g. a voice in a room perceived as empty or a sudden change in the note of a car engine when driving) and sounds that have particular personal significance for us (e.g. someone speaking our name) are likely to 'grab' our attention, and we are likely to relinquish our immediate focus of concern to search for and locate the source of the sound.

We possess remarkable powers for monitoring many aspects of our situation without being fully conscious of doing so (e.g. Underwood, 1976), and any sudden, important or 'unexpected' change in the environmental activities that are in the background of our conscious awareness is likely to distract and relocate our interest.

The fact that we are often 'unconsciously' in touch with the world through its sounds gives us a constant source of information about the activities of objects and people in parallel with our own concerns. Vision and hearing are our major 'distance' receptors. Touch and taste demand direct personal contact with the objects that occasion them. Smell can provide cues to distance and even to spatial position, but, in humans, this sense is rudimentary and limited in scope. Thus, the argument proceeds, deaf people, lacking the parallel worlds afforded by sight and sound are, of necessity, more ego-centred and psychologically self-contained. Their sphere of attention is more likely to be limited to their own immediate concerns since it is not expanded by the sounds of others. Their attention will be more fixed and less flexible since unexpected changes usually signalled by sound changes are impercept-ible. Similarly, the world will be more 'personal' since consciousness will be limited to one's own concerns. Even where one deliberately scans the environment to keep check on the actions of others, this will be a deliberate and conscious personal act, not a subconscious and continuous process of monitoring that occasionally 'demands' attention. Thus viewed, the deaf person is, in one sense, more the master of his own attentions, but also more likely to be left out of and behind changes occurring in the world that he has not thought to look at. More poetically, the deaf person is often alone in a crowd.

So, egocentrism and a lack of flexibility and anticipation are likely to be natural products of the 'organismic shift' caused by deafness. The deaf person is not stupid; nor is he consciously selfish or egocentric. Indeed, to the extent that he is aware of others, he can often take more 'credit' than the hearing since he must *choose* to be aware, but the lack of sound robs him of the continuous, *natural* and, indeed, for the hearing, inevitable awareness of others and their activities.

Within this theoretical analysis, it is the lack of access to *sound in general* that leads to such effects. A lack of access to *speech* occasions more specific effects on psychological functioning. In considering the impact of poor language on the development of abstract, flexible and reflective thinking, Myklebust's theory shares some similarities with that of the Soviet psychol-ogists, Vygotsky (1962) and Luria (e.g. Luria and Yudovich, 1971). Very briefly, the Soviet theorists provide a very special place for language (and, more specifically, speech) in the development of abstract, intelligent thinking. In this respect, their analysis of the nature of thinking is diametrically opposed to the views of Piaget and Furth.

Let us consider two important functions proposed for the influence of language on thought. First, it is argued that words 'free' us from domination by our immediate perceptual impressions. When we can name objects and events in our ongoing activities, we produce bridges and connections with our past and our potential futures. To name is to classify. To classify is, implicitly, to relate what we are seeing to all other things that have names. A dog is not a cat but both are animals. A man is also an animal but bipedal, social and linguistic. A woman is also bipedal, social and linguistic but capable of bearing young, and so on. Lacking words, Luria and Yudovich (1971, p. 32) write:

... the deaf mute who has not been taught to speak ... does not possess all those forms of reflection which are realised through speech ... (he) indicates objects or actions with a gesture; he is unable to form abstract concepts, to systematise the phenomena of the external world with the aid of abstracted signals furnished by language but which are not natural to visual, practically acquired experience.

In terms of this theory, deaf people are not intellectually incompetent, but only lack some forms of thought and reflection. But their thinking is more likely to be limited to their immediate concerns because they lack the power of 'inner speech' that serves as a vehicle for relating the present to the past and the future in highly articulated and specific ways. This is not to say that the deaf lack memories, imagination or aspirations. Rather, they lack the highly specific, disciplined and, above all, *socialized* forms of reflection that are the product of language. Thus, their thinking is likely to be more idiosyncratic. Sharing words, people can draw attention to, think about and relate situations in similar ways. Lacking these, the (non-speaking) deaf person's attention, memory and thought will be more idiosyncratic and concrete.

According to Vygotsky and many contemporary psychologists (Wood, 1980) language not only 'distances' us and frees us from immediate experience but also enables us to construct plans and models of the world which can be operated on mentally and evaluated intellectually. The symbol system provided by language (together with other systems, such as mathematics) is generative and creative. We can, through words, describe and, in part at least, understand experiences and even possible ways of living that we have not directly experienced. Since words and the structures of language are relatively formal (i.e. rule-governed) and shared with others, we can also communicate about those hypothetical worlds and may even decide to build them and try to live in them. Language also provides a vehicle for 'taking thought'. When, during the course of development, we provide children with the names for the things that they are perceiving, doing and feeling, we help to structure their intentions, attentions and memories. We literally tell them what aspects of experience are worthy of note and how these aspects interrelate, interact, influence and cause each other. But we help to structure not only the 'content' of experience but also the structure or manner in which they receive and direct it.

Reflect upon the importance, within this theory, of mundane conversations or dialogues that are a characteristic feature of interactions between adults and children in everyday life. We help to shape children's feelings of efficacy or incompetence. We extend the scope of their anticipations, offer them a sense of optionality and guide their evaluations of possible outcomes of given lines of activity. We caution and encourage, enliven or depress, remind and prompt, connect the moment to the past and so on. The many ways in which we help children to structure and reflect upon their own past, present and possible futures often rest on the ways in which we *talk* to them. We might say 'Remember what you did last time', 'Do you think that looks right?', 'I don't think that will work', 'If you do that, Daddy will be angry when he gets home', 'If you put that there, I think it might get broken'. Implicit in such dialogues, for the Soviet psychologists and others, are externalizations of the structures of mind. They represent the cultural transmission of ways of thinking and technologies of intelligence. Whereas Piaget and Furth see symbolism, abstraction and rational thought emerging from the child's own actions in the world, these theorists regard ways of thinking as historical and cultural inventions, passed on and developed from one generation to another by processes of informal and formal teaching which take place largely in interactions involving speech.

As the child discovers speech and, literally, begins to 'talk to himself', he inherits far more than words and grammar. He is inducted into ways of being and thinking. Intelligence, thus viewed, is not the direct outcome of universal stages of individual development, but a cultural product, in which the organic potential of the child interacts with ways of living, thinking and talking to shape the structure of knowing and being.

To the extent that he has not been 'taught how to speak', in the Soviet view, the deaf child's thinking remains more-or-less unsocialized. More specifically, the 'inner dialogues' that urge caution, reflection, recollection or planning, that suggest alternatives and options, will be largely unformed. Lacking the technologies of thinking passed on through language, the options open to the child will be relatively few. He will tend to be impulsive because he does not have the structure of alternatives nor the processes of self-control and reflection that language provides.

In the following sections, we will look at some recent developments in the study of abstract thinking in both deaf and hearing people to see how far claims for a 'special psychology' of deafness such as those we have just considered seem reasonable in the face of current evidence. We then move on to explore studies of mathematical abilities in the deaf and consider the implications of this work for hypotheses about the concrete, inflexible and impulsive nature of thought without speech.

CONCRETE AND ABSTRACT THINKING

If a five-year-old child is shown two identical beakers filled with water and asked if either contains 'more to drink' or if both contain the 'same to drink' he will usually decide that both have the same. Then, in full view of the child, we empty the contents of one of the containers into a third with a different shape (say it is taller and thinner). We ask the child the same question, and this time he announces that the tall thin one contains more to drink.

This now widely known demonstration of the young child's 'failure to conserve quantity' was first presented by Piaget as one line of evidence showing that young children cannot reason logically (Piaget and Inhelder, 1969). Failures in other logical tasks by children at the same age demonstrates, for Piagetians, that all children go through a 'pre-operational' or pre-logical stage of development. When the child is older, at the age of seven or so, he will probably have advanced to the stage of 'concrete operations' and display logical thinking. This older child 'sees' that pouring the liquid from one container to another may lead to changes in its appearance but he also realizes that it must leave the quantity unchanged. Thus, he can appreciate that changes in height are offset by equivalent changes in other dimensions. Further, he understands that by reversing the pouring operation he must recreate the original state of affairs. The younger child is unable to 'perceive' the simultaneous changes that occur in more than one dimension during the process of pouring. He attends to the 'end state' of the change but cannot conceptualize the compensating, simultaneous changes in height, width and depth that occur during pouring. Nor can he hold in mind different judgements made over time in order to coordinate them and appreciate any logical inconsistencies. The rather static thinking of the pre-logical child and his inability to perceive and encompass two mental acts or judgements simultaneously makes him the victim of his immediate perceptions, and hence, renders him illogical (or, better, pre-logical).

Many alternative explanations have been put forward to explain why young children fail in this task (which they almost universally do), and these refute Piaget's conclusion that young children are illogical (e.g. Bryant, 1974; Donaldson, 1978). However, our aim is not to explore such issues here. We have considered an example of Piaget's studies to illustrate the type of experimental task adapted by Hans Furth in his work with deaf children. Basically, Furth modified several of Piaget's experiments so that they could be presented non-verbally to deaf children, avoiding any 'contamination' by poor linguistic understanding. His work, in company with that by other researchers (notably Oleron, 1977), led him to conclude that, whilst often developing more slowly, deaf children's eventual success with such problems demonstrates powers of logical thought. However one chooses to interpret such results with hearing children, it seems reasonable to suggest that deaf children should be credited with whatever logical competence we claim for the hearing child. So, Furth concluded, deaf children achieve rational thought and pass through the same stages that hearing children do. He also concluded, more controversially, that the success of deaf children showed that language is not a necessary basis for logical thinking.

But there is another stage beyond concrete operational thinking in Piagetian theory. This, the stage of 'formal operations', is evident when (around thirteen or fourteen years, usually) children are able to apply logical operations to hypothetical, abstract or imagined situations. For example, formal operations are demanded to appreciate that, 'If all x's are y's and all y's are z's, then it follows logically that all x's are z's but not that all z's are x's'. Like all Piaget's proposed stages, the status of this one as a specific and distinct structure in the development of human thought has been questioned (e.g. Wason and Johnson-Laird, 1972).

Attempts to demonstrate formal operational thinking in deaf subjects usually fail. Consider the following example cited in Quigley and Kretschmer (1982). Deaf children were given a series of premises such as 'The shirt is dirty. The shirt is under the bed. The cat is on the shirt. The cat is white' and asked 'Where is the white cat?'. These were presented in speech, sign and writing. The deaf children were less likely than hearing children to make the inference that 'The cat is under the bed' (Wilson, 1979).

Numerous explanations have been put forward for such findings. One is that deaf children are naturally more concrete in their thinking. Another, proposed by Furth, is that they suffer from an 'experiential deficit' that slows down but does not affect the essential structure of their intellectual development.

Generally speaking, whilst deaf children do relatively well on problems to do with concrete events and physical objects (e.g. being able to classify, group and count objects, noting similarities and differences between them) wherever they are asked to work with more abstract materials or to reason analogically (i.e. in terms of abstract, structural relations rather than with specific, concrete ones) they tend to fail (see Quigley and Paul, 1984, Chap. 2 for a detailed review).

Compelling interpretations of such experimental studies are difficult to achieve. In addition to problems of communication—which become increasingly difficult as a task becomes more abstract and, hence, less easily explained—there are deeper problems. These really revolve around the position different theorists adopt in relation to basic questions about the relationships between logical thinking and everyday reasoning. We will not dwell upon these complex issues here, but will illustrate how such results question any attempt to draw firm conclusions from studies of logical thinking in deaf children.

Because Piaget's theory proposes universal stages in the development of human intelligence, despite very great differences, say, in language or cultural experience, it has stimulated a great deal of comparative cross-cultural research. Do people in all cultures think in the same way and pass through the same stages of development? The answer to such questions is not clear-cut (e.g. Berry and Dasen, 1973; Cole and Scribner, 1974). For example, whilst the sequence of development in infancy (the sensori-motor stage) of children from different cultures seems to fit Piaget's predictions, the status of the later stages is more problematic, and nowhere more so than in the proposed formal operational stage. Consider the following example from studies of a Central African tribe called the Kpelle, taken from Cole et al. (1971). Non-schooled members of the tribe were posed the following logical problem (in their own language, of course!).

Experimenter:	Flumo and Yakpalo always drink cane juice (rum) together. Flumo is drinking cane juice. Is Yakpalo drinking cane juice?
Subject:	The day that Flumo was drinking the cane juice Yakpalo was not there on that day.
Experimenter:	What is the reason?
Subject:	The reason is that Yakpalo went to his farm on that day and Flumo remained in town on that day.

Are the Kpelle, like many deaf people, incapable of formal operational thinking? Or is it the case, as Cole and his colleagues conclude from wider ranging and more 'naturalistic' observations, that making inferences from hypothetical statements about implausible situations is a peculiarly Western activity—one developed for certain, rather special purposes? It seems that formal, logical thinking does not come 'naturally' but is a rather special way of thinking invented by technological societies to perform certain functions. If so, then such ways of thinking must be *culturally transmitted* and are not an inevitable product of general experience or intelligence. One view is that such forms of thinking are the products of schooling and literacy (e.g. Donaldson, 1978).

The relationships between formal logical rules and procedures of everyday reasoning are, then, complex and indirect. Reasoning logically about abstract or 'non-sensical' propositions—suspending reality and common sense—is a rather specialized activity that requires experience and the development of what Russell (1981) has called 'propositional attitudes'.

In our experience, linguistic interactions with deaf children tend to be literal and concrete. Talk is often about the names of things and their attributes (shared descriptions) or about everyday events that 'really happened'. Getting speech and language 'right' is at a premium. We cannot, therefore, rule out the possibility that the propositional attitude demanded by hypothetical, abstract reasoning is simply not fostered in the deaf. Abstract reasoning and analogical thinking are not an inevitable stage of development that the deaf, by their nature, fail to achieve. Rather, as Piaget himself acknowledged (1972), it may be that such ways of thinking demand specific cultural experiences and, in particular, the sorts of experience that normally take place in schools. Perhaps the deaf are not inevitably concrete. Maybe we treat them too 'literally', so they remain literal.

Let us consider one final example that takes us to the main focus of the chapter—the study of arithmetical and mathematical abilities in deaf children. Imagine a group of children posed the following (not atypical) mathematical problem: 'If it takes two men three days to dig a hole, how many days does it take three men to dig the same hole?' Suppose the youngsters respond with observations like 'Well, if the hole has already been dug, then the earth will be soft' or 'Well, with three men, one can take a rest, so the two working can work harder'. What have they got 'wrong'? In mathematical and logical discourse, one must often suspend such pragmatic and 'irrelevant' ideas, but in solving everyday problems (someone about to dig up your drive at home), such pragmatic concerns could prove more vital than the 'pure' mathematical calculations. Like logical discourse, mathematical thinking operates in an idealized problem space stripped of many everyday implications that have to be ignored so that the formal mathematical elements involved can be manipulated to reach idealized solutions. Children must learn—usually without explicit guidance—that what appear to be concrete and 'relevant' problems in school are, in fact, discussed according to specific and special 'ground rules' that are different from those governing everyday behaviour and discourse. Herein lie learning problems for many children (Mercer and Edwards, 1981).

In summary, whilst there is experimental evidence to suggest that deaf people, in comparison to the hearing, tend to be more literal and concrete, less abstract and hypothetical in their thinking, the basis for such differences remain unclear and problematic. We should be cautious about accepting such features as general attributes of a special 'deaf intelligence' when experiential factors that might also account for the differences have yet to be explored. We return to this issue after we have discussed studies of mathematical abilities in deaf children.

MATHEMATICAL REASONING, LANGUAGE AND DEAFNESS

One advantage of studying intellectual processes through mathematics, rather than formal experimental tests, is that mathematical experiences form a part of children's everyday activities in school. Consequently, some of the problems associated with the artificial and arbitrary nature of many experimental tasks can be avoided.

A number of studies of mathematical attainment in deaf people have demonstrated that they lag behind their hearing contemporaries. The question we address is why this should be the case. One obvious explanation is that language is involved in the mental processes underlying mathematical thinking. If, as some suggest (Hitch, 1978), internal speech or subvocalization is a necessary basis for some aspects of mathematical thinking (holding different numbers and operations in memory, for example) we would expect that deaf children, with generally poor linguistic abilities, should show low levels of mathematical competence and specific difficulties in learning how to do mathematics.

This proposition is difficult to sustain, however. Studies of the mathematical achievement of deaf children in the United States, for example, provide no evidence for any simple relationships between degree of deafness, language ability and mathematical achievement. Profoundly deaf children often do as well or better than their less deaf peers on some mathematical tests. Whilst, as one would expect, less deaf and more verbally able children do better when problems are stated in linguistic form and demand some degree of literacy (and a propositional attitude?), where problems are presented in mathematical symbols with no demands for reading, such differences are not nearly so marked.

However, in our discussions of reading test performance of deaf children, we argued that similar scores by deaf and hearing children do not necessarily reflect the same things. This conclusion, recall, was based on an examination of scoring patterns and errors on different test items. In this chapter, we discuss similar analyses performed on a test of mathematical and arithmetical ability. Basically, we ask if the patterns of success and error shown by deaf and hearing children are similar or different. If we find marked differences, then this invites us to explore the basis for these and to entertain the hypothesis that deaf children think differently in mathematics.

In the reading tests, we found that deaf children tended to try more items than hearing children, and that they made more errors, suggesting that they might be less aware of their own strengths and weaknesses. This result might be specific to reading tests (i.e. language-based ones) or it might be a general feature of the way in which deaf children tackle problems. If the latter, it would imply that deaf children are generally less aware of the state of their own knowledge and abilities. In contemporary jargon, they would have poor 'meta-cognitive skills'. In relation to Soviet theory, it would support the notion that the deaf are more impulsive (having a go at almost anything) and less reflective (not stopping, for example, to consider whether a given item should be attempted or whether it would be better to find an item more likely to produce a correct answer). We have also explored this feature of children's test-taking strategies in mathematics. Would they, as they had in reading tests, be less selective and less accurate than their hearing peers?

Before trying to answer these questions, we need to say a little about the study upon which these answers are based. Since full accounts of procedure and analysis have already been reported (Wood, Wood and Howarth, 1983a; 1983b; Wood et al., 1984) we will concentrate here on the main results and their implications.

The test we used was the Vernon–Miller Graded Arithmetic–Mathematics Test (1976). One reason for selecting this test was that it contains two complementary versions, 'Senior' and 'Junior', which, together, cover a wide age-range of mathematical abilities (from five to seventeen years). The study involved a total of 1,005 children of whom 540 were hearing-impaired. Of these, 269 were attending special schools, 136 were attending partially hearing units attached to ordinary schools and 135 were being educated in classrooms for normally hearing children (i.e. they were 'mainstreamed'). We also included 465 hearing children both to provide an up-to-date comparison group and to obtain a database for analysing scoring patterns and errors.

The children involved in the study were all in their final year at school. Their average hearing losses and average maths ages are shown in Table 9.1.

Table 9.1   Mean maths ages

Type of school	Hearing loss	Maths age
Special schools	92 dB	12.1
Partially hearing units	68 dB	12.8
Mainstream	48 dB	14.0
Hearing children	—	15.5

In addition to the theoretical questions addressed by this research, our work was also motivated by more practical educational issues. Basically, we wanted to find out if children being educated in different school environments (having made allowances for any differences in hearing loss) were performing better than those in others. In England and Wales, as in other parts of the world, the issue of school placement and questions about the effectiveness of different forms of provision are currently the subject of debate. We hoped that this survey might produce some much-needed empirical evidence to help inform these debates and also that it might provide a baseline against which future performances of hearing-impaired children might be compared. We attempted to obtain completed test papers from every hearing-impaired school leaver in England and Wales. Whilst we do not suppose that we did reach every child (no comprehensive records are available) we have no reason to believe that our sample is not a representative one.

What of the results in Table 9.1? Well, two things need to be said by way of background. First, the test we used was selected, amongst other reasons, because it involved relatively little written language. We wanted to minimize any confounding effects due to different levels of reading ability across the different groups of children. However, it should be borne in mind that tests which do include more verbally stated problems would probably produce a very different pattern of results. The test involves a wide range of arithmetical and mathematical procedures including the basic operations of addition, subtraction, multiplication and division together with algebra, manipulation of decimals and fractions, and problems involving graphical representation.

The initial analysis involved a comparison of the performances of deaf and hearing children. Hearing children did significantly better than deaf children from all three school backgrounds. Children in special education (schools and units) were, on average, about three years behind their hearing peers on this test. The integrated or mainstreamed children were about eighteen months behind. Why did the deaf children perform less well than the hearing children?

Well, the first question we asked, not surprisingly, was 'How important a factor is degree of deafness in influencing test achievement scores?' The answer is: 'not very important'. This conclusion can be illustrated in a number of ways. The first, most powerful but abstract, involves statistical analyses for determining how much of the 'variance' in maths scores can be accounted for by relative degrees of deafness. For those not familiar with this rather technical measure, an example might be of help. If deafness was the only factor that influenced the test scores, then knowing how deaf a child is would be a perfect guide to his or her ability relative to all the other children. The measure of deafness would account for all 100 per cent of the variance in maths scores. The closer the amount of 'variance accounted for' approaches the 100 per cent figure then the more important that factor is. Conversely, the more it approximates to 0 per cent the less important it is. Despite the fact that children in our study ranged in hearing loss from 30 to 120 dB, the amount of variance in maths scores accounted for by degree of deafness was only 7 per cent. Though statistically significant for the group as a whole (i.e.

unlikely to be an effect of chance), this value indicates that degree of deafness is not a good predictor of maths age for individual children.

Another way of approaching the analysis is to ask if children from different school backgrounds (special schools, units and mainstream) perform differently. The average hearing losses of children from different environments vary substantially. If hearing loss and/or school environment itself are important factors in the determination of test scores, then we should find significant differences. The scores of children from schools and units were not significantly different. Although they differed in mean hearing loss, and hearing loss related (albeit weakly) to maths scores, the difference in degree of deafness was evidently not great enough to lead to a significant difference in average scores. The mainstreamed children did score significantly higher, on average, than the children from the other settings but were still outscored by their hearing peers. Was the better performance of the mainstreamed children attributable (amongst other things) to differences in amount of hearing or to school environment (e.g. being taught alongside hearing children or with a different curriculum) or both? It is possible to separate the effects of hearing loss and school background statistically. When we did this, we found that school background was not a significant factor *per se*. Hearing loss accounted for nearly all the differences between the mainstreamed children and those from special schools and units. A more concrete illustration of the same result can be gained by comparing the scores of children from different settings who have similar hearing losses. Although the average hearing loss of children from the three environments was very different, there was a reasonable number of children in all three with losses in the 50 to 70 dB range. When we looked at their scores, we found no significant differences. Again, this suggests that the sort of school attended did not influence performance to any great degree. Note, however, that this is not to say that children from all schools did equally well; rather, there was no difference associated with the *type* of school environment over and above that due to differences in the deafness of the children in them. We found, for example, that children from one special school obtained average maths ages that were equivalent to those of the mainstreamed (much less deaf) sample, whereas children in other special schools had average maths ages well below nine years.

These lines of analysis suggest that deafness as such is not a barrier to the development of mathematical competence. Another way of making a somewhat similar point is to look at the highest scores achieved by children with different levels of hearing loss. We divided the whole sample into nine, 10-dB hearing loss bands to find that within each 'band' were children who reached the 'ceiling' (highest attributable maths age on the test). There was *no* correlation between hearing loss and the 'top scores' achieved within each band. There was, however, a significant correlation between hearing loss and 'lowest scores' in each band, suggesting that it is at the lower end of the mathematical ability range that hearing loss is exerting most effect, a point we return to later.

But if hearing loss is relatively unimportant and the type of school attended does not seem to exert much effect on average levels of achievement, why do deaf children lag so far behind hearing children? The relatively small influence of hearing loss suggests (but does not prove) that language is not an important factor in maths achievement in the deaf. If so, why are there differences between them and the hearing? The answer to this question, we believe, cannot be explained by a single factor but involves several, interacting ones. Before we consider the issue further, we need to return to one of our central questions—is the mathematics test measuring the same thing in deaf and hearing samples?

DEAF MATHEMATICIANS—DELAYED OR DIFFERENT?

We approached an answer to this question in three ways. First, we looked at all the test items and asked if deaf and hearing children tended to get different items correct and incorrect. There were some minor differences (see below) but no suggestion of any marked variation in scoring patterns. Second, we asked if the sorts of errors made by the two groups of children were different in kind. Again, we found no evidence that they were. The mistakes made by deaf and hearing children were similar (though the frequencies of different types varied somewhat). Third, we asked if deaf children were more likely than hearing children to 'persevere senselessly' on the test. For example, did the deaf children tackle questions in great numbers but only achieve a few right answers? The answer to this question is rather more complex. However, in general, we found no marked overall differences between the deaf and hearing children.

We return to each of these results and their more detailed implications later. For the moment, the important finding is one of general similarity across the groups of children. There is no reason to suppose that, on this test at least, deaf children's mathematical reasoning (though retarded) was different in kind from that of hearing children. Nor did we gain any evidence that the deaf children were necessarily less selective in tackling the test items nor, by implication, any more 'impulsive' in their test-taking approach than the hearing children were. This suggests that any such impulsivity by the deaf (e.g. on reading tests) is relatively task specific and is not a general aspect of their personality or intellectual 'style' of thinking.

In the next sections, we look first at the relationships between deaf children's error patterns and predictions made by their teachers about where such errors might lie. This analysis is informative both because it helps us to gauge the predictability of children's problems and also because it raises issues about the ability of deaf children to tackle maths problems that involve some written language. The second section examines questions that 'deceived' children. These were problems that relatively large numbers of children tried but relatively few got right. We examine the questions that deceived deaf and hearing children as another, more focused way of exploring similarities and differences in the mathematical knowledge of the two groups of children. Finally, we explore the errors that deaf children made on specific problems in an attempt to reveal some aspects of their mathematical 'logic'. The main hypothesis that arises from this final section is that children's errors are often systematic and symptomatic of different 'stages' in the achievement of correct mathematical operations. Finally, we return to a consideration of the central theoretical issue to speculate about the possible reasons for deaf children's slower development in mathematics and to consider the implications of our findings for future research and curriculum development.

TEACHER PREDICTIONS AND PUPIL PERFORMANCE

As part of our survey, we asked all the teachers of the hearing-impaired children (in special schools and units) to identify questions which they thought their children would find difficult. We also asked them to specify whether any such difficulties would occur for mathematical reasons or linguistic ones. Although the test involved little written language in comparison with other tests that we examined, it did still contain problems with up to thirty-three words in them. Consequently, we felt that there might be a 'linguistic' element in the test which might produce special problems for deaf children and could explain some or all of the differences in test scores across different groups of children. Teachers might help identify any such 'verbal' factors.

To derive a rough measure of the predicted difficulty of problems, we found the sum total, for each problem, of teachers who identified it as a likely source of difficulty for either linguistic or mathematical reasons (or both). We then compared these 'predictions' with children's levels of success on the problems. The measure of difficulty is a crude one, in that different children in any group might have different problems. Any such differences would be eradicated when we added the predictions of all teachers together. However, there was enough agreement across teachers to make the endeavour seem sensible and worthwhile.

We found extremely high correlations between teacher predictions of *mathematical difficulties* and children's success rates, and, in fact, these predictions applied equally well to both deaf and hearing children. However, when we looked at their predictions of difficulties due to *linguistic problems*, we found the relationship with children's success was far weaker on the Senior test and non-existent on the Junior version. Although teachers tended to agree about where such linguistic problems would lie (in fact, their predictions related to the number of words in questions) their judgements did not agree at all closely with what children did. In fact, generally speaking, children found the linguistic problems *considerably easier* than the teacher predictions would suggest. Two examples are given below of problems that teacher predictions suggested should have proved difficult but which children found (relative to other problems) easy.

> Tom had some toy cars. He gave 5 to Jim and still had 16 left. How many cars had he to begin with?
>
> This graph shows the times and distances of someone walking 12 kilometres between 10 a.m. and 3 p.m. How long did he rest for lunch?

The way in which we calculated teacher predictions is, as we have already acknowledged, crude and could be misleading. However, since this measure did identify a number of 'wordy' questions which were expected to cause difficulties, we undertook other analyses. First, we correlated the number of words in questions with children's success rates, to find no significant relationship. Next we determined, for every deaf child, the number of right answers to the most wordy questions. We then correlated these scores with children's hearing loss. If these items did lead to purely linguistic difficulties, we argued, then hearing loss should correlate more highly with success rate with these questions than with the remaining, 'non-verbal' questions. They did not.

To sum up, teachers' predictions of mathematical difficulties were more accurate than their predictions about linguistic ones. Children did better than teachers predicted with wordy questions. This does not mean that there may not be other, less obvious, influences of written language on test scores (see later section on errors), but it does raise questions both about teacher expectations and their influence on curriculum and teaching styles. Could deaf children do much more with linguistically based mathematical problems than we currently expect or demand of them? How do they use a knowledge of mathematics either to read or bypass the need for reading in solving some mathematical problems?

QUESTIONS THAT DECEIVE—OR I'M HARDER THAN YOU THINK!

Generally speaking, both deaf and hearing children displayed similar test-taking behaviour in the sense that nearly all the children tackled the easy questions (which nearly all who made the attempt got right) and progressively fewer tackled items as they got harder (when relatively few children who made the attempt were correct). But some questions were deceptive, in that a much smaller proportion of children who tried them got them right than would be expected from comparisons with other problems. Put another way, suppose we know that, on average, 50 per cent of children tackle a problem which 70 per cent of children making the attempt get right. We then discover that on one problem, although 90 per cent of the children had a go at it, only 40 per cent (of those trying) get the correct answer. This we would designate a deceptively hard question. By picking out such deceptive problems for deaf and hearing children we can get some insight into the issue of whether or not deaf and hearing children are 'deceived' in similar ways. We consider here the results of just one such analysis in which we compared the performances of deaf children from special schools and units with those of the hearing children. All these children had completed the Senior version of the paper.

We picked out, for both deaf and hearing children, the ten most deceptively hard questions. We then examined the two lists to see if there was any agreement. There was. Seven problems appeared on both lists. Since the test involves sixty-five problems, the probability that seven should appear in common simply by chance is astronomically small. Consider the common core of seven most deceptive problems.

$$\frac{3}{4} + \frac{1}{2} = \dots$$

Write in numbers: one hundred thousand and fifty-six. .....

What was the greatest number of kilometres he walked in any single period of 60 minutes? .....

Write fifteen thousandths as a decimal. .....

$$20 \div \frac{1}{5} = \dots$$

How many minutes between 10.40 a.m. and 1.20 p.m.? .....

One room in my house measures 2 metres by 3 metres, and it cost £50 to carpet it. Another room measures 4 metres by 6 metres. How much would it cost to carpet it at the same rate?

Whatever aspect or aspects of problems led the group of *hearing* children to tackle questions that relatively few were to get right also, generally speaking, did the *same* to the deaf. But why were these questions deceptive for both groups?

Had this list been drawn up for the deaf alone, one might have been tempted to say that some of the items proved difficult simply because they involved words. However, as we have seen, wordiness *per se* is not an important factor on this test. Some wordy questions were relatively easy, others relatively difficult. A good deal of research with hearing children (see Bell, Costello and Kuchemann, 1983, for a recent review) has shown that relatively simple mathematical procedures which children can handle when they are stated in familiar, mathematical nomenclature and format are solved far less successfully when stated even in simple language.

Our list contains several wordy problems, and it may be that both deaf and hearing children found them more difficult than they expected because they knew the mathematical operations needed for the problem but many could not transform the problem into a workable mathematical format without making errors. Another feature of this deceptive list is a failure to handle relatively straightforward problems involving fractions. We discuss the sorts of errors children make on fractions in the next section.

Although we can only speculate about the reasons why these questions should provoke relatively large numbers of mistakes from children, the main reason for presenting them is to underline the fact that deaf and hearing children responded in very similar ways to them.

If we had only considered the problems that deaf children found deceptive and had not explored those that deceived hearing children, we might have been tempted to conclude that deaf children were facing problems because they were deaf and linguistically weak rather than because they were experiencing 'normal' difficulties in learning mathematics. The fact that many problems are shared by deaf and hearing children implies that their remediation lies in attempts to help them overcome the *mathematical* problems they face.

THE ANALYSIS OF CHILDREN'S ERRORS

In Chapter 6, where we compared the performances of deaf and hearing children on reading tests, the analysis of errors proved a useful way of gaining some insights both into the different performances of the two groups and into the features of the test items that deaf children exploited in answering questions. We found, recall, that the error patterns of deaf children were consistent in that many children gave the same wrong answers and that those of the hearing children were not (implying that, as a group, hearing children found the various distractor items equally distracting).

When we analysed the errors on the mathematics test, we found a quite different pattern of relationships to that found on the reading tests. Clearly, on maths items, where children can make one or more mistakes in attempting an item, the scope for error is wide and the number of possible wrong answers is non-determinate. Although, in theory, one could obtain a different wrong answer to a given question from every child who gets it wrong, in practice, there were *common* errors on most questions. This, in turn, suggests that errors are not *random* but the product of *systematic but invalid or incomplete* mathematical procedures.

When we compared the errors of deaf and hearing children, two main findings emerged. First, on the vast majority of the questions the same common errors appeared in both deaf and hearing groups. Thus, any systematic procedures involved in the production of errors were likely to be evidenced by both of them. Put another way, any 'logic' involved in producing errors was the same for deaf and hearing children. This, in turn, would imply that the ways in which children conceptualize and/or work through mathematical problems to produce errors were similar.

A second finding was that although similar patterns of errors occurred in both groups, the actual *proportions* of errors of each type tended to vary. So, for example, there might be three errors that occurred frequently in response to a given item for both groups, but the relative frequencies of these three errors would differ between groups. How are we to interpret this finding? Well, one important factor is likely to be that the deaf children were less mathematically advanced than the hearing sample. Consequently, their error patterns, as a group, might be less 'sophisticated'. We can explore this possibility in two ways. One is to compare the deaf group with a sub-group of the hearing children who achieved the same average maths score. The second, more time-consuming and speculative, is to attempt to produce an analysis which 'explains' how errors are produced and generates some insights and hypotheses as to why some errors are more sophisticated than others. We turn now to consider these two analyses.

ERRORS BY DEAF AND HEARING CHILDREN WITH SIMILAR SCORES

As we have already said, the test we used involves two, complementary forms—a Junior test which was used with the mathematically less able children and a Senior one used with the more able. For this analysis, papers from 188 children were used—94 deaf and 94 hearing. Of these, 48 deaf and 48 hearing had taken the Junior version whilst 46 children in each group had taken the Senior test. A number of analyses were undertaken on these tests.

First, we looked at how many children attempted each test item and at their average level of success in doing so. On the reading tests, recall, we found that deaf children were likely to tackle more items and that they made more errors in doing so. On the Senior test, the hearing children attempted an average 78 per cent of the questions, the deaf group 77 per cent. The average success rate of the deaf children who tackled an item was 79 per cent and the hearing figure was also 79 per cent. On this measure, then, there was no difference between the two groups. In mathematics, unlike reading tests, deaf and hearing children of nominally similar test ages score in a similar way. This reinforces our general argument, which is that deaf children are delayed but not deviant or different in their mathematical reasoning.

With the 'Junior' samples, there were, however, some differences. For example, the deaf group attempted on average 77 per cent of the questions and 65 per cent of the children who tried an item got it right. The corresponding figures for the hearing children were 67 per cent attempts and 76 per cent success. The deaf 'Juniors' stand out, in that their pattern of test-taking behaviour is different from all the other groups, including the more able deaf. Basically, they obtained their maths scores at the cost of more errors than any other group of children. We speculate about possible reasons for the 'odd' performance of the less able deaf children later. The question we turn to now is whether the errors of this 'odd' group are different in kind from hearing children or whether they simply make more errors of a similar nature.

THE 'LOGIC' OF ERROR

The analysis and classification of errors on a relatively long maths test taken by so many children involves a great deal of time and demands attention to a lot of detail. Consequently, we will concentrate here on a discussion of a few questions.

Overall, as we said above, we found that deaf and hearing children made the same types of error but in different proportions. So we begin by illustrating errors of varying degrees of sophistication and by considering how they relate to overall test performance. This analysis is *post hoc* (i.e. took place after the study and was not planned) and therefore speculative. However, we present it to illustrate how the detailed examination of children's errors can be used to gain insights into their thinking and understanding.

Consider the following question:

$$3 \times 4 = 6 \times \ldots$$

Common errors on this problem were (our 'explanation' in brackets):

$$72 \ (3 \times 4 \times 6)$$
$$12 \ (3 \times 4)$$
$$18 \ (3 \times 4 + 6)$$
$$6 \ (3 \times 4 - 6)$$

If our 'explanations' are right, then we can make a number of predictions. For example, 72 as an answer involves ignoring the equation sign. However, if our explanation is valid, it also involves getting a quite difficult multiplication problem right. Children who make this error get higher test scores, on average, than those who give the answers 12 and 18. Is this because they are better at multiplication? Does their error actually reveal a 'hidden' strength in comparison to children making the errors 12 or 18?

If a child gives an answer of 12, it suggests that he both ignores more relevant information than one who answers with 72 and also does less computation. Thus, we classify 12 as a less sophisticated error than 72. Of the deaf children making an error on this question, 18 per cent gave an answer of 12 and 18 per cent gave an answer of 72. For the hearing children, the relevant figures were 0 and 4 per cent respectively. If it is the case that the children who give an answer of 72 are relatively good at multiplication, then it might follow that they will do well on a 'straight' multiplication sum. To test this possibility, we compared the '72 group' with the '18 group' on the following problem:

$$\text{Multiply: } 4 \times \pounds 3.37 = \ldots$$

In fact, 85 per cent of the '72 group' got the answer to this question right. Children making errors 12 or 18 only achieved a success rate of 42 per cent, a highly significant difference. Thus, the better test scores of the '72 group' is due, at least in part, to their better abilities in multiplication.

The most common error on this problem by hearing children was 6, an answer given by a third of the children who got the problem wrong. The same error was made by deaf children, too, but only 7 per cent gave this answer. If our interpretation of this error is valid, then it suggests a relatively sophisticated understanding of equations (in relation to other errors, that is). Children seem to be working on the rule 'When you bring numbers over from one side of an equation to the other, then subtract that number'. If this interpretation is correct, these children should be quite likely to get the following sum right:

$$\boxed{4 + 3 = 2 + \,.\,.\,.\,.\,.}$$

In fact, 94 per cent of the children who made the '6' error did get this sum right. The children making errors on this item which ignored the '=' sign achieved only 7 per cent correct answers on this second sum.

These examples are given to illustrate a general feature of the results. First, many of the errors that children made were systematic and they related in interpretable ways to the answers given on other problems. There is a certain 'logic' underlying many errors. Further, these errors can usually be classified as more-or-less sophisticated on the basis of the number of elements in the problem they involve (e.g. the equals sign, number of numbers to be processed, etc.). The more an error reflects attention to all the problem elements, the more sophisticated it is. Children who made more sophisticated errors on a given item tended to score higher on the test than those who made less sophisticated ones. Finally, although the less able deaf children made more errors than hearing children or more able deaf children, the errors they made were usually found in the performance of hearing children too. The errors are sometimes more numerous and often less sophisticated but rarely 'abnormal'. Thus, we suggest, deaf children go through the same 'stages' as hearing children en route to mastery of mathematical processes, but their progress is slower. The reasons why they are slower concern us in the next section.

DISCUSSION AND IMPLICATIONS

Whatever the reasons for deaf children's relatively slow progress in mathematics, the evidence we have reviewed shows, we argue, that their reasoning processes are similar to hearing children's. The similarities in patterns of items attempted, success rates and error types all point to delay rather than difference.

This conclusion is, of course, compatible with Furth's arguments about the rationality of deaf people and the essential normality of their logical development. Furth, however, usually attributes delays in deaf children to a rather nebulous concept of 'experiential deficit'. Language, in his view, is not an important determinant of the *structure* of intelligence nor the capacity for rational thought. The very low correlation between hearing loss and mathematical achievement in our study *is* compatible with the conclusion that speech is not a *necessary* condition for problem solving in mathematics. If it was, we would have expected the relationship between hearing loss and maths scores to be far higher than it was. Other research, using more focused, experimental techniques has led to similar hypotheses (Hitch, Arnold and Phillips, 1983). However, there *is* a relationship between degree of deafness and level of achievement which, though relatively weak, cannot be ignored, and we have still to explain why deaf children are delayed.

Where we depart from Furth concerns the importance of *language and communication* in the *transmission* of knowledge. Furth, in his early work, often referred to deaf children as though they completely *lacked* any functional linguistic competence. However, throughout this book we have emphasized the fact that pre-verbal and verbal communication with deaf children does take place and, furthermore, that deaf children possess a generative linguistic system, albeit, often a limited one. Pre-school deaf children, as we saw in Chapter 3, can be taught how to perform a complex task and similar principles of effective teaching influence deaf and hearing children's success or failure. But we also pointed to specific problems facing both teacher and child due to the child's limited auditory awareness and the ensuing problems of divided attention. We suggest that the deaf child's relatively slow progress in learning mathematics (and other things) resides in the difficulties involved in teaching–learning processes. Thus, whereas Furth's explanation for delay rests on the child's limited access to general experience, we argue that its basis is social and communicative. The deaf child may not reason about mathematics in words, but he must acquire the concepts, procedures and symbols of mathematical processes through communication. Thus, we suggest, slow progress results from impaired teaching–learning processes.

Our study also touched upon various ways of exploring deaf children's awareness of their own knowledge and of their often-cited 'impulsivity'. What evidence we have suggests that many deaf children are just as selective in attempting and avoiding problems as their hearing peers. If, as Luria argued, deaf children are often impulsive and non-reflective, then we suggest this is not a generalized cognitive style or part of a general characteristic of 'deaf psychology', but is far more task specific. It seems to us, quite simply, that deaf children are only likely to appear impulsive and non-selective where their knowledge of the task at hand (e.g. reading) is limited. Where, as in the maths tests, deaf children reveal relatively normal (if delayed) levels of functioning, they are no less selective and no more impulsive than hearing children.

Another important, but problematic, result came from the comparison of patterns of attempt, success and error made by the more mathematically able and less able deaf children. Although less able hearing children (by definition) scored lower than their more able peers, their pattern of test-taking behaviour (e.g. relative error rates) on the problems they tackled were very similar. The less able deaf children tackled more items but got fewer right and, hence, made more errors. The errors, however, were not usually 'random' ones, though the analysis upon which this conclusion is based was illustrative and not empirically compelling. We cannot explain this difference with any confidence, but it does illustrate an important general argument. Deaf children are more *variable* as a population than hearing children. When we apply a common label such as deafness to children, there is an implicit invitation to regard them as somehow more alike than is the norm. Other research, by Norden (1975) in Sweden, reaches similar conclusions. In a wide-ranging series of studies of deaf adolescents, Norden found that the deaf group was less homogeneous than hearing controls. She also investigated claims about the concrete, rigid and egocentric thinking of deaf people. Whilst she found one group of deaf children who did tend to be more rigid (and so on) than the hearing sample, there were many deaf children who were not. She argues, in fact, that such intellectual consequences are not inevitable effects of the handicap as such. Her research, in company with studies in the United States (e.g. Jensema, 1975), and our own work on mathematics point to *cause* of deafness as an important determinant of differences *within* the deaf population. As we noted above, children who are deafened by factors such as maternal rubella tend to present more behavioural and emotional problems and achieve less in school than children, for example, whose deafness is inherited. Even within the 'difficult' groups, however, there are children who do not evidence such additional problems. It seems likely that both the greater variability in deaf children's development and, in part, the lower average scores of deaf children in comparison to hearing children may be attributable to aetiological factors. These, we suspect, exacerbate the teaching–learning problems that we have been discussing.

EDUCATIONAL IMPLICATIONS

Teachers in our study tended to overestimate the amount of difficulty deaf children would face with the mathematical problems employing relatively large numbers of words. Although, in common with hearing children, deaf children tended to make more errors on *some* problems that involved mathematical operations embedded in written examples, their performance was relatively good in comparison to the predictions derived from teacher judgements. Further, the lack of any correlation between hearing loss and performance on 'wordy' questions also suggests that wordiness *per se* is *not necessarily* a barrier to success for deaf children. To be sure, we could probably find other, more verbal problems on which deaf children would fail, thus both increasing the correlation between performance and hearing loss and also magnifying the differences between children from different school environments. The question we put before teachers is whether or not they make too many 'allowances' in teaching maths to deaf children because of an overinflated sense of the language problems involved. For example, seventeen out of sixty-one deaf children who got the following non-verbal subtraction sum *wrong* got the more verbal problem *right*.

Subtract: 560
          -192
          .....

Mary bought a record for £1.69. How much change did she get from £2.00?

Although the straight subtraction problem is numerically more difficult than the verbal one, it was interesting that teachers were accurate in predicting the relative difficulty of the first but greatly underestimated children's abilities in the latter. Although the problem involves an auxiliary verb, pronoun and prepositions, all of which children have trouble with, many presumably used their knowledge of mathematical problems and key words such as 'bought' and 'change' to identify the nature of the computation needed. This raises questions about the extent to which a far more systematic and careful use of language and reading in mathematics might provide an avenue for the development of children's knowledge of language. Such comments are obviously speculative, but the mismatch between teacher perceptions and pupil performance in our study suggests that there is a need for educators to reexamine their assumptions about the relationships between maths and language and ask themselves whether they may be failing to exploit deaf children's capacities.

In contrast to predictions of linguistic difficulty, teacher judgements about likely sources of mathematical problems were very accurate. Two possible reasons are involved here. First, teachers might have a good sense of where deaf children are likely to misunderstand/miscompute using mathematical procedures that the children have been *taught*. This would involve a number of things. First, many children should encounter the same computational difficulties (otherwise there would be nothing to predict) and, second, many teachers should recognize those problems (otherwise there would be no predictions). If these implications are borne out they would have vital educational significance. It would follow that teachers have an explicit or implicit theory of children's computational problems that they share and that is valid.

An alternative explanation for the accuracy of teacher predictions is less benign but equally important. Perhaps teachers can predict what children cannot do because they know the children have never been taught those things. For this to hold true, it should follow that many teachers teach the same, somewhat limited curriculum to deaf children.

Although we have yet to gain empirical evidence on this issue, our suspicion, having worked in many schools for the deaf, is that the vast majority of deaf children are not taught such things. Rather, teaching tends to concentrate on the basic operations (addition, subtraction, etc.) and on topics such as buying and change with some work on fractions and, perhaps, a bit on decimals and a little on simple graphical representation. More complex mathematics (e.g. algebra, trigonometry), more demanding uses and analyses of graphs, etc., seldom seem to be taught. This gives rise to the now familiar issue of cause and effect. If deaf children learn or develop more slowly, then this could explain why they never reach more complex maths. Alternatively, part of the reason why deaf children score less well than hearing children may be explained by the fact that they are not taught so much. We cannot choose between these two alternatives on the basis of our existing evidence. However, a large-scale research project in the United States (Suppes, 1974) showed that, given computer-assisted teaching in mathematics, deaf and hearing children of similar maths ages showed different rates of progress. The deaf made more rapid gains. Thus, perhaps because of fewer problems of communication, greater demands, motivation or a combination of such factors, deaf children were catching up with their (younger) hearing peers.

This study indicates that deaf children have greater potential for rapid mathematical learning than we currently exploit. On our tests, we also found that deaf children were doing somewhat better than maths-age-matched hearing children on basic numerical operations. This suggests to us that they may well have been more thoroughly, extensively taught in these things. The question is, have they been taught them 'too well'? Couldn't teaching time have been better spent in moving on to new areas of mathematics? A response to this might, of course, be that language becomes more difficult as the mathematics gets more complex, but we have already argued that we tend to underestimate children's capacities to handle or 'bypass' linguistic difficulties in mathematics.

In conclusion, we suggest that the time is right to consider whether, particularly in the later years of schooling, our concern for the linguistic development of deaf children leads us to underestimate and undervalue their potential and needs in other areas of the curriculum. Indeed, it may well be the case that linguistic development itself would be better served by *using* language to teach and instruct in subjects such as mathematics.

CHAPTER 10

Modes, Methods and Manner of Communication

For the benefit of those readers who have decided to read this concluding chapter first and for those who would appreciate a general overview of the contents of earlier chapters, we begin this one with a resumé of the main arguments, findings and suggestions put forward throughout the book. Those who want to move on can skip the next section.

RESUMÉ

We began this book by asking why, after so many years in school, the majority of deaf children leave with what look like depressing levels of linguistic and academic achievement. We argued that some answers to this question would be found not in the 'organic' nature of the handicap nor in any 'special psychology' of deafness but in disrupted teaching–learning processes. We believe that the evidence reviewed in this book provides support for the value and plausibility of this theory. There *are* special learning problems that emerge as a 'natural' consequence of severe and profound deafness. However, the nature and magnitude of the effects these have on a child's personal, intellectual and linguistic development are determined, in part, by the reactions of other people to the handicap, both in formal and informal teacher–learner interactions. Throughout the book, we have attempted to demonstrate the plausibility of this view and to explore its educational implications. We have been critical of many aspects of educational practice but we hope that these have been tempered by our attempts to understand the problems that schools and teachers face. We have also made a number of specific suggestions about changes in teaching practice and curriculum design that were intended to help ameliorate or overcome the problems and counter-productive strategies we have identified.

By studying individual differences between both teachers and children, and exploring the connections between teaching methods and children's performance, we have tried to isolate approaches to communication, conversation and teaching that are relatively successful. Where feasible, we have explored the 'cause–effect' problem in an attempt to demonstrate that such differences between strategies help to *create* individual differences in children's achievements.

The main findings and conclusions we reached are summarized below:

***The disruption of mother–child and teacher–child interactions often associated with deafness arises because of the impact of specific communication difficulties that permeate the deaf child's experiences. For example, young deaf children experience a problem of 'divided attention' brought about by the fact that they must learn how to use the visual modality to attend to both *acts* and *objects* of communication. Because of this problem deaf children need and take more time to master the pre-verbal foundations of spoken language. During this time, however, they often meet with unhelpful and even counter-productive reactions from hearing adults that exacerbate their difficulties. Indeed, we have shown that some of the strategies used by teachers in our experimental teaching situation effectively robbed the children of 'natural' non-verbal sources of communication which normally aid hearing children in developing an understanding of speech. More generally, the usual effect of infant deafness on hearing adults is to lead them into spirals of increasing control over the child, creating mutual frustration and a non-contingent social learning environment.

***The transition from pre-verbal to the beginnings of verbal communication in deaf children involves five main stages. The development of both their understanding and production of speech rests on prior achievements in which the child discovers how to distribute his attention between his partner in interaction and the objects of talk. Our analyses emphasized the central role played by adults in promoting a child's development through these stages, but observation and experiment showed that many encounters between deaf children and their teachers in schools do not fulfil such roles nor facilitate the emergence of language. Longitudinal studies of the development of communication in deaf children provided some ideas about how one can set about the creation of a more contingent and productive social learning environment in nursery school.

***When older deaf children are involved in conversations with teachers the non-contingent, overly controlling styles of adult interaction often found with deaf preschoolers continue. Control is now manifested in adults' *verbal* control over a child's attempts at communication and by their frequent attempts to 'repair' his efforts. Conversation plays an important role in social and linguistic development but the question–answer exchange, which typifies most adult–child 'conversations' in school, does not promote but actively inhibits such development. Having observed teachers as they experimented with several different strategies for managing conversations with their children, we investigated the disadvantages of both 'didactic' and 'laissez-faire' teaching styles in discourse and outlined more effective ways of holding conversations.

***Although writing is not simply speech in written form, conversation plays an important role in developing the foundations for literacy. Most deaf children do not achieve functional levels of literacy but the relationships between their written and spoken language shows that the two abilities are related and governed by a generative but limited grammatical system. However, tests of reading designed for use with hearing children are insensitive to deaf children's linguistic abilities and limitations and, hence, are a poor guide to their competence and needs.

***Observations and analyses of reading lessons demonstrated that the 'gap' between deaf children's linguistic knowledge and the demands of text often lead to teaching strategies that do not facilitate the development of literacy but, rather, may 'teach' children special and non-productive strategies for trying to make sense of the written word. The problems faced by both teachers and children in reading lessons help to explain why years of effort in attempts to teach reading yield disappointing results. It seems clear that we need new approaches to the teaching of reading. Whilst it is not yet clear just what such approaches would entail, our view is that productive conversation and discourse lay the necessary foundations for literacy.

***Analyses of structural features of teachers' language in the classroom indicated that teachers do not make any greater linguistic demands of older than of younger children. Teacher talk to older children does not 'challenge' children's linguistic knowledge, implying that teachers may, unwittingly, be limiting children's knowledge of language by keeping their *own* language too *simple*. What is needed is greater and more detailed attention to the content and structure of discourse as a basis for linguistic development.

***Deaf children, though retarded in mathematical attainment, show similar processes of mathematical reasoning to hearing children. Their relatively slow progress in learning mathematics is due, in part, to the special teaching–learning problems deaf children face and is not the product of a level of intelligence that is somehow more limited, 'concrete' or 'literal' than that of hearing children. Further, deaf children's lower attainments in mathematics may be due to the fact that they are taught less intensively. We were critical of the view that the teaching of mathematics should be so constrained (as it currently appears to be) by the assumption that it is 'too difficult' to communicate mathematical concepts to children with low levels of expressive and receptive language.

***Throughout the book, we have emphasized marked individual differences in the attainment of children and in the philosophies and styles of teachers. These differences, and the relationships we found between them, were used to inform our suggestions for future developments in the way teachers try to teach deaf children.

ALTERNATIVE APPROACHES AND VIEWS

One argument about the needs of deaf children is that many of their problems could be avoided or ameliorated if they were provided with good hearing aids early in life and subjected to a 'normal' range of child-rearing and educational practices (e.g. Tucker and Nolan, 1984). If functional levels of hearing can be restored to a child then, almost by definition, such an argument is valid, in that he will no longer be functionally deaf. However, the promises held out by such views had not been fulfilled for the majority of children discussed in this book. If current and future generations of deaf children *can* be provided with sufficient amplification then it should follow that the teaching–learning problems that we have identified may be attenuated or overcome. We suggest that by using the measures and observational techniques we have developed it is possible to provide a basis for evaluating the extent to which any new developments or changes in practice *do* restore a 'normal' range of functioning. We provide some examples of the questions we would ask in such an evaluation exercise below.

Another familiar argument also concerns the issue of what is 'normal' for the deaf child, but entails a very different definition of what normality is. This arises from the assumption that the eye, and not the ear, is the natural avenue of communication for him. Those who subscribe to this view argue that deafness beyond a certain level (Conrad puts the figure at 85 dB while others, e.g. Meadow, 1980, suggest that the 'cut-off' may be 70 dB) precludes the possibility of functional hearing for speech and, hence, access to language by ear for all but a tiny minority. Consequently, for children beyond this rather blurred audiological threshold, communication will depend upon vision, whether this is for purposes of lip-reading or sign language.

There are many variations on this theme, as there are on the oral one (Quigley and Paul, 1984), and several quite different systems of 'manual' communication are currently in use throughout the world (see Quigley and Kretschmer, 1982, for an overview). In our current research, for example, we are studying the use of both Signed English and Sign Supported English in schools, and other research is taking place into the nature of British Sign Language (e.g. Brennan, 1981). Advocates of various methods offer different promissory notes. The aspiration behind Signed English, for example, is to capitalize on the perceptual salience of signs but to embody these in English syntax, thus, in prospect, helping children to develop a better understanding of spoken and written language by eye.

Advocates of indigenous sign languages (such as British Sign Language) argue, however, that sign languages have grammatical structures that are different from and not compatible with those of spoken languages. In the past, differences between spoken and signed communication were taken as evidence that sign systems were non-grammatical. However, more recent research has led an increasing number of linguists and psycholinguists to the conclusion that sign languages are governed by syntactic rules which, though different in nature from those of spoken languages, are no less grammatical (e.g. Stokoe, 1978). Some educators, particularly in the United States, now advocate the use of indigenous sign language with all deaf children, with English being taught as a second language. To support such calls for a bilingual approach in schools, empirical evidence is cited showing that deaf children of deaf parents, who acquire sign language as a mother tongue and learn English as a second language, do better on some tests of literacy and understanding of spoken English (though not speech intelligibility) than deaf children taught orally (e.g. Brasel and Quigley, 1977). Studies of the benefits of 'mother tongue' teaching in the education of hearing children whose language at home is different from that in their 'host' culture is also consistent with the call for bilingualism.

The divide between those who view deaf children as like all others but with specific problems of hearing (which can be ameliorated or overcome) and those who see the deaf child's perception of the world as quite different from that of hearing people creates only one of the chasms that splits opinion amongst those concerned with the education of the deaf (e.g. Meadow, 1980; Freeman, Carbin and Boese, 1981; Quigley and Kretschmer, 1982; Quigley and Paul, 1984).

These and other philosophies are often presented with ardour and ferociously defended. Many promises about the future possibilities for educational achievements of deaf children have been held out by their advocates. However, when comprehensive surveys have been mounted in an attempt to evaluate the general effectiveness of different forms of provision in terms of children's communicative abilities in English, their literacy and other aspects of academic achievement, what emerges gives no unequivocal support to any one school of thought. Jensema and Trybus (1978), for example, after an extensive review of the achievements of deaf children in various educational regimes in the United States, conclude that the major factors influencing children's performances do *not* include the mode(s) of communication experienced by children. Rather, the list comprises degree of hearing loss, intelligence, cause of deafness, ethnic background and the economic circumstances of a child's family. In short, deaf children, like their hearing peers, are influenced by demographic and social factors as well as by 'organic' factors such as aetiology, but not by the 'type' of educational provision they encounter *per se*.

This does not mean, of course, that *schools* have no influence on the achievements of their children. Rather, when we *group* schools together under a common heading such as 'oral' or 'manual' no differences seem to emerge between any of the categories so formed. However, *within* categories there are marked variations. We have cited some evidence to this effect and research in the United States has produced similar results (e.g. Quigley and Kretschmer, 1982). The implication, then, is that grouping schools according to the mode of communication they use is not a suitable strategy if we are attempting to define the nature of educational excellence and the factors that influence it. The individual school rather than the type of school might well be a better unit of analysis if we are to discover if and to what extent the effects of deafness can be ameliorated or overcome by educational factors. Put another way, we might do well to suspend arguments about *modes* of communication and concentrate more on the *process* of communication and the *strategies* of education found in different schools. We fully subscribe to the recommendations made by Jensema and Trybus (1978) in the conclusion to their survey. They write (p. 19):

Large amounts of effort in our field have been devoted to the consideration of the educational effects of using one group of muscles rather than another to convey messages to hearing-impaired children. Our work has convinced us, however, that relatively fixed and unchangeable factors presently have the greatest influence on the educational achievement of hearing-impaired children. If this report encourages any of its readers to shift their attention and efforts to materials, TEACHING methods, attitudinal and cognitive factors, and the like in an attempt to undo the influence of the fixed factors, we shall consider our work here a success.

Amen to that.

In our various analyses, we have identified what we believe to be important dimensions that need to be considered in attempts to describe and evaluate educational processes. To date, we have not extended these analyses to the use of methods of communication other than oral ones, though such research is currently under way. We end this book by posing a series of questions that we feel could be addressed in studies of educational practices with deaf children, whatever medium, mode or manner of communication they are experiencing. The answers to such questions may help us to move forward in the truly Herculean task of trying to describe and evaluate not simply the modalities within which communication takes place but also the teaching methods employed and the manner in which these are exercised in the home and classroom.

QUESTIONS AND ISSUES IN EDUCATION

1: Early Childhood

In Chapters 2 and 3, we reviewed some of the research relating both to parent–child and teacher–child interactions with preschool deaf children. Generalizations emerging from the literature such as the didactic, controlling and non-contingent nature of hearing adults' likely responses to young deaf children were drawn out and related to the difficulties many face in the development of intersubjectivity, reciprocity and communication. In particular, we laid stress on the problem of divided, visual attention for the child and the effects this has on the development of pre-verbal and verbal communication. There are now arguments in the literature about the 'inevitability' of such disruptions in adult–child relationships, coupled with the claim that early provision of good amplification and skilled parental support overcome such problems. What we need now are systematic, longitudinal studies of children who are diagnosed early and whose parents are provided with support and advice based upon new insights into the processes of language acquisition. We *have* found groups of children in our work, as have others in their research, who do far better than the norm. We have argued, but by no means demonstrated conclusively, that the education of the children who were successful was based on processes that minimize some of the interpersonal problems we have identified. If future research can establish clear causal relationships between systems of parental support and educational provision, on the one hand, and such 'success' stories on the other, then this will reinforce the thesis that attention to the nature of the infant's social and linguistic experiences can lead to much better levels of functioning in deaf children. But we need evidence that indications of success arising from studies of early development are actually maintained in the later years.

One hotly disputed argument about the introduction of any form of manual communication with deaf children is that it will 'distract' their attention from residual hearing and impede the acquisition of speech. We identified five stages in the transition from pre-verbal to verbal communication in Chapter 3 which could be used to adjudicate such issues early in development. If the use of Signed English, for instance, does have such consequences we could make two predictions. One is that the development of structured attention would not be followed by an increase in verbal responses in Stage 4. Rather, signs but not words would emerge in turn-taking. If both words and signs or words alone emerge, however, this would weaken the assertion that the use of signs detracts from the acquisition of speech and the development of auditory awareness.

There is an increasing body of knowledge about the effects of sign language on early development. Studies of deaf children of deaf parents, where sign language is the mother tongue, indicate that the interactions between parent and child are less stressful, more positive in emotional tone, more reciprocal and successful than is usually the case with hearing parents of deaf children (e.g. Schlesinger and Meadow, 1972). Studies of the use of some form of sign support for communication by hearing parents of deaf children have also led to generalisations to the effect that the process of early communication can be eased by inclusion of a signed component (e.g. Greenberg, 1980). It is interesting to note that, in these lines of research, no one has noted or commented upon any problems of divided attention facing the young deaf child. It may be that the problem still exists, but the relevant, very detailed analyses have not been carried out to identify it. Alternatively, the fact of signing to a child, either in parallel or in sequence with his activities, may help young babies to overcome the problem. Signs may be more perceptually salient and easier to imitate. They may be more 'memorable' because they are iconic or represent actions associated with objects (although Bonvillian *et al.*, 1982, argue that many signs used by deaf children are not iconic in nature). However, whatever the reason, if the deaf infant is able to associate the adult's act of communication with his own intentions and actions, if he can remember and reenact signs at a very early stage, then the impact of signs on the problem of divided attention should be measurable in the pre-verbal stages of development.

Another explanation for the relative ease with which deaf parents communicate with their young deaf babies has been put forward by Mogford, Gregory and Hartley (1980). They argue that deaf mothers of deaf babies are more sensitive to the ebb and flow of their young child's attention and, hence, are more contingent upon his actions. This, in turn, facilitates the development of turn-taking and reciprocity with the child. If this view is correct, then it may be that the more rapid development of communication skills in such children does not rest on the use of signs *per se* but on the greater empathy of the deaf mother and the more contingent interactions she can sustain. Others (Brasel and Quigley, 1977) have also pointed out that the better-than-average (though still not startling) achievements of deaf children of deaf parents in, for example, literacy may reside not simply in the exposure to sign language but in social and interpersonal factors. Evidence cited by Jensema and Trybus (1978) is compatible with such a view. They found that deaf children with one deaf and one hearing parent also did relatively well on a number of measures of achievement, even though these children tended to be one of the most 'oral' groups in their sample. Thus, it may not be the 'mode' of communication that underlies success so much as the 'manner' in which communication takes place.

The effects of introducing sign language into hearing homes could be evaluated by examining its impact on the early stages of pre-verbal communication. For example, will hearing mothers still find it difficult to interact with the deaf baby because they, unlike deaf mothers, fail to use signs contingently? If so, this would imply that more attention to the *structure* of interactions rather than to the mode of communication being employed would be more profitable and useful.

We cannot yet evaluate the relative importance of manner and mode of communication. What we suggest, however, is that detailed studies along the lines we have just outlined could help to evaluate them. Large-scale attempts to compare different 'methods' of communication have proved inconclusive. Perhaps the reason is their neglect of the process of communication.

2: The Classroom Experience

We have drawn attention to a number of 'abnormal' and counter-productive features of many interactions between teachers and their children, and provided some explicit, empirical measures to identify such features. We suggest that any method of communication can be measured against and evaluated in terms of how far they help to overcome such features. Thus, we should seek answers to the following questions:

(a) How far does any given mode of communication result in more reciprocal interactions in discourse? Are interactions characterized by signs of initiative and loquacity from the child? Who introduces, develops and extends themes of conversation? How far does the child ask questions and go beyond the force of teacher questions to elaborate on his answers? Does the child take up openings to initiate readily? Such questions can be answered.

(b) Degree of deafness is often correlated with the frequency of teacher repair. If a given mode of communication is more 'natural' and accessible to deaf children, then this incidence should decrease. If repair remains abnormally high, it serves as a signal that communication is *not* easily established and that both receptive and expressive communication from the child are ambiguous and uncertain. However, if repair is low (our estimate of 'normal' frequency of repair in hearing classrooms is around 5 to 10 per cent) while evidence of mutual comprehension is high, then, providing the topic is 'normal' and interesting for the age group in question, this provides evidence that communication is proceeding smoothly.

(c) How far does the use of any mode of communication involve the use of complex utterances displaying structural features that deaf children find difficult? Does the use of such structures by both teachers and children increase over time? Are they associated with a high incidence of breakdown in understanding and repair? If communication involving complex linguistic expressions takes place without a high incidence of breakdown in communication this provides further evidence that the mode of communication involved is proving effective. Clearly, to explore such ideas in relation to sign language demands insights into its syntactic structure and a system for describing it.

(d) How far do assessments of reading in children suggest that the child is actually *reading* and understanding structural aspects of language? If school-leavers are obtaining reading ages of around seven or eight years by exploiting special 'strategies' it is unlikely that literacy is developing along normal and functional lines. How is any given mode of communication exploited in the teaching of reading? Is the child's reading rate increased beyond forty words per minute? Is the lesson genuinely concerned with the decoding of print or is it also a 'language' lesson? Does the child provide evidence that he recognizes and understands the structural aspects of text?

(e) Finally, how effective is any given mode of communication in teaching complex ideas in disciplines such as mathematics? If, as we have argued, processes of mathematical reasoning in the deaf are essentially normal but delayed, does the use of any given mode of communication accelerate the communicative process and result in more sophisticated mathematical understanding?

The answers to such questions would shed fresh light on the value and use of different methods and modes of communication with deaf children. We might find that one or more modes of communication do overcome some of the problems we have identified. Alternatively, it may prove to be the case that the basis for successful communication and learning lies in the 'manner' rather than, or in addition to, the mode of communication. If we look systematically at *processes* of communication and teaching, we believe that answers to these questions will be forthcoming to complement and extend those we have tried to provide in this book.

A Teacher Trainer's Perspective: From Research to Practice

SUE LEWIS
Formerly of Lady Spencer Churchill College, Oxford Polytechnic

Introduction to Sue Lewis

We (members of the Deafness Research Group) met Sue Lewis several years ago when we began to present our early research findings to conferences for teachers of the deaf. Sue was then a tutor at the Lady Spencer Churchill College in Oxford. She already shared our interest in studying styles of communication between teachers of the deaf and their pupils, and was beginning to adapt some of our observational schedules for use in training.

When we decided to write this book, we thought it would be useful to explore the transition from 'research' to 'practice' by asking her to reflect upon our research and outline the use she has made of it in her own work. Here she describes how she has turned the coding systems into 'self-assessment' procedures for use by teachers in training. She explains how this approach has been integrated within the training course and how it relates to her own philosophy both as an educator of deaf children and a trainer of teachers.

INTRODUCTION

The one year certificate course for teachers of the deaf offered at Lady Spencer Churchill College (now Oxford Polytechnic) was established in 1969. Student recruits are all qualified teachers who, for varying reasons, have elected to specialize as teachers of hearing-impaired children. Some come as newly qualified teachers with no formal continuous teaching experience, whilst others may have taught hearing or hearing-impaired children in a variety of settings.

Students spend a great deal of their time studying the theoretical and practical aspects of the management of hearing loss in children. They must draw on current knowledge on speech, acoustics, audiology, psychology, linguistics and education. We have designed the course to help them to integrate this knowledge into their own teaching practice. This is achieved by exposure to very different philosophies and styles of teaching, 'self-observation' studies and a child language study which I will describe later.

PRECONCEPTIONS AND RECONCEPTUALIZATION

All the teachers who embark on a course such as ours have already formed views on the educational process and an image of their own role as a teacher. They have developed their own styles of interacting with children informed by implicit theories of child development and learning. They may well have an 'image' of the deaf child. Depending upon their previous experiences, these are based on 'lay' stereotypes, background reading or direct experience of working with hearing-impaired children. Whatever the source of their preconceptions, we try to help them to challenge and, if they are prepared to do so, reconceptualize their views and experiences. We do this through practical work and theoretical study and, in particular, by encouraging them to reflect upon, describe and analyse their own styles of interaction with children.

There is clear evidence from many sources, including the studies in this book, that certain features of adult–child interaction with infants, preschool and school-aged children exert enhancing or depressing effects, not only on the children's linguistic skills but also on their self-concepts, academic performance, and personal and social growth. An important element of our training is an exploration of these aspects of adult–child interaction. This book has made a case for examining the practice of individual teachers and has shown that it is usually the *pupils* who adapt to teaching style rather than the other way around. In other words, it looks as though the children 'learn the system' and play it; they adapt their behaviour to styles of teaching. Because of the asymmetry of power in the classroom, as discussed in this book, we feel it is necessary for teachers in training to be helped to view events from the *pupils'* point of view. We try to train them to become more sensitive to children's interests and to manage their interactions and communication with this knowledge in mind.

EXPLORING 'GOOD' PRACTICE

My own observations of hearing-impaired children in a wide variety of placements have convinced me that their educational management is of greater significance than previous research (e.g. Conrad, 1979) has suggested. On school admission, we see very similar three-, four- and five-year-olds who present themselves very differently at eight, nine and ten when their education has been in different settings. These differences cannot be explained entirely by appeals to the traditional 'methods of communication' arguments. Indeed, there is now a clear acknowledgement of the range of approaches and practices previously subsumed (and confused) under all embracing terms such as 'the oral' or 'the manual' method.

Given my role and the many school contacts it has created, I have been able to observe and gain an overview of many differences in philosophy and practice. They are to be observed between schools and within schools, similarly between units and main schools. Even a change of teacher in a classroom can lead to dramatic effects. Though the same 'method' may still be employed, teacher orientation, expectations and philosophy can have far-reaching effects on the children concerned. The children's perception of the teacher, the way in which roles are negotiated in the classroom and the 'locus of control' may alter dramatically and, with them, opportunities for learning and the 'climate' of the classroom. We have also been able to make video-recordings of teachers practising on the basis of very different philosophies, and these are used to give students a sense of the very wide range of options open to them, as I explain later.

Evidence provided in this book has shown how certain features of teacher and parent interaction are more facilitative of communication and learning than others with both hearing and hearing-impaired children. This is an important addition to our knowledge and understanding of the educational process.

Many believe that hearing-impaired children can benefit from techniques and styles of interaction that differ from those that help hearing children. However, such differences must surely be justified by *results* and *not* by untested assumptions. We try to encourage our trainees to *test* their assumptions and provide them with tools to do so.

Another goal as trainers is to try to promote styles of interaction which are the most facilitative for meeting an individual child's needs. If certain styles of interaction appear to be more effective in encouraging children to 'open up' in conversation or in promoting linguistic development then an understanding by teachers of how these styles can be effected is most important. We acknowledge, along with the authors of this book, the vital role that both a certain level of linguistic attainment and *confidence* in language use play in the personal, social and cognitive growth of the child. An attempt to foster such skills forms part of our aim to encourage prospective teachers to consider language learning as a whole, how it differs from other types of learning and what impact a hearing loss may have on these processes.

It is in pursuit of these general objectives that we have been working with students on ways of evaluating their teaching styles in terms of the linguistic environment they provide for children. We do this by concentrating not only on the students' own teaching styles but also on the interaction styles of mothers with their young hearing children. We draw heavily from published research on 'motherese' (e.g. Cross, 1977; Snow, 1979) and on teacher interaction with hearing and hearing-impaired children (Wells, 1981; Huntington and Watton, 1981, 1982; Wood, 1982; Wood et al., 1982). An examination of one's own teaching style, judged in the light of one's objectives for individual and groups of hearing-impaired children is, we think, an important part of evaluation in the classroom for both experienced and inexperienced teachers.

We recognize that children at different stages of development may need a more or less controlling style of teaching. We also acknowledge that aims over and above linguistic ones might dictate a particular style of interaction in some situations that may not be appropriate in others. We try to help students to evaluate and improve the 'fit' between their objectives and their styles.

During a full-time course such as ours, students have time to adopt a 'longitudinal' approach in evaluating their teaching style. Using some of the techniques outlined earlier in this book, they can assess any changes and improvements that occur in their techniques over the year of training. We encourage students to *experiment* with the adoption of slightly differing styles according to the identified aims of the session and to evaluate their effects.

OBSERVATION AND ASSESSMENT

How, then, do we try to make more explicit those aspects of teaching style which we hope student teachers of the deaf will incorporate into their own styles in insightful, rather than mechanical, ways? Perhaps I should emphasize here the fact that we are not in the business of attempting to produce batches of teachers who all converse in the same way. But how can we ensure that the more counter-productive elements of teacher style are minimized as students evolve their own teaching strategies? We have found that for many students it is not so much a case of knowing what to do, rather to be aware of what it is *not* helpful to do and why.

We have found videorecordings an indispensable tool for teaching, observation and assessment. They provide an excellent vehicle for exploring teaching styles and help students to identify characteristics of teacher talk that seem most productive. Students are shown videotapes of individual tutors or teachers designed to demonstrate both facilitative and less facilitative styles, and which reflect very different educational philosophies. Initially the more extreme styles are demonstrated, but gradually a broader spectrum, underpinned by different images of the deaf child, are explored. Within the category termed 'oral' education, for example, one can observe very different forms of interaction, particularly with relation to the 'locus of control'.

Amongst the different approaches we expose students to are two very different 'oral' philosophies. We also show them examples of the teacher–child interactions these philosophies are designed to promote. We attempt to illustrate both the intended rewards and potential pitfalls of both approaches (which differ dramatically in techniques of control and repair).

One approach, that has been termed 'natural aural' (e.g. Harrison, 1981), draws heavily on research data on maternal and teacher interaction to make the case for a less controlling, more contingent teaching style. At its best, it promotes a mutually accepting and interesting interaction where teachers listen carefully as well as talk, inform and discuss. They ask for opinions and reasons and try to interpret what their children might be thinking, seeing and feeling. With a child at the very earliest stages of linguistic development, they monitor the to and fro of attention and ask relevant questions. They have ideas about what they want to share and, like the teacher described in Chapter 3, they are prepared to relinquish their own topic or comment to follow up a child's contribution.

Of course, not everyone who subscribes to this approach manages to succeed in creating interactions that are sensitive and purposeful. There is, in particular, a danger of becoming too 'laissez-faire'. Initial aims and objectives may well be to 'get the child talking' and 'to give him confidence in himself as a communicator'. However, fostering and extending the child's linguistic skills is not just a case of fostering loquacity. It involves extending his broader conversational and thinking skills, such as sustaining a topic over a number of turns and being sensitive to the needs of his conversational partner.

In contrast, a 'structured' oral approach relies more heavily on imitation, elicitation of language patterns and controlled exposure to language form and function. Such an approach reflects the view that the rules of language should be made more explicit for the hearing-impaired. Input may be rich and varied but the philosophy defines the adult's role as one of model and leader. In the best hands, this approach may encourage child interest, motivation and communication, selectively reinforcing and modelling child utterances. It can both challenge and stimulate. On the other hand, it can degenerate into drill, with the 'manner' of control and the content of the lesson only serving to deter initiative.

Students will observe and experiment with a range of such styles. In particular, they are encouraged to identify their *aims* in terms of content, curriculum and identification of child need and also to recognize the degree to which their style of interaction may or may not be facilitative in meeting those needs.

The gap between aims and performance can indeed be a wide one! Here is a brief illustration of one trainee's attempt to hold a conversation with a ten-year-old profoundly deaf child.

T. Hello Peter.
C. Hello Miss Black.
T. Lovely. What's this?
C. Train.
T. 'It's a train.'
C. It a train.
T. 'It's a train.'
C. It a train.

T. It's a train, yes.
C. Is a train.
T. What kind of train?
C. Pardon?
T. What kind of train?
C. Green.
T. Can you remember? What's this?
C. Smoke, smoke.
T. It's smoke. What's another name for it?
C. That, that a –––.
T. Smoke or . . . ?
C. White, white.
T. Yes, it's white. What is it? Can you remember? It begins with an 's'. Ssssss.
C. Smoke, smoke.
T. Look (writes 'st').
C. Smoke, st.

We often find that even when a student's intentions are to be 'non-controlling' in conversation, uncertainty and insecurity about possible break-down in communication can still result in a very tightly structured repairing conversation, with little initiative being left to the child and often little substance to the conversation. Similarly, very specific aims for a session (such as vocabulary) can also lead to such an approach. As students grow in confidence and experience, however, they usually begin to appreciate the child's perspective more. Here is an extract of a more successful attempt by a student, now fully trained, to engage an eight-year-old profoundly deaf child in conversation.

C. What's that? Mmm, that?
T. Let's have a look.
C. Look!
T. Oh yes, there's your tummy button. Can you see it?
C. Button.
T. Yes, it's got smaller and smaller, hasn't it?
C. Yes, watch.
T. As you've grown. Yeah, you can see the inside. Ooh! Don't pull it out!
C. What's that?
T. That's where it was cut when you were a very small baby.
C. Man cut or lady cut?
T. Well, I don't know. It could have been a nurse or it could have been a doctor.
C. I haven't seen!
T. No, well you were very small. You didn't see.
C. Have you seen?
T. I didn't see.
C. Adam seen (his brother)!
T. You'll have to ask your Mummy if she can remember if it was . . . uhm . . . a lady or a man, a nurse or a doctor who cut your umbilical cord when you were a baby.
C. Nurse.
T. You think it was a nurse?
C. ⟨nods⟩

T. It could have been a nurse. And you'll have to ask Mummy 'Was I born in hospital or was I born at home?'
C. What?
T. You'll have to ask Mummy if you were born at home or in hospital.
C. Hospital.

CHILD LANGUAGE STUDY

A major element of the course involves students in a longitudinal, comparative study of one hearing (one- to two-year-old) and one hearing-impaired (school-aged) child. This involves observation, description and comparison of the linguistic development of the two children using a range of linguistic analyses and developmental schedules.

One of the linguistic measures used to compare and contrast the interactions these children experience is based on the 'Moves Matrix' developed by Wood and his group. This matrix provides an overall summary of the relationships between adult moves and children's responses in discourse. It is a diagrammatic analysis which allows the 'pattern' of child responses to be easily grasped with the 'naked eye'. By listing the various types of possible adult moves down the left-hand side of the diagram and the possible types of child responses across the top, we can plot the 'fate' of each adult move type and the origins of each child move type. In this way it is easy to observe, for example, the 'clusters' of child contributions that usually result from adult contributions and other low control moves. We have found the 'Moves Matrix' to be very useful in assessing the locus of control in conversation and other aspects of interaction. Such a system enables students to compare the role of adults in conversations with hearing and hearing-impaired children. It also enables them to analyse their own style of interaction objectively since they also record themselves in interactions with these children.

Studying a hearing child in the 'throes' of his language development also provides opportunities to observe not only the child and his emergent language but the way adults respond to his developing abilities in communication. We are particularly concerned that our students should be able to identify factors in the mother's style of interaction that foster the child's motivation to communicate and his understanding of how effective a tool language can be. In other words, we want them to be aware not only of the emerging *structure* of language but also of its capacity to express a range of meanings and intentions in certain contexts.

The students see their two children regularly throughout the year in various contexts and with different people. They thus build up a detailed knowledge of the child and are able to explore the impact of different situations and people on the children's interactions and use of language. One of the valuable lessons learned by students in this study is how far a perfectly normal hearing child can differ from the 'norm'! Written down, some children's utterances look odd, yet may seem perfectly acceptable *in context* for a child who is still developing his language. Errors of word order, omissions, substitutions, strange juxtapositions abound, and yet meaning is retrievable and 'errors' are rarely if ever repaired by parents. This, as we have seen, differs from the experiences of many hearing-impaired children in school.

The two children's experiences in various interactions are compared in several ways. Comparisons are made of developmental patterns in phonology, semantics, syntax, receptive and functional language. The effects of different people and settings on the child's language are examined using the 'Matrix' approach just outlined. Students take into account the differing ages, cognitive levels and social demands placed on the children they are observing but their major task is, within this context, to identify and describe those features of situations and styles which facilitate and promote (or impede and inhibit) the child's use of language. The final report on their work includes a comparison of the linguistic data amassed on the two children and enables an objective appraisal of the 'normality' or otherwise of the hearing-impaired child's linguistic interactions.

In general, the students find that their results follow the patterns identified in Chapters 4 and 5, with hearing-impaired children receiving a larger proportion of high controlling moves from adults than the younger hearing children. The balance of power is much more weighted in the teacher's direction in the hearing-impaired setting. The implications of excessive repair have already been explored in this book; students often observe and experience this themselves as they struggle to build up a child's confidence in expression, only to knock it down again at the first repairing hurdle. Such constant repair (as we also saw in Chapter 4) is often the result of the multiplicity of goals the teacher of the deaf sets herself, using 'conversation' as a setting for speech correction, reinforcement of vocabulary, checking on information taught in group sessions and so on. It is this multiplicity of goals and the anxiety to achieve them that dictates the interactional style of many teachers of the deaf.

CONCLUSIONS

Arguments concerning the linguistic and academic achievements of hearing-impaired children have for too long centred on the 'method' of communication alone. The research outlined in this book allows us to go beyond this and focus on the *style* and *quality* of the linguistic and educational environment, together with implications for the educational process. We have found this to have direct relevance to the training of teachers of the deaf.

Over four years of examining data on nearly two hundred hearing children and the same number of hearing-impaired children, we have worked with students trying to tease out those features of adult–child interaction that might influence their teaching style. Our major assumption in this endeavour is that their primary aim in conversation is to foster the child's linguistic skills as a basis for his later learning. We believe that several features of mother–child (as opposed to the usual teacher–child) interaction are crucial in this respect: the way conversation tends to revolve around subjects meaningful to the child, the low incidence of highly controlling moves from the adult and the low incidence of repair. These seem to help the child to have confidence in the value of his own contributions. Mothers of hearing children do not often consciously attempt to 'teach' their children to talk, though they instinctively provide the best language learning situations. They do not force the child to talk. Questions may be asked, opinions sought, comments offered, but if no response is forthcoming mothers will often fill the child's turn themselves. We consider that hearing children are, usually, in an ideal language learning situation and that these are exactly the conditions which must be provided for a hearing-impaired child if he is going to use language confidently. How do we ensure that these conditions are provided? They are provided by fostering in new teachers the type of interactional style that incorporates these features of mothers' speech to young hearing children.

It is through research of the sort described in this volume that we, as teacher-trainers, can identify what we consider to be important aspects of the practising teacher's role and ensure that we alert new teachers to the wide variety of possibilities open to them when they move into their own class-rooms.

Further Information about Conversation Studies

CODING SYSTEM FOR ANALYSIS OF CONVERSATIONS: LEVELS OF CONTROL

Table A.1 Levels of teacher control and child response

Level of control	Examples
1. Enforced repetitions	Say 'I have one at home'.
2. Two-choice questions	Did you have a good time?
	Did you go with Jim or Pete?
3. Wh-type questions	What happened?
	Tell me about Sunday.
4. Personal contributions	That must have been awful!
	They call it a zoom lens.
	I love the lakes in Scotland.
5. Phatics	Oh lovely! Super! I see. Hmm.
5.1 Requests for repetition	Pardon?
	You had a what?
5.2 Tag phatics	Did you?
	It was green, was it?
4.2 Tag contributions	You like those, don't you?
	Strawberries are delicious, aren't they?

√	Appropriate answer to a question (even if wrong!)
√4	Appropriate answer plus elaborating contribution
×	Clear misunderstanding of what is required in question
×4	Clear misunderstanding but C goes on to add contribution
nr	No response
?	Unintelligible and/or not codable
ch	Chairing move, e.g. 'OK Sharon, tell us about it'
Other	Any move not covered above, e.g. teacher pointing to picture, or 'management' in the form of 'Turn around, we can't hear you'

TABLES OF CHILD RESPONSE TO TEACHER MOVES

Table A.2   Levels of child response to teacher moves I
(averages of four conversation sessions in percentages)
(From Wood *et al.*, 1982)

T.move	√	√4	2/3	4	5	×	Other
1	96	0	0	0	0	3	1
2	61	21	0	1	0	8	9
3	74	3	0	1	0	12	10
4	0	2	2	69	22	0	5
5	0	0	1	75	19	0	5
5.2	56	32	0	1	0	7	4

Table A.3   Levels of child response to teacher moves II
(averages of eight conversation sessions in percentages)
(From Griffiths, 1983)

T.move	√	√4	2/3	4	5	×	Other
1	98	0	0	0	0	1	1
2	54	25	1	2	0	4	14
3	69	4	2	2	1	11	11
4	0	0	8	67	21	0	4
5	0	0	5	74	20	0	1
5.2	62	36	0	1	0	0	1

References

Anderson, R. J., and Sisco, F. H. (1977). *Standardisation of the WISC-R Performance Scale for Deaf Children*, Office of Demographic Studies, Gallaudet College, Washington DC.

Baddeley, A. D. (1979). Working memory and reading. In *Processing of Visible Language* (Eds. P. A. Kolers, N. E. Wrolstad and H. Bouma), Vol. 1, Plenum Press, New York.

Beggs, W. D. B., and Breslaw, P. I. B. (1983). Reading retardation or linguistic deficit? (III): A further examination of response strategies in a reading test completed by hearing-impaired children. *Journal of Research in Reading*, **6**(1), 19–28.

Beggs, W. D. B., Breslaw, P. I. B., and Wilkinson, H. P. (1982). Eye movements, reading achievement and reading test validity. In *Cognition and Eye Movements* (Eds. R. Groner and P. Fraisse), North-Holland Publishing Co., Amsterdam.

Bell, A. W., Costello, J., and Kuchemann, D. (1983). *A Review of Research in Mathematical Education. Part A Research on Learning and Teaching*. NFER-Nelson, Windsor.

Berry, J. W., and Dasen, P. R. (1973). *Culture and Cognition: Readings in Cross-cultural Psychology*, Methuen, London.

Bishop, J., and Gregory, S. (in preparation). *The Young Hearing-Impaired Child at Home and School* (working title).

Blank, M., Rose, S. A., and Berlin, L. J. (1978). *The Language of Learning: The Preschool Years*, Grune and Stratton, New York.

Bonvillian, J. D., Orlansky, M. D., Novack, L. L., and Folven, R. J. (1982). Early sign language acquisition and cognitive development. In *The Acquisition of Symbolic Skills* (Eds. D. R. Rogers and J. A. Sloboda), Plenum Press, New York and London.

Bowerman, M. (1979). The acquisition of complex sentences. In *Language Acquisition* (Eds. P. Fletcher and M. Garman), Cambridge University Press, Cambridge.

Bowerman, M. (1982). Reorganisational processes in lexical and syntactic development. In *Language Acquisition: The State of the Art* (Eds. E. Wanner and L. R. Gleitman), Cambridge University Press, Cambridge.

Brasel, K. E., and Quigley, S. P. (1977). Influence of certain language and communication environments in early childhood on the development of language in deaf individuals. *Journal of Speech and Hearing Research*, **20**, 95–107.

Brazelton, T. B. (1982). Joint regulation of neonate–parent behaviour. In *Social Interchange in Infancy. Affect, Cognition and Communication* (Ed. E. Z. Tronick), University Park Press, Baltimore.

187

Brennan, M. (1981). Grammatical processes in British Sign Language. In *Perspectives on British Sign Language and Deafness* (Eds. B. Woll, J. Kyle and M. Deuchar), Croom Helm, London.

Breslaw, P. I. B., Griffiths, A. J., Wood, D. J., and Howarth, C. I. (1981). The referential communication skills of deaf children from different educational environments. *Journal of Child Psychology and Psychiatry*, **22**, 269–282.

Brimer, A. (1972). *Wide-span Reading Test*, Nelson, London.

Brown, G., Anderson, A., Shillcock, R., and Yule, G. (1984). *Teaching Talk. Strategies for Production and Assessment*, Cambridge University Press, Cambridge.

Brown, R. (1973). *A First Language: The Early Stages*, Penguin, Harmondsworth.

Brown, R. (1977). Introduction to C. E. Snow and C. A. Ferguson, *Talking to Children. Language, Input and Acquisition*, Cambridge University Press, Cambridge.

Bruner, J. S. (1966). *Toward a Theory of Instruction*, W. W. Norton and Co., New York.

Bruner, J. (1983). *Child's Talk. Learning to Use Language*, Oxford University Press, Oxford.

Bryant, P. (1974). *Perception and Understanding in Young Children*, Methuen, London.

Bryant, P., and Bradley, L. (1985). *Children's Reading Problems*, Basil Blackwell, Oxford.

Butterworth, G., and Cochran, E. (1980). Towards a mechanism of joint visual attention in human infancy. *International Journal of Behavioral Development*, **3**, 253–270.

Cazden, C. B. (1977). Concentrated versus contrived encounters: suggestions for language assessment in early childhood education. In *Language and Learning in Early Childhood* (Ed. A. Davies), Social Science Research Council, London.

Chomsky, C. S. (1969). *The Acquisition of Syntax in Children from 5 to 10*, MIT Press, Cambridge, Mass.

Chomsky, N. (1965). *Aspects of a Theory of Syntax*, MIT Press, Cambridge, Mass.

Chomsky, N. (1980). *Rules and Representations*, Basil Blackwell, Oxford.

Churcher, J., and Scaife, M. (1982). How infants see the point. In *Social Cognition. Studies of the Development of Understanding* (Eds. G. Butterworth and P. Light), Harvester Press, Brighton.

Clark. E. V. (1978). From gesture to word: on the natural history of deixis in language. In *Human Growth and Development* (Eds. J. S. Bruner and A. Garton), Oxford University Press, Oxford.

Cohn, J. F., and Tronick, E. Z. (1982). Communicative rules and the sequential structure of infant behaviour during normal and depressed interaction. In *Social Interchange in Infancy: Affect, Cognition and Communication* (Ed. E. Z. Tronick), University Park Press, Baltimore.

Cole, M., Gay, J., Glick, J. A., and Sharp, D. W. (1971). *The Cultural Context of Learning and Thinking*, Methuen, London.

Cole, M., and Scribner, S. (1974). *Culture and Thought. A Psychological Introduction*, Wiley and Sons, London.

Collis, G. M., and Schaffer, H. R. (1975). Synchronization of visual attention in mother–child pairs. *Journal of Child Psychology and Psychiatry*, **16**, 315–320.

Commission of the European Communities (1979). *Childhood Deafness in the European Community*, ESSC-EEC-EAEC, Brussels-Luxembourg.

Conrad, R. (1979). *The Deaf School Child*, Harper and Row, London.

Conrad, R. (1981). Sign language in education: some consequent problems. In *Perspectives on British Sign Language* (Eds. B. Woll, J. Kyle and M. Deuchar), Croom Helm, London.

Crassini, B., and Broese, J. (1980). Auditory–visual integration in neonates: a signal detection analysis. *Journal of Experimental Child Psychology*, 29, 144–155.

Cross, T. G. (1977). Mothers' speech adjustments: the contribution of selected child listener variables. In *Talking to Children: Language Input and Acquisition* (Eds. C. E. Snow and C. A. Ferguson), Cambridge University Press, Cambridge.

Cross, T. G. (1978). Motherese: its association with rate of syntactic acquisition in young children. In *The Development of Communication* (Eds. N. Waterson and C. E. Snow), Wiley, Chichester.

Department of Education and Science (1978). *Special Educational Needs; Report of the Warnock Committee of Enquiry into the Education of Handicapped Children and Young People*, Her Majesty's Stationery Office, London.

De Villiers, P. A., and De Villiers, J. G. (1979). *Early Language*, Fontana/Open Books, London.

Dillon, J. T. (1982). The effect of questions in education and other enterprises. *Journal of Curriculum Studies*, 14, 127–165.

Dodd, B., and Hermelin, B. (1977). Phonological coding by the prelingually deaf. *Perception and Psychophysics*, 21, 413–417.

Donaldson, M. (1978). *Children's Minds*, Fontana, London.

Edinburgh Reading Tests (1977). *Manual of Instructions*, Hodder and Stoughton, London.

Elias, G. (1983). *Structure and Content of Mother–Infant Vocal Encounters*, PhD Thesis, University of Queensland.

Ewoldt, C. (1981). A psycholinguistic description of selected deaf children reading in sign language. *Reading Research Quarterly*, 17, 58–59.

Freeman, R. D., Carbin, C. F., and Boese, R. J. (1981). *Can't Your Child Hear? A Guide for Those Who Care about Deaf Children*, Croom Helm, London.

French, P., and MacLure, M. (1981). Teachers' questions: pupil's answers. An investigation of questions and answers in the infant classroom. *First Language*, 2(1), 31–45.

Furth, H. G. (1966). *Thinking without Language: Psychological Implications of Deafness*, The Free Press, New York.

Furth, H. G. (1971). Linguistic deficiency and thinking: research with deaf subjects 1964–69. *Psychological Bulletin*, 76(1), 58–72.

Gleitman, L. R., Newport, E. L., and Gleitman, H. (1984). The current state of the motherese hypothesis. *Child Language*, 11, 43–79.

Gleitman, L. R., and Wanner, E. (1982). Language acquisition: the state of the state of the art. In *Language Acquisition: The State of the Art* (Eds. E. Wanner and L. R. Gleitman), Cambridge University Press, Cambridge.

Goss, R. N. (1970). Language used by mothers of deaf children and mothers of hearing children. *American Annals of the Deaf*, 115(3), 93–96.

Greenberg, M. (1980). Social interactions between deaf preschoolers and their mothers: the effects of communication method and communicative competence. *Developmental Psychology*, 16, 465–474.

Gregory, S. (in preparation). *Achieving Understanding. The Development of Communication in Deaf Babies* (working title).

Gregory, S., and Mogford, K. (1981). Early language development in deaf children. In *Perspectives on British Sign Language and Deafness* (Eds. B. Woll, J. Kyle and M. Deuchar), Croom Helm, London.

Griffiths, A. J. (1983). *The Linguistic Competence of Deaf Primary School Children*, PhD Thesis, University of Nottingham.

Gross, H. (in preparation). *Language and Play in the Deaf Nursery School*, PhD Thesis, University of Nottingham.

Harrison, D. (1981). The effects of parent guidance on educational management in

Leicestershire. *Report of the Proceedings of the Conference for Heads of Schools and Services for Hearing-Impaired Children*, University of Manchester, September 1981.
Heider, F., and Heider, G. M. (1941). Studies in the psychology of the deaf: the language and social behaviour of young deaf children. *Psychological Monographs*, 53, No. 242.
Hitch, G. J. (1978). Developing the concept of working memory. In *Cognitive Psychology* (Ed. G. Claxton), Routledge and Kegan Paul, London.
Hitch, G. J., Arnold, P., and Phillips, L. J. (1983). Counting processes in deaf children's arithmetic. *British Journal of Psychology*, 74, 429–437.
Howarth, S. P., Wood, D. J., Griffiths, A. J., and Howarth, C. I. (1981). A comparative study of the reading lessons of deaf and hearing primary-school children. *British Journal of Educational Psychology*, 51, 156–162.
Hung, D. L., Tzeng, O. J. L., and Warren, D. H. (1981). A chronometric study of sentence processing in deaf children. *Cognitive Psychology*, 13, 583–610.
Huntington, A., and Watton, F. (1981). Language and interaction in the classroom. Part 1: Teacher talk. *Journal of the British Association of Teachers of the Deaf*, 5(6), 162–173.
Huntington, A., and Watton, F. (1982). Language and Interaction in the Classroom. Part 2: Pupil talk. *Journal of the British Association of Teachers of the Deaf*, 6(1), 18–21.
Hutt, C. (1972). *Males and Females*, Penguin, Harmondsworth.
Ivimey, G. P. (1976). The written syntax of an English deaf child; an exploration of method. *British Journal of Disorders of Communication*, 11(2), 103–120.
Jensema, C. J. (1975). *The Relationship between Academic Achievement and the Demographic Characteristics of Hearing-Impaired Children and Youth*, Series R, Number 2, Office of Demographic Studies, Gallaudet College, Washington.
Jensema, C. J., and Trybus, R. J. (1978). *Communication Patterns and Educational Achievement of Hearing-Impaired Students*. Series T, Number 2, Office of Demographic Studies, Gallaudet College, Washington.
Kaplan, E. J. (1969). Cited in P. Menyuk (1971). *The Acquisition and Development of Language*, Prentice-Hall, Englewood Cliffs, New Jersey.
Karmiloff-Smith, A. (1979). *A Functional Approach to Child Language*, Cambridge University Press, Cambridge.
Kingdon, J. (1983). *Face-to-Face Instruction in Relation to Teaching-Strategies and Children's Perceived Ability*, MPhil Thesis, University of Nottingham.
Lees, J. M. (1981). *Conversational Strategies with Deaf Children*, MPhil Thesis, University of Nottingham.
Leybaert, J., Alegria, J., and Fonck, E. (1983). Automaticity in word recognition and in word naming by the deaf. *Cahiers du psychologie cognitive*, 3(3), 255–272.
Lock, A. J. (1980). *The Guided Reinvention of Language*, Academic Press, London.
Luria, A. R., and Yudovich, F. (1971). *Speech and the Development of Mental Processes in the Child*, Penguin, Harmondsworth.
McNeill, D. (1966). Developmental Psycholinguistics. In *The Genesis of Language* (Eds. F. Smith and G. A. Miller), MIT Press, Cambridge.
McNeill, D. (1979). *The Conceptual Basis of Language*, Erlbaum, New Jersey.
Meadow, K. P. (1980). *Deafness and Child Development*, Arnold, London.
Menyuk, P. (1971). *The Acquisition and Development of Language*, Prentice Hall, Englewood Cliffs, New Jersey.
Mercer, N., and Edwards, D. (1981). Ground rules for mutual understanding: a social psychological approach to classroom knowledge. In *Language in School and Community* (Ed. N. Mercer), Arnold, London.
Milne, A. A. (1926). *Winnie-the-Pooh*, Methuen, London.
Mogford, K., Gregory, S., and Hartley, G. (1980). Deaf children with deaf parents and deaf children with hearing parents: a study of adult–child interaction. *Paper*

presented at the *XXIInd International Congress of Psychology*, Leipzig, East Germany.

Murphy, C. M., and Wood, D. J. (1982). Learning through media: a comparison of 4- to 8-year-old children's responses to filmed and pictorial instruction. *International Journal of Behavioral Development*, **5**(2), 195–216.

Myklebust, H. (1964). *The Psychology of Deafness*, Grune and Stratton, New York.

Norden, K. (1975). *Psychological Studies of Deaf Adolescents*, Gleerup, Studia Psychologica et Pedagogica, Seria Altera, 39, Lund.

Oleron, P. (1977). *Language and Mental Development*, Erlbaum, New Jersey.

Piaget, J. (1972). Intellectual evolution from adolescence to adulthood. *Human Development*, **15**, 1–12.

Piaget, J., and Inhelder, B. (1969). *The Psychology of the Child*, Routledge and Kegan Paul, London.

Prosser, G. V. (1974). Questions as an aid to learning. In *Education, Curiosity and Questions* (Ed. W. P. Robinson), Schools Council Report, Southampton. Cited in W. P. Robinson and S. J. Rackstraw (1975).

Quigley, S. P., and Kretschmer, R. E. (1982). *The Education of Deaf Children: Issues, Theory and Practice*, Edward Arnold, London.

Quigley, S. P., and Paul, P. V. (1984). *Language and Deafness*, Croom Helm, London.

Quigley, S. P., Steinkamp, M. W., Power, D. J., and Jones, B. W. (1978). *The Test of Syntactic Abilities*, Dormac, Beaverton, Oregon.

Quirk, R., and Greenbaum, S. (1980). *A University Grammar of English*, Tenth Impression, Longman, London.

Raven, J. C. (1958). *Standard Progressive Matrices*, H. K. Lewis & Co. Ltd., London.

Robinson, E. J. (1976). Conversational tactics and the advancement of the child's understanding about referential communication. In *Communication in Development* (Ed. W. P. Robinson), Academic Press, London.

Robinson, E. J., and Robinson, W. P. (1982). The advancement of children's verbal referential communication skills: the role of metacognitive guidance. *International Journal of Behaviour Development*, **5**(3), 329–355.

Robinson, W. P., and Rackstraw, S. J. (1975). *Questioning and Answering of School Children*, Joseph Rowntree Memorial Trust Project.

Romaine, S. (1984). *The Language of Children and Adolescents*, Basil Blackwell, Oxford.

Russell, J. (1981). Propositional attitudes. In *Children's Thinking Through Language* (Ed. M. Beveridge), Edward Arnold, London.

Scaife, M., and Bruner J. S. (1975). The capacity for joint visual attention in the infant, *Nature*, **253**(5489), 265–266.

Schlesinger, H. S., and Meadow, K. P. (1972). *Sound and Sign: Child Deafness and Mental Health*, University of California Press, Berkeley.

Skinner, B. F. (1957). *Verbal Behaviour*, Appleton-Century-Crofts, New York.

Snow, C. E. (1979). Conversations with children. In *Language Acquisition* (Eds. P. Fletcher and M. Garman), Cambridge University Press, Cambridge.

Snow, C. E. and Ferguson, C. A. (1977). *Talking to Children. Language Input and Acquisition*, Cambridge University Press, Cambridge.

Southgate, V. (1962). *Group Reading Test*, Test 2, Form A—Sentence Completion, Hodder and Stoughton, London.

Springer, S. P., and Deutsch, G. (1981). *Left Brain, Right Brain*, W. H. Freeman, San Francisco.

Stanovich, K., and West, R. (1979). Mechanisms of sentence context effects in reading: automatic activation and conscious attention. *Memory and Cognition*, **7**, 77–85.

Stokoe, W. C. (1978). *Sign Language Structure: The First Linguistic Analysis of American Sign Language*, Linstock Press, Silver Spring, Maryland.

192

Suppes, P. (1974). Cognition in handicapped children. *Review of Educational Research*, **44**, 165–176.

Swift, J. N., and Gooding, C. T. (1983). Interaction of wait time feedback and questioning instruction on middle school science teaching. *Journal of Research in Science Teaching*, **20**, 721–730.

Sylva, K., Roy, C., and Painter, M. (1980). *Child Watching at Playgroup and Nursery School*, Basil Blackwell, Oxford.

Tait, D. M. (1984). *The Role of Singing in the Social and Linguistic Development of Nursery-Aged Deaf Children*, PhD Thesis, University of Nottingham.

Tait, D. M. (1985). *Reaching Our Children through Song*, Booklet available from the Psychology Department, University of Nottingham.

Tizard, B., and Hughes, M. (1984). *Young Children Learning. Talking and Thinking at Home and at School*, Fontana, London.

Tough, J. (1977). *The Development of Meaning*, Allen and Unwin, London.

Tucker, I., and Nolan, M. (1984). *The hearing-impaired child developing language*, AEP Journal. *Association of Educational Psychologists*, **6**(5), 39–45.

Underwood, G. (1976). *Attention and Memory*, Pergamon Press, Oxford.

Underwood, G. (1979). Memory systems and the reading process. In *Applied Problems in Memory* (Eds. M. M. Gruneberg and P. E. Morris), Academic Press, London.

Vandenberg, D. M. (1971). *The Written Language of Deaf Children*. New Zealand Council for Educational Research, Wellington.

Van Uden, A. (1970). *A World of Language for Deaf Children. Part 1: Basic Principles*, 2nd revised ed., Rotterdam University Press, Rotterdam.

Vernon, P. E., and Miller, K. M. (1976). *Graded Arithmetic–Mathematics Test*, Hodder and Stoughton, Sevenoaks.

Vygotsky, L. S. (1962). *Thought and Language*. MIT Press, Cambridge, Mass.

Wales, R. (1979). Deixis. In *Language Acquisition* (Eds. P. Fletcher and M. Garman), Cambridge University Press, Cambridge.

Wanner, E., and Gleitman, L. R. (Eds.) (1982). *Language Acquisition: The State of the Art*, Cambridge University Press, Cambridge.

Wason, P. C., and Johnson-Laird, P. N. (1972). *Psychology of Reasoning*, Batsford, London.

Webster, A., Wood, D. J., and Griffiths, A. J. (1981). Reading retardation or linguistic deficit? (I) Interpreting reading test performances of hearing-impaired adolescents. *Journal of Research on Reading*, **4**(2), 136–147.

Wechsler, D. (1974). *Wechsler Intelligence Scale for Children*, Revised ed., Psychological Corporation, New York.

Wells, G. (1979). Variation in child language. In *Language Acquisition* (Eds. P. Fletcher and M. Garman), Cambridge University Press, Cambridge.

Wells, G. (1981). *Language through Interaction*, Cambridge University Press, Cambridge.

Wells, G. (1983). The language experiences of five-year-old children at home and school. Draft manuscript, Centre for the Study of Language and Communication, University of Bristol School of Education, Bristol.

Wells, G. (1984). *Language Development in the Pre-school Years*, Cambridge University Press, Cambridge.

Wilson, K. (1979). Cited in S. P. Quigley and R. E. Kretschmer (1982), *The Education of Deaf Children: Issues, Theory and Practice*, Edward Arnold, London.

Wolk, S., and Schildroth, A. (in press). Consistency of an associational strategy used on reading comprehension tests by hearing-impaired students. *Journal of Research in Reading*.

Wood, D. J. (1980). Teaching the young child: some relationships between social interaction, language and thought. In *Social Foundations of Language and Cognition: Essays in Honor of J. S. Bruner* (Ed. D. Olson), Norton, New York.

Wood, D. J. (1982). The linguistic experiences of the prelingually, hearing-impaired child. *Journal of the British Association of Teachers of the Deaf*, **6**, 86–93.

Wood, D. J. (1984). Social and educational adjustment of deaf children in relation to mental retardation. In *Scientific Studies in Mental Retardation* (Ed. J. Dobbing), Royal Society of Medicine/Macmillan, London.

Wood, D. J. (in press). Aspects of teaching and learning. In *Children of Social Worlds: Parts of the Main* (Eds. M. Richards and P. Light).

Wood, D. J., Griffiths, A. J., and Webster, A. (1981). Reading retardation or linguistic deficit? (II) Test-answering strategies in hearing and hearing-impaired school children. *Journal of Research on Reading*, **4**(2), 148–156.

Wood, D. J., McMahon, L., and Cranstoun, Y. (1980). *Working with Under Fives*, Basil Blackwell, Oxford.

Wood, D. J., and Wood, H. A. (1985). Teacher questions versus student initiative in classroom discussions, Paper to the American Educational Research Association, Chicago, April 1985.

Wood, D. J., Wood, H. A., Griffiths, A. J., Howarth, S. P., and Howarth, C. I. (1982). The structure of conversations with 6- to 10-year-old deaf children. *Journal of Child Psychology and Psychiatry*, **23**, 295–308.

Wood, D. J., Wood, H. A., and Howarth, S. P. (1983a). Mathematical abilities in deaf school leavers. *British Journal of Developmental Psychology*, **1**(1), 67–74.

Wood, D. J., Wood, H. A., and Howarth, S. P. (1983b). Language, deafness and mathematical reasoning. In *The Acquisition of Symbolic Skills* (Eds. D. R. Rogers and J. A. Sloboda), Plenum Press, New York and London.

Wood, D. J., Wood, H. A., and Middleton, D. J. (1978). An experimental evaluation of four face-to-face teaching strategies. *International Journal of Behavioural Development*, **1**, 131–147.

Wood, H. A., and Wood, D. J. (1983). Questioning the preschool child. *Educational Review*, **35**(2), Special Issue 15, 149–162.

Wood, H. A., and Wood, D. J. (1984). An experimental evaluation of the effects of five styles of teacher conversation on the language of hearing-impaired children. *Journal of Child Psychology and Psychiatry*, **25**(1), 45–62.

Wood, H. A., Wood, D. J., Kingsmill, M. C., French, J. R., and Howarth, S. P. (1984). The mathematical achievements of deaf children from different educational environments. *British Journal of Educational Psychology*, **54**, 254–264.

Author Index

Subject Index